Teachers Leading Educational Reform

Teachers Leading Educational Reform explores the ways in which teachers across the world are currently working together in professional learning communities (PLCs) to generate meaningful change and innovation in order to transform pedagogy and practice. By discussing how teachers can work collectively and collaboratively on the issues of learning and teaching that matter to them, it argues that through collective action and collaborative agency, teachers are leading educational reform.

By offering contemporary examples and perspectives on the practice, impact and sustainability of PLCs, this book takes a global, comparative view showing categorically that those educational systems that are performing well, and seek to perform well, are using PLCs as the infrastructure to support teacher-led improvement.

Split into three sections that look at the macro, meso and micro aspects of how far professional collaboration is building the capacity and capability for school and system improvement, this text asks the questions:

- Is the PLC work **authentic**?
- Is the PLC work being **implemented** at a superficial or deep level?
- Is there evidence of a **positive impact** on students/teachers at the school/ district/system level?
- Is provision in place for **sustaining** the PLC work?

Teachers Leading Educational Reform illustrates how focused and purposeful professional collaboration is contributing to change and reform across the globe. It reinforces why teachers must be at the heart of the school reform processes as the drivers and architects of school transformation and change.

Alma Harris is Professor of Educational Leadership at the University of Malaya, Malaysia.

Michelle Jones is Assistant Professor of Education at the University of Bath, UK.

Jane B. Huffman is Emeritus Professor of Educational Leadership at the University of North Texas, USA.

Teacher Quality and School Development Series
Series Editors: Christopher Day and Ann Lieberman

The Teacher and the World
A Study of Cosmopolitanism and Education
David T. Hansen

Raising Achievement in Schools
Learning to Succeed
Alma Harris, David Crossley, Graham Corbyn and Tracey Allen

Self-Study and Inquiry into Practice
Learning to teach for equity and social justice
Linda Kroll

The New Lives of Teachers
Christopher Day and Qing Gu

Teacher Education Around the World
Changing policies and practices
Linda Darling-Hammond and Ann Lieberman

The Professional Identity of Teacher Educators
Career on the cusp?
Ronnie Davey

Resilient Teachers, Resilient Schools
Building and sustaining quality in testing times
Christopher Day and Qing Gu

Promoting Early Career Teacher Resilience
A socio-cultural and critical guide to action
Bruce Johnson, Barry Down, Rosie LeCornu, Judy Peters, Anna Sullivan, Jane Pearce, and Janet Hunter

Teachers and Academic Partners in Urban Schools
Threats to professional practice
Lori Beckett

Teacher Learning and Leadership
Of, By, and For Teachers
Ann Lieberman, Carol Campbell and Anna Yashkina

Teachers' Worlds and Work
Understanding Complexity, Building Quality
Christopher Day

Teachers Leading Educational Reform
The Power of Professional Learning Communities
Edited by Alma Harris, Michelle Jones and Jane B. Huffman

Teachers Leading Educational Reform

The Power of Professional Learning Communities

Edited by Alma Harris, Michelle Jones and Jane B. Huffman

Routledge
Taylor & Francis Group

LONDON AND NEW YORK

First published 2018
by Routledge
2 Park Square, Milton Park, Abingdon, Oxon OX14 4RN

and by Routledge
711 Third Avenue, New York, NY 10017

Routledge is an imprint of the Taylor & Francis Group, an informa business

British Library Cataloguing in Publication Data
A catalogue record for this book is available from the British Library

Library of Congress Cataloging in Publication Data
Names: Harris, Alma, 1958- editor. | Jones, Michelle S., editor. | Huffman, Jane Bumpers, 1950- editor.
Title: Teachers leading educational reform : the power of professional learning communities / edited by Alma Harris, Michelle Jones & Jane B. Huffman.
Description: Abingdon, Oxon ; New York, NY : Routledge, 2017. | Series: Teacher quality and school development series | Includes bibliographical references.
Identifiers: LCCN 2016056458| ISBN 9781138641051 (hardback) | ISBN 9781138641068 (pbk.) | ISBN 9781315630724 (ebook)
Subjects: LCSH: Professional learning communities. | Teachers--Professional relationships. | Educational change.
Classification: LCC LB1731 .T41987 2017 | DDC 370.71/1--dc23
LC record available at https://lccn.loc.gov/2016056458

ISBN: 978-1-138-64105-1 (hbk)
ISBN: 978-1-138-64106-8 (pbk)
ISBN: 978-1-315-63072-4 (ebk)

Typeset in Bembo
by Saxon Graphics Ltd, Derby

Contents

Contributors

Editors

Dr Alma Harris has held professorial posts at the University of Warwick, Institute of Education, University College London, the University of Malaya and, latterly, the University of Bath. She is internationally known for her research and writing on educational leadership and school improvement. In 2009–2012, she was seconded to the Welsh Government as a senior policy adviser to assist with the process of system-wide reform. She co-led the professional learning communities (PLC) programme with Dr Michelle Jones and also led on the development and implementation of a Master's qualification for all newly qualified teachers in Wales. Since 2009, she has worked for the World Bank, contributing to development and research programmes aimed at supporting schools in challenging contexts in Russia. Dr Harris is a Visiting Professor at the Moscow Higher School of Economics. Dr Harris is Past President of the International Congress for School Effectiveness and School Improvement (ICSEI), which is an organization dedicated to enhancing quality and equity in education. In January 2016, she received the ICSEI honorary lifetime award. She was appointed as an international adviser for the Scottish Government in 2016.

Dr Michelle Jones is an internationally recognised expert in school leadership, professional learning communities and blended learning. Before taking up her most recent academic post at the University of Bath, she was Associate Professor and Deputy Director of the Institute of Educational Leadership, University of Malaya, where her work focused upon Academic Development and Internationalization. Dr Jones' commitment to educational excellence has driven her entire career. In 2008 she was seconded to the Welsh Government, UK as an Education Adviser assisting with the national implementation of the 'Professional Learning Communities' programme in over 2000 schools. She has been an Education Consultant for the World Bank since 2010. Most recently, she has also been working with government agencies in England, Russia, Singapore, Australia and Malaysia to contribute to the design and delivery of their leadership and professional learning programmes. Dr Jones is a Research Fellow of the Hong Kong Institute of

Education and the Moscow Higher School of Economics. She is currently leading a research project that is exploring instructional leadership practices and is co-leading a project focused upon 'turnaround schools'.

Dr Jane B. Huffman, Professor Emeritus, enjoyed 20 years at the University of North Texas (UNT), Denton, Texas. As Mike Moses Endowed Chair in Educational Leadership, Dr Huffman led research initiatives, chaired 55 doctoral dissertations, taught courses in leadership, change management, and professional learning communities (PLCs) and sponsored the annual Leadership Conference at UNT. In 2014 she received the Research Leadership Award from UNT. Since 2009 Dr Huffman has worked with researchers in Taiwan, Hong Kong, China and Singapore on the topic of professional learning communities. In 2013 she was Visiting Scholar at the University of Canberra, Australia. These collaborative efforts resulted in the formation of the Global PLC Network whose members work to achieve common goals and coordinated implementation strategies towards re-culturing educational systems. Dr Huffman has published numerous international and national peer-reviewed articles, book chapters and books. Along with her co-author, Kristine Hipp, and research team, she published two books on PLCs: *Reculturing Schools as Professional Learning Communities* (2003) and *Demystifying Professional Learning Communities: School Leadership at its Best* (2010).

Authors

Dr Anthony E. Brazouski is Whitnall School District Executive Director of Academic Achievement. He serves as an adjunct staff member at the graduate level in the School of Education and Leadership at Cardinal Stritch University. He has co-authored a book chapter with Dr Kristine Kiefer Hipp titled 'Teachers at the forefront: A comprehensive, systematic process for creating and sustaining a district-wide culture of learning'.

Dr Chris Brown is a Senior Lecturer at UCL Institute of Education. With an interest in how evidence can aid education policy and practice, Chris has written four books (including *Leading the Use of Research and Evidence in Schools*) and several articles. Chris has led a range of projects, and received Education Endowment Foundation funding to support 100+ primary schools in England in increasing their use of research. Chris has been awarded the AERA's 'Emerging Scholar' award (Education Change SIG) and 'Excellence in Research to Practice' award (Research Use SIG), and also the UCEA Jeffrey V. Bennet Outstanding International Research Award.

Dr Carol Campbell is Associate Professor of Leadership and Educational Change at OISE, University of Toronto. She is also Director of the Knowledge Network for Applied Education Research – Réseau d'échange des connaissances pour la recherche appliquée en education (KNAER-RECRAE), a tripartite partnership between the Ontario Ministry of Education, University of Toronto and Western University to advance the mobilization and application of research for educational practice in Ontario.

Dr Christopher Chapman is Professor and Co-Director of the Robert Owen Centre for Educational Change at the University of Glasgow and also of What Works Scotland. He has led over 50 research projects and has over 100 publications in the areas of leadership, improvement and change. He is a Senior Academic Advisor to the Scottish Government and is a member of the First Minister's International Council of Education Advisors.

Dr Peiying Chen is Associate Professor in the Graduate Institute of Policy and Administration at National Taiwan Normal University (NTNU). Her doctoral thesis was awarded the CIES Gail Kelly Award and published by Routledge Falmer in 2004. She specializes in research on school improvement, school leadership, PLCs, and gender and education. Her work has been published in *School Effectiveness and School Improvement, Educational Review, Asia Pacific Journal of Education* and domestic journals. She is currently leading the national school improvement programme. She is also the main developer of PLC and NLC workshops for building school leaders' and teachers' capacity for change.

Hannah Chestnutt is a doctoral candidate at the University of Glasgow. Previously she was a teacher in Canada, the United States and Scotland. Her experiences of teaching children from diverse backgrounds led to her current work which uses social network analysis to explore the use of networks of educational professionals to ameliorate educational inequity. Her other interests include mathematics education, teacher professional development and educational governance.

Dr Fiona Ell is a Senior Lecturer in the Faculty of Education and Social Work at the University of Auckland. Fiona's research is concerned with how people learn in complex social settings, such as schools, universities and communities. In particular she is interested in the development of adaptive expertise in teachers, both in teacher preparation and while they are teaching. Fiona is involved in several national and international research projects that are investigating different elements of how new understandings, ideas and attitudes are developed and adopted by teachers and teacher candidates. Fiona is fundamentally interested in research focused on questions that will improve educational outcomes for all learners.

Dr Niamh Friel is a Research Assistant at the Robert Owen Centre, University of Glasgow.

Dr Jonathan W.P. Goh is Associate Professor at the National Institute of Education, Nanyang Technological University, Singapore. His research interests and publications include school leadership, work values, assessment, measurement and psychometrics including Rasch Analysis. He teaches educational marketing and management-related courses for various in-service and higher degree programmes.

Dr Mark Hadfield is Professor of Education in the School of Social Sciences at Cardiff University. Mark's interest in researching professional development has involved him in setting up a range of school networks both nationally and internationally. Over the last ten years Mark has written and researched extensively on the leadership of improvement efforts. He has advised and supported national and local governments in developing collaborative approaches to school improvement and professional learning.

Dr Salleh Hairon is Assistant Professor at the National Institute of Education, Nanyang Technological University, Singapore. His research interests and publications include distributed leadership, teacher leadership, teacher learning in communities (e.g. professional learning communities), and education change and reform. He teaches on graduate and in-service courses pertaining to leadership development.

Dr Judy Halbert and **Dr Linda Kaser** are co-leaders of the Networks of Inquiry and Innovation and the Aboriginal Enhancement Schools Network in British Columbia, Canada.[1] They have served as teachers, principals, district leaders and senior policy advisors with the Ministry of Education in the areas of innovative leadership, district change, rural education, literacy and Aboriginal education. They are Canadian representatives to the OECD international research programme on Innovative Learning Environments. They are currently faculty members at the University of British Columbia where they lead the Transformative Educational Leadership Program for system-level leaders. They have worked extensively with leadership groups in British Columbia as well as in Australia, New Zealand and England.

Dr Stuart Hall is a Senior Researcher in the Robert Owen Centre for Educational Change at the University of Glasgow. He has been involved in more than 70 policy-related research or evaluation projects and has undertaken work for organizations including the Scottish Government and the European Union and a number of major charities. He has a wide range of experience in both quantitative and qualitative research methods and has a particular interest in the use of research for organizational development.

Dr Kristine Kiefer Hipp is a Professor Emerita in the Doctoral Leadership Department at Cardinal Stritch University in Milwaukee, Wisconsin, USA. Hipp taught in the Doctorate in Leadership for the Advancement of Learning and Service, the Master's in Leadership and the District Administrative Licensure programmes for 18 years. In 2010 she co-edited *Demystifying Professional Learning Communities: School Leadership at Its Best*, an extension of her first co-authored book, *Reculturing Schools as Professional Learning Communities*.

Dr Deidre Le Fevre is a Senior Lecturer in the Faculty of Education and Social Work at the University of Auckland where she is the programme leader for postgraduate studies in educational leadership. Her research and teaching focus on leadership and learning for educational change and improvement. She has undertaken research and developed practices that support educational organizations to be increasingly effective in responding to the interests, needs and growth of all learners. Her research focuses on professional learning and organizational change. She examines both cognitive and affective aspects of learning that influence professional capability and organizational change.

Dr Ann Lieberman is an Emeritus Professor from Teachers College, Columbia University. She is now a Senior Scholar at The Carnegie Foundation for the Advancement of Teaching and a Visiting Professor at Stanford University. She received her BA and Ed.D at UCLA. She got her Master's Degree at California State University at Northridge, where she also received an honorary degree. Dr Lieberman was the President of the American Educational Research Association (AERA) in 1992. She is widely known for her work in the areas of teacher leadership and development, collaborative research, networks and school-university partnerships and, increasingly, on the problems and prospects for understanding educational change.

Kevin Lowden is a Senior Researcher at the Robert Owen Centre for Educational Change, University of Glasgow and member of the What Works Scotland team. He has 30 years' experience researching and leading national and international research projects, including those on partnership working and collaborative action research to inform educational change.

Dr Mike Mattingly serves as the Assistant Superintendent for Curriculum and Instruction with Denton ISD, Denton, TX. He has formerly been a teacher, principal and executive director for schools in Texas and Georgia. Dr Mattingly has taught instructional supervision as a part-time Assistant Professor for the University of Georgia and currently teaches education leadership courses for the University of North Texas. He received his B.S. from the University of Texas at Austin, his M.Ed. from the University of North Texas and his Ed.D. from the University of Georgia. He is a past president of the Georgia Association of Curriculum and Instructional Supervision.

Dr Dianne F. Olivier, Ph. D., Professor in Educational Foundations and Leadership at the University of Louisiana at Lafayette, serves as Coordinator of the Doctoral Program and holds the Joan D. and Alexander S. Haig/BORSF Endowed Professorship in Education. Dr Olivier's research focuses on professional learning communities, educational leadership, school culture and teacher self- and collective efficacy. She has developed several assessments and has authored/coauthored book chapters and articles relating to her research interests. Her PLC research has transitioned from the domestic national level to a global perspective as a member of a Global PLC Network. (dolivier@louisiana.edu)

Dr Wen-Jung Peng is a researcher mainly interested in various aspects of school effectiveness in different cultural contexts. She previously worked at the Graduate School of Education, University of Bristol (2002–2014), and was a co-applicant (with Sally M. Thomas) on two ESRC/DFID-funded projects – Improving Educational Evaluation and Quality in China and Improving Teacher Development and Educational Quality in China. Her other research interests include motivation of physical activity, service science in management and educational research methods.

Dr Patrice B. Pujol is the President of the National Institute for Excellence in Teaching and the former Superintendent of Schools for the Ascension Parish School System. She is a 40-year educator who has long been at the forefront of school and district improvement efforts. Her focus has been on improving teaching and learning processes throughout the school system to assure that students are prepared to compete in the global economy. She has most recently worked to develop system-wide processes for collaboration and support to advance educator effectiveness and district collective efficacy. She holds a doctoral degree in Educational Leadership.

Karen Spence-Thomas is a Programme Leader at UCL Institute of Education. She has previously held teaching and leadership roles in London schools. She specializes in designing and facilitating tailored professional development programmes within and across schools and other public sector organizations. Recent and current projects include: the EEF-funded Research Learning Communities (with Chris Brown), ESRC-funded Middle Leaders as Catalysts for Change (with Louise Stoll) and the NCTL Research Themes Project (which she co-led with Carol Taylor). Recent publications include 'Understanding Impact and the Cycle of Enquiry' with Carol Taylor in C. Brown's (Ed., 2015) *Leading the Use of Research and Evidence in Schools*.

Dr Louise Stoll is Professor of Professional Learning at the UCL Institute of Education. Her research and development activity focuses on how schools and local and national systems create capacity for learning and improvement, through creative leadership, leadership development, professional learning communities (PLCs) and learning networks. A Fellow of the Academy of the Social Sciences, she is an OECD expert and international consultant. Louise's books are translated into five languages. She is committed to finding ways to help 'animate' research findings, including developing PLC materials, a networking simulation and an *Improving School Leadership Toolkit* for the OECD.

Carol Taylor is a Strategic PD Programme Leader at UCL Institute of Education. She is involved in supporting schools across London to embed practitioner research and enquiry into organization and individual practice. She co-led the NCTL's Teaching Schools R&D project involving over 60 schools across England, and worked on the ESRC-funded middle leadership knowledge exchange project. She works with and designs bespoke leadership programmes for national and international contexts. Recent publications include 'Understanding Impact and the Cycle of Enquiry' with Karen Spence Thomas in C. Brown's (Ed., 2015) *Leading the Use of Research and Evidence in Schools*.

Dr Sally M. Thomas is Professor of Education at the Graduate School of Education, University of Bristol, UK. For 25 years she has published widely on the topics of educational quality, effectiveness and improvement using both qualitative and quantitative research methods. In particular, she has led numerous research studies using 'value-added measures of school effectiveness' for different purposes including school improvement and self-evaluation, assessing educational quality, international indicators and academic knowledge-based research. Her key research interests are also focused on Professional and School Learning Communities, pupil learning, citizenship and education in developing countries including East Asia, Africa and South America.

Dr Helen Timperley is Professor of Education at The University of Auckland and has worked extensively internationally and in New Zealand with schools and education systems that are innovating in ways that make a difference to the outcomes for learners, particularly those not well served by our education systems. Much of this work has focused on building both the professional and evaluative capacity to enable those involved to both innovate and check if their efforts are making the difference they desire. She is widely published internationally in her specialist areas with her most recent book titled *Realising the Power of Professional Learning* published by the Open University Press.

Pat Triggs recently retired from a post as Research Fellow in the Graduate School of Education, University of Bristol. She has been involved in a range of projects including ESRC-funded studies: PACE (a six-year longitudinal study of the impact of the introduction of the National Curriculum on primary schools), ENCOMPASS (a comparative study of student experience in secondary schools in Denmark, France and England) and Interactive Education (on the uses of information technology for learning in schools). She has a particular interest in teacher development, the experience of learners and school improvement.

Dr Jennifer G. Tuttleton, Executive Director of Talent Pipeline for Louisiana's Department of Education, has served in multiple leadership roles over her 23 years at the local and state level. She has gained an appreciation for the professional growth needs of educators. Improving the system of support for teacher and leader collaboration and evaluation is a priority for Dr Tuttleton. She strives to create and support high-quality teaching and learning experiences inclusive of all educational talent – pre-service teachers and beyond. Dr Tuttleton earned her Bachelor's and Master's degrees from Southeastern Louisiana University, as well as a doctoral degree in Educational Leadership.

Dr Steve V. Westbrook is Director of Educator Evaluation and Professional Development for the Louisiana Department of Education. He has been an educator for 28 years, beginning his career as a high school social studies teacher, and from there becoming a middle school assistant principal, high school principal and assistant superintendent for Ascension Parish in Louisiana. Dr Westbrook earned his Bachelor's and Master's degrees from Louisiana State University and his Doctor of Education degree from Southeastern Louisiana University. Implementing and moving toward sustainability of professional learning communities has been a major focus of his work as an educational leader.

Dr James K. Wilson is Superintendent of Schools, Denton, TX. During his 25-year career in education he has focused on public education advocacy, growth management and finances and instructional innovation. Dr Wilson, who earned his graduate degrees at the University of North Texas, has forged partnerships with local businesses, universities and organizations. In 2016, the National School Public Relations Association named Dr Wilson in the 'Top 25 Superintendents to Watch' list for his innovative practices in the area of public engagement and outreach.

Dr Anna Yashkina is an Instructor and Researcher working with the Department of Leadership, Higher and Adult Education at the Ontario Institute for Studies in Education (OISE), University of Toronto.

Note

1   www.noii.ca

Foreword

Teachers Leading Education Reform provides much welcomed evidence of the power of professional learning communities to influence the mindsets of teachers themselves and, indirectly, the attitudes and achievements of their students. Much has been published and much claimed for the benefits of proximity 'power with' collaboration rather than 'power over' relationships in schools through, for example, teacher leadership and professional learning communities.

The aim of the editors of this collection of papers from British Columbia, Ontario, two contrasting provinces in mainland China, England, USA, New Zealand, Singapore, Scotland, Taiwan and Wales is to 'position' the development of collective, collaborative leadership roles of teachers within the mainstream of the discourse about school and system improvement in the context of policy reforms. In doing so, they use the work of Andy Hargreaves and Michael Fullan (2012) to ask the question, 'What kind of professional learning and action can mobilize professional capital?' The answer, repeated and reinforced throughout each chapter, is to advocate cultural and context-specific manifestations of professional learning communities (PLCs) which are known to contribute to improved school and system outcomes. The key cross-cultural features of successful PLCS identified in the 'good news' accounts are teacher agency, teacher leadership, teacher voice and, alongside these, the facilitating role played by combinations of system and school leaders and university colleagues – all people who work at the interface of policy and practice.

Whilst much has been written, especially over the last 20 years, about the virtues of PLCS, this collection of accounts reminds us of the importance of understanding the complex and often fragile processes of building and sustaining them, especially in contexts of central government reforms which are dominated by the influence of the programme for international student assessment (PISA). For example, the importance of being able to change the culture of schools and systems which by tradition separate and isolate teachers; the need for teachers to mediate and internalize externally instituted change; the need for teachers to move from 'routines' to 'adaptive' expertise and re-align their professional identities in changing practice landscapes in managing continuing tensions between pressures of drives for more competition alongside contractual accountabilities and the drive for more creativity, and collaboration within and between schools and systems. The editors, rightly, are quick to point out that without such positive management, there can be no guarantee of 'authentic, effective collaboration', that 'deep collaboration' requires time and the growth of trust and that reform from within cannot be achieved without changing the culture of schools. The importance of this is well illustrated in the final case which provides a salutary illustration of the difficulties of achieving professional learning communities when they appear to challenge long-held, deeply embedded values, cultures and practices in schools themselves.

This book differs from others previously published in a number of important ways. First, its 'coverage' of different countries and cultures is broader. Second, it provides powerful testimonies of the benefits of collaboration. Third, building processes of sustained collaboration at macro, meso and micro level is complex and requires particular values and mindsets, equal power relationships, mutual respect and a disposition to trust among participants. In short, it reminds us of the accrued benefits to the education system, schools, teachers and, not least, students themselves that teacher leadership in professional learning communities can bring and the complex challenges that those who advocate these through their practices face.

Christopher Day and Ann Lieberman, Series Editors

Reference

Hargreaves, A., & Fullan, M. (2012). *Professional capital: Transforming teaching in every school.* USA: Teachers College Press.

Introduction

The critical issue of improving schools and school systems continues to preoccupy policy makers around the globe. This book considers the role of teacher collaboration and teacher leadership within education reform, improvement and change. The purpose of the book is to position the collective and collaborative work of teachers centrally within the contemporary discourse about improving schools and school systems. All too often teachers are the passive recipients of mandated reform rather than the active instigators of innovation and change. This book argues that through their collective action and collaborative agency teachers are, in fact, leading educational reform.

The failure of a great deal of contemporary education reform and change largely stems from the fact that practitioners' views are not adequately considered and teachers are not leaders of the reform process. There are two additional reasons why so much investment in well-intentioned reform tends not to provide the expected returns. First, there is a tendency to policy borrow without adequate attention to evidence or outcomes. Second, in too many education systems teachers sit on the sidelines of the process of educational reform and change.

While 30 years of evidence from the school effectiveness and school improvement field (Townsend, 2007) has undoubtedly shaped and influenced education policy making for the better, there are still significant challenges facing those charged with raising educational attainment and achievement. At present, these challenges manifest themselves, predominantly, in the form of big data, as large-scale international assessments tend to dominate and overshadow the global discourse about educational transformation and change. These large-scale comparative assessments, most notably PISA, have radically re-defined the international educational policy discourse in both positive and negative ways (Morris, 2012; Harris, Jones & Adams, 2016).

On the positive side, large-scale data sets afford detailed comparisons across education systems in ways that were simply not available before. This comparative perspective can be both illuminating and useful in evaluating policies and interventions aimed at school and system improvement. Indeed, as the field of comparative education has demonstrated very ably over several decades, there is much that can be learned and gained from grounded, evidence-based international comparisons. Conversely, however, it has been argued that large-scale international assessments, in particular PISA, have far moved beyond their intended remit (Luke, 2011). PISA is now the main player in global discussions about education policy and remains a hugely influential force in the contemporary debate about school and system improvement (Harris et al., 2016; Shirley, 2017).

In policy terms, the contemporary debate about school and system improvement has become increasingly polarized. On the one hand, the 'Global Education Reform Movement', or GERM as it has been called (Sahlberg, 2011, p. 99), characterized by accountability, standardization and competition continues to exercise a tight grip over policy development in a large number of countries. This inherently 'top-down' approach to educational improvement and change has also been associated with a move towards greater private involvement in education and, some have argued, the systematic erosion of public education (Ravitch, 2013). Despite numerous critiques and relatively little evidence of sustained success, this particular 'top-down' model of educational change and improvement remains persuasive and prevalent. As Sahlberg (2011, p. 102) notes, 'GERM relies on an assumption that competition between schools, teachers and students is the most productive way to raise the quality of education'.

In direct contrast to this particular brand of school and system reform is a movement that endorses professional collaboration, professional agency, teacher engagement and collective action as the main levers of productive educational change. Hargreaves and Shirley (2009) talk about the 'Fourth Way' where the path to improvement is less concerned with standards and accountability and more preoccupied with professional involvement and engagement. Similarly, the 'Finnish Way' outlines 'a professional and democratic path to improvement that grows from the bottom, steers from the top and provides support and pressure from the sides' (Sahlberg, 2011, p. 105).

There is a wealth of evidence that underlines the potential of concerted, collective, collaborative teacher–led activity to improve school and system performance (Hattie, 2015; Moller & Pankake, 2006; Timperley, Wilson, Barrar & Fung, 2007; Hargreaves & Shirley, 2009; Harris & Jones, 2010). At the heart of this approach to reform and change is the fundamental premise that the teacher is the key to lasting school and system improvement. As Hargreaves and Fullan (2012, p. 22) note,

> High performing systems have virtually all of their teachers on the move. It is a school thing, a professional thing and a system thing. The only solutions that will work on any scale are those that mobilize the teaching force as a whole – including strategies where teachers push and support each other.

The debate about educational change and reform, at scale, is currently polarized between two very different positions. On the one hand, GERM endorses and typifies mechanistic and heavily interventionist approaches to large-scale improvement based on a core assumption that teachers are the problem to be fixed. The direct alternative to this position is a more organic approach to school and system reform that presupposes that teachers, through their professional capability, professional collaboration and professional capacity, offer a potent solution to improvement at scale.

Professional capital

In their writing, Hargreaves and Fullan (2012) propose that the group is far more powerful than the individual in school and system change. They suggest that the system won't change unless 'development becomes a persistent collective enterprise' (Hargreaves & Fullan, 2012, p. 3). In this collective endeavour, the idea of 'professional capital' is centre-stage and is characterized in three ways: human capital, social capital and decisional capital. As the OECD (2014) report summarized:

> Human capital refers to the quality of teachers' initial training and on-going professional development; their skills, qualification and professional knowledge. Social capital refers to the impact that teachers and other learning professionals have on each other through collaboration and professional learning communities. Decisional capital refers to the development of teachers' professional judgment and careers, especially as they reach the middle level. These three factors work in combination with the leadership capital of head teachers and other leaders to define the quality of the education system as a whole.
>
> (OECD, 2014, p. 67).

Essentially, this approach to educational change and improvement endorses teacher-led reform and advocates that education professionals should take greater ownership of school and system improvement. Hargreaves and Fullan (2012, p. 9) suggest that this movement can be defined as a move from 'power over to power with' where those best placed to improve teaching and learning are given the opportunity and the collective responsibility to do so. The main rationale for this approach to educational change and reform is that those working within schools and with schools are best placed to mobilize productive, lasting and impactful school and system change (Campbell, Lieberman & Yashkina, 2016). The question remains, however, what particular form of professional learning and action can maximize professional capital?

The broader literature on professional learning offers some useful pointers. In particular, the synthesis of the evidential base on professional learning by Timperley et al. (2007) highlights the potential impact of professional learning communities (PLCs) as one powerful form of teacher collaboration. They note that to be most effective professional learning communities require two conditions: first, participants need to be supported to process new understandings and to assess their implications for teaching; second, the main focus of the PLC has to be upon making a positive impact to student learning.

It is recognized that a great deal of professional collaboration in schools is informal and this has clear benefits particularly in terms of building a strong cohesive culture. Professional learning communities tend to be a more formal, structured approach to professional collaboration where a clear model or set of principles or values guides the collective work (Cordingley, 2016). As highlighted later on in the book, definitions of PLCs tend to vary quite significantly. Simply put, a PLC is where teachers inquire together and learn together in order to develop new practices that will improve learner outcomes (Harris & Jones, 2010). Another definition of a PLC sees it as a framework of 'Professional educators working collectively and purposefully to create and sustain a culture of leaning for all students and adults' (Hipp & Huffman, 2010, p. 12). In essence, a PLC is not a talking shop or a therapy group; its prime aim is to engage professionals in *disciplined collaborative enquiry* in order to generate new approaches to learning and teaching that will have a positive impact on student outcomes (Harris and Jones, 2010).

The evidence about professional learning communities shows that, if properly constructed and enacted within and between schools, this form of professional collaboration can contribute to improvements in student achievement (Hord, 1997; Lomos, Hofman & Bosker, 2011; Vescio, Ross & Adams, 2008). The research evidence also underlines that professional learning teams (PLTs) or communities have the potential to change teachers' practice in ways that impact directly and positively on student learning outcomes (Campbell, 2015; Jones & Harris, 2014; Hipp & Huffman, 2010). Hord and Sommers (2008) describe the work of PLCs as 'continuous and intentional staff learning, so that staff always are increasing their effectiveness leading to students' increased successful learning' (p. 20).

In summary, the evidence on professional learning highlights that, where teachers are part of a well-functioning professional learning community, they tend to be more reflective on their professional practice and more willing to innovate in the classroom (Stoll and Seashore Louis, 2007; Day, 2000). Under the right conditions, therefore, a professional learning community can improve teachers' professional learning and can make a positive contribution to improved classroom and school performance (Lomos et al., 2011).

This book focuses specifically on how professional learning communities within, between and across schools are contributing to improved student and system outcomes. It illustrates how focused and purposeful professional collaboration is contributing to change and reform in a range of different countries and contexts.

Professional learning communities

As so much has been written about professional learning communities, it is important to be clear at the outset of this book about origins and definitions.

The original idea of a professional learning community, within an education context, came from the seminal work of Shirley Hord (1997). Subsequent interest in the idea of professional learning communities was generated by a number of influential writers espousing their virtues and value (e.g. Little & Horn, 2007; Louis & Marks, 1998; Talbert, 2010; Kruse & Louis, 2007; Hord, 2004). Largely, this group of commentators and academics conceptualized a PLC as a set of collaborative norms and practices at the whole school level. Here the PLC was characterized by certain core principles, such as shared values, a focus on student learning, reflective dialogue and action enquiry (Hord, 2004; Stoll & Seashore Louis, 2007; Hipp & Huffman, 2010). This 'whole-school' notion of a professional learning community is one that still tends to characterize much of the contemporary writing on this topic.

What constitutes a PLC tends to vary and wander considerably in the international literature, often to the point where, as DuFour (2004) proposes, 'it is in danger of losing all meaning'. Therefore, this book acknowledges and accepts that there are alternative models or interpretations of PLCs, but essentially it differentiates between three models. Firstly, there is the *whole school* model, as already mentioned, where the entire school is considered to be operating as an entire learning community by adhering to certain shared norms and values (DfES, 2005; Hipp, Huffman, Pankake & Olivier, 2008). Secondly, there is a *within school* model of PLCs where collaborative groups, sometimes called professional learning teams (PLTs) or teacher learning communities (TLCs), take responsibility for leading research, improvement and innovation (Harris & Jones, 2010; DuFour & DuFour, 2013; Wiliam, 2016). Thirdly, there is an *across school* model where the collaborative activity between teachers is 'school to school', embodying and reflecting network learning (Hadfield & Chapman, 2009; Kaser & Halbert, 2006). In the chapters that follow, these different manifestations of PLCs in action are represented and illuminated at the macro, meso and micro levels of different education systems.

The evidence from the various chapters shows that successful PLC work requires teachers to be clear about two things. First, they have to be clear about the particular model or models of PLCs they are adopting or adapting (i.e. whole school, within school or across schools). Where there is confusion about what a PLC is or what it does, even the best efforts at implementation could be derailed (Harris and Jones, 2010). Secondly, a clear PLC operational model, targeted support material, external expertise and adequate resources need to be in place for the PLC work to have a chance of being properly embedded and sustained.

The main purpose of this book is to outline the various ways in which collective agency and teacher leadership, in the form of professional learning communities, are enacted and realized to affect school-, district- and system-level change and improvement. The book aims to illuminate and demonstrate how teacher-led reform is being mobilized across very different countries, jurisdictions and contexts.[1] The book explores the various ways in which teacher-led reform is being nurtured, supported and realized through professional collaboration, supportive structures and trusting relationships. In particular, the book provides examples of effective professional collaboration and impactful professional learning in action. It also highlights emerging evidence about the ways in which teacher-led collaboration is positively influencing school, district and system improvement.

Over the past two decades, researchers in the field of professional learning have increasingly focused attention upon individual teachers, schools and networks of schools, engaging in collective learning within and across educational systems. Ideas of effective professional learning have increasingly been moved towards 'job-embedded' models, in which educators in various roles collaborate on core problems of practice through evidence-based inquiry (Stoll & Seashore Louis, 2007). These collaborative professional learning activities have been described at the macro (systemic and state or provincial), meso (district and region) and micro (individual and school) level. Consequently, this book is organized into these three sections.

The first section focuses on the macro level and explores how teacher collaboration is contributing to educational reform *within and across systems*. The second section looks at the meso level and considers professional collaboration *within and across schools, districts and localities*. The third and final section looks at the micro level and investigates *within and across school collaboration*. Collectively, the three sections explore how far professional collaboration is building the capacity and capability for school and system improvement.

Each section will be introduced separately with a brief outline of the chapters that follow. In some cases, the PLCs represented are part of a national initiative or district programme, in others they are project based or locally generated and driven. While the nature, focus and manifestation of the PLCs inevitably vary from context to context, there are four questions or tests to bear in mind when reading these accounts:

1   Is the PLC work *authentic*?
2   Is the PLC work being *implemented* at a superficial or deep level?
3   Is there evidence of a *positive impact* on students/teachers at the school/district/system level?
4   Is provision in place for *sustaining* the PLC work?

While a great deal of work takes place within and across schools every day under the label of professional learning communities, these four tests – *authenticity, implementation, impact and sustainability* – provide a basis for distinguishing between well-meaning, worthy, co-operative work and focused and impactful professional collaborative activity. If PLCs are worth the time and effort of busy professionals, it is important to think about how far these tests will be met and demonstrated. In the chapters that follow there are not only plenty of illustrations of exactly how these four tests are being met but also rich examples of teacher-led reform and improvement in action.

Note

1 www.dylanwiliamcenter.com/changing-what-teachers-do-is-more-important-than-changing-what-they-know/

References

Campbell, C. (2015). Teachers as leaders of professional learning: Lessons from Ontario's Teacher Learning and Leadership Program (TLLP). *Education Canada, 55*(1), 1–3.

Campbell, C., Lieberman, A. & Yashkina, A. (2016). Developing professional capital in policy and practice: Ontario's Teacher Learning and Leadership Program. *Journal of Professional Capital and Community, 1*(3), 219–236.

Cordingley, P. (2016). Knowledge and research use in local capacity building. In T. Burns, & F. Köster (Eds.), *Governing education in a complex world*. Paris: OECD Publishing.

Day, C. (2000). *The life and work of teachers: International perspectives in changing times*. London and New York: Psychology Press.

Department for Education and Skills (DfES). (2005). *Creating and Sustaining Effective Professional Learning Communities, Research Report RR 637*. London: Bolam, R., McMahon, A., Stoll, L., Thomas, S., Wallace, M., Greenwood, A., . . . Smith, R.

DuFour, R. (2004). What is a professional learning community? *Educational Leadership, 61*(8), 6.

DuFour, R., & DuFour, R. (2013). *Learning by doing: A handbook for professional learning communities at work TM*. Bloomington, New York: Solution Tree Press.

Hadfield, M. & Chapman, C. (2009). *Leading school-based networks*. London: Routledge.

Hargreaves, A. & Fullan, M. (2012). *Professional capital: Transforming teaching in every school*. USA: Teachers College Press.

Hargreaves, A. & Shirley, D. (2009). *The fourth way: The inspiring future for educational change*. Thousand Oaks, CA: Corwin Press.

Harris, A. & Jones, M. (2010). Professional learning communities and system improvement. *Improving Schools, 13*(2), 172–181.

Harris, A., Jones, M., & Adams, D. (2016). Qualified to lead? A comparative, contextual and cultural view of educational policy borrowing. *Educational Research, 58*(2), 166–178.

Hipp, K. & Huffman, J. (2010). *Demystifying professional learning communities: School leadership at its best*. Lanham, MD: Rowman & Littlefield Education.

Hipp, K. K., Huffman, J. B., Pankake, A. M. & Olivier, D. F. (2008). Sustaining professional learning communities: Case studies. *Journal of Educational Change, 9*(2), 173–195.

Hord, S. M. (1997). *Professional learning communities: Communities of continuous inquiry and improvement*. Austin, TX: Southwest Educational Development Laboratory.

Hord, S. M. (Ed.). (2004). *Learning together, leading together: Changing schools through professional learning communities*. USA: Teachers College Press.

Hord, S. & Sommers, W. (2008). *Leading professional learning communities: Voices from research and practice*. Thousand Oaks, CA: Corwin Press.

Jones, M. & Harris, A. (2014). Principals leading successful organisational change: Building social capital through disciplined professional collaboration. *Journal of Organisational Change Management, 27*(3), 473–485.

Kaser, L. & Halbert, J. (2006). An approach to school-wide action research: Sustaining inquiries in networked learning communities. *BC Educational Leadership Research, 6*, 1–13.

Kruse, S. D. & Louis, K. S. (2007). Developing collective understanding over time: Reflections on building professional community. In L. Stoll & K. Seashore Louis (Eds.), *Professional learning communities: Divergence, depth and dilemmas* (106–118). Berkshire, England: Open University Press.

Little, J. W. & Horn, I. S. (2007). 'Normalizing' problems of practice: Converting routine conversations into a resource for learning in professional communities. In L. Stoll & K. Seashore Louis (Eds.), *Professional learning communities: Divergence, depth and dilemmas* (79–92). Berkshire, England: Open University Press.

Lomos, C., Hofman, R. & Bosker, R. (2011). Professional communities and student achievement – a meta analysis. *School Effectiveness and School Improvement, 22*(2), 121–148.

Louis, K. S. & Marks, H. M. (1998). Does professional community affect the classroom? Teachers' work and student experiences in restructuring schools. *American Journal of Education*, 532–575.

Luke, A. (2011). Generalizing across borders: Policy and the limits of educational science. *Educational Researcher, 40*(8), 367–377.

Moller, G. & Pankake, A. (2006). *Lead with me: A principal's guide to teacher leadership.* Larchmont, NY: Eye on Education.

Morris, P. (2012). Pick'n'mix, select and project; policy borrowing and the quest for 'world class' schooling: An analysis of the 2010 schools White Paper. *Journal of Education Policy, 27*(1), 89–107.

OECD. (2014). *Improving schools in Wales: An OECD perspective.* Retrieved from www.oecd.org/edu/Improving-schools-in-Wales.pdf

Ravitch, D. (2013). *The reign of error: The hoax of the privatization movement and the danger to America's public schools.* New York: Knopf.

Sahlberg, P. (2011). *Finnish lessons.* USA: Teachers College Press.

Shirley, D. (2017). *The new imperatives of educational change.* London: Routledge.

Stoll, L. & Seashore Louis, K. (Eds.). (2007). *Professional learning communities: Divergence, depth and dilemmas.* Maidenhead, UK: Open University Press.

Talbert, J. E. (2010). Professional learning communities at the crossroads: How systems hinder or engender change. In *Second international handbook of educational change* (pp. 555–571). Springer: Netherlands.

Timperley, H., Wilson, A., Barrar, H. & Fung, I. (2007). *Teacher professional learning and development: Best evidence synthesis.* Auckland, New Zealand: University of Auckland.

Townsend, T. (Ed.). (2007). *International handbook of school effectiveness and improvement: Review, reflection and reframing* (Vol. 17). Springer Science & Business Media.

Vescio, V., Ross, D. & Adams, A. (2008). A review of research on the impact of professional learning communities on teaching practice and student learning. *Teaching and Teacher Education, 24*(1), 80–91.

Wiliam, D. (2016). The secret of effective feedback. *Educational Leadership, 73*(7), 10–15.

Section 1

Teachers leading educational reform within and across systems

Section 1 considers the idea of professional collaboration at the system or macro-level. The chapters in this section look specifically at the deployment of professional learning communities as a deliberate strategy to secure change and improvement *within* and *across* systems. Collectively, the chapters map out the different ways in which PLCs, as a form of structured and systematic professional collaboration, can generate agency, energy and the impetus for lasting change and improvement, at scale.

The first chapter by Chris Chapman et al. focuses on a major investment in school-to-school collaboration in Scotland. The School Improvement Partnership Programme (SIPP) is a system-wide, evidence-based approach to educational change premised upon systematic and focused collaborative enquiry. The chapter reports on the progress of the project to date and highlights evidence about positive impact and outcomes. In particular, the chapter highlights the importance of teacher leadership in significantly promoting and enhancing the work of the school-to-school partnerships.

In their chapter, Kaser and Halbert build upon the theme of system-wide change and sustainable collaborative professional learning by describing their work with networks of schools in British Columbia. For the past sixteen years, voluntary networks of schools have been supported in an inquiry-orientated approach to collaborative professional learning. The chapter reinforces the importance of common goals as the key foundation for effective collaborative learning and presents a model of inquiry that the networks use to guide their collective work. Importantly, the chapter ends with a commentary on evidence of impact, which offers some insights into the way in which the various networks have positively affected teacher and student outcomes. The chapter also underlines that, while financial support matters, it is professional will, skill and persistence that matters more in creating, maintaining and sustaining effective networks of professional learning and collaboration.

The next chapter by Stoll, Brown, Spence-Thomas and Taylor explores the way in which professional learning communities are being deployed in England as a systematic way of generating improvement. The authors note that a great amount of collaborative activity is in evidence within England but also caution that unless this activity is underpinned by deep collegiality then the term 'professional learning community' is simply inappropriate. The chapter reflects on three different projects that were all designed to build system capacity for change and improvement through extensive professional collaboration and offers insights into their impact.

In their chapter, Campbell, Lieberman and Yashkina outline a teacher-led approach to developing a community of professional learners within the province of Ontario in Canada. Once again, this is a project-based initiative aimed at building capacity and mobilizing change within the system. The Ontario Teacher Learning and Leadership Program (TLLP) commenced in 2007 and is a good example of how collaborative professional learning can be sustained, even at scale. The chapter draws upon research evidence to illustrate the way in which the TTLP has impacted positively at the school, district and provincial level. As the chapter notes, the TLLP is teacher led and, like the SIPP in Scotland, is part of a wider system approach to building teachers' collective and collaborative professional development.

The last chapter in this section takes a look at professional learning in Singapore. It considers the possibilities and the challenges of developing teacher leadership through PLCs in Singapore as a whole-system strategy. Within Singapore, PLCs are mandated and therefore all teachers are engaged in this form of professional collaboration. The chapter explores the relationship between teacher leadership and professional learning communities within the Singaporean context by drawing upon contemporary data. The chapter highlights a number of difficulties facing teacher leaders working within PLCs and points towards the importance of middle leaders as facilitators in the process of professional collaboration.

Overall, the chapters in this section present a powerful case for professional collaboration, at scale, along with evidence of the clear benefits of school-to-school collaboration through professional learning communities or networks. The chapters also offer an important reminder that, to be most effective as a whole-system strategy, professional collaboration has to be 'disciplined, focused and purposeful', supported by a common model along with a shared intention to make a positive difference to learner outcomes (Harris and Jones, 2014).

Reference

Jones, M. & Harris, A. (2014). Principals Leading Successful Organisational Change: Building Social Capital through Disciplined Professional Collaboration. *Journal of Organisational Change Management, 27*(3), 473–485.

1 Taking the lead

Teachers leading educational reform through collaborative enquiry in Scotland

Christopher Chapman, Hannah Chestnutt, Niamh Friel, Stuart Hall and Kevin Lowden

Introduction

Education systems around the world are continually striving to improve their overall standard of educational provision and also to close the gap in outcomes between children from more and less advantaged backgrounds. The well-used term 'raising the bar and closing the gap' dominates the policy-making discourse in many systems. This chapter focuses on a three-year initiative designed to place teachers at the centre of reform efforts and to lead the change in closing the attainment gap in Scotland. The initiative is used to exemplify the possibilities for teachers to lead change and highlights the challenge of rethinking roles and responsibilities to promote distributed and teacher leadership both within and between schools. The chapter is structured into four sections. This section provides a background context by offering an overview of the key concepts of leadership and collaborative teacher action. The second section builds on the introduction to outline the principles and practice associated with the initiative, while the third explores the initiative's impact. In conclusion, the final section offers some reflections and speculations related to placing teachers at the centre of reform.

Sammons and colleagues (1995) identified 'professional leadership' as a key characteristic of effective schools. The elements of professional leadership were summarized as being 'firm and purposeful', having 'a participative approach' and being 'the leading professional' (p. 8). More recently, it has been claimed that leadership is second only to teaching and learning in terms of influencing student outcomes (Day, Sammons & Leighwood, 2011). Specifically, a review of the relationship between leadership practice and activity and student outcomes identified that promotion and participation in teacher learning and development had around twice the effect size (0.84) compared to other leadership practices such as 'planning, coordinating and evaluating, teaching and curriculum' (0.42) or 'establishing goals and expectations' (0.42). Practices such as 'resourcing strategically' (0.31) and 'ensuring an orderly and supportive environment' (0.27) were identified as having even smaller effects (Robinson, Hohepa & Lloyd, 2009).

West-Burnham (2009) highlights the importance of learning-centred leadership as a collective capacity rather than an individual pursuit, where collective responsibility is supported by an appropriate collegial infrastructure. West-Burnham notes that it is crucial to develop leaders who *'are confident in abandoning many of the norms that have informed the practice of leadership in the past and learn to lead with authenticity in new ways'* (p. 25) and that leadership of innovation and change requires head teachers who are able to ensure that leadership and management activities are distributed throughout the school, and can model collaborative approaches.

Distributed leadership has become a popular concept within contemporary leadership circles and in particular has been used to argue for developing the leadership capacity of educators (Harris, 2013), teacher agency supporting school improvement and reform (Spillane & Coldren, 2015). The idea within education can be traced back to the early papers presented by Peter Gronn in the late nineties that argued for distributed leadership as the new unit of analysis (Gronn, 2002) and by Jim Spillane and colleagues (2001) who argued that distributed leadership practice is extended across the social and situational context. Since this early work, distributed leadership has become part of the educational lexicon, widely known and enacted in various ways in different schools and systems (Harris, 2010). There has been much discussion and debate about the various merits, limitations and challenges of the concept (Harris, 2013) and Gunter and colleagues (2013) have attempted to 'map' distributed leadership and knowledge formation into functional (descriptive and normative), critical and socially critical dimensions.

The concept of teacher leadership has emerged from the broader ideas associated with distributed leadership (Spillane, 2015), and from teacher networks and professional learning communities (Harris & Muijs, 2003; Lieberman, 2000). In practice, teacher leadership tends to be exercised by teachers who want to remain in classrooms, working with students, but are minded to play a role in leading change by working with colleagues to support the professional learning of others and creating professional learning communities. In a similar vein to distributed leadership, teacher leadership challenges assumptions about *'the nature of leadership, the community within which it occurs and the relationships about power, authority and influence'* (Harris & Muijs, 2003, p. 26). Reporting a study of Union learning representatives, Stevenson (2012) takes an alternative position on teacher leadership to argue that an alternative understanding, not rooted in traditional managerialist hierarchies, is required. Stevenson argues that this alternative should not be concerned with 'vision' but with establishing a democratic professional voice to lever genuine transformative possibilities.

Collaborative teacher action for school improvement

Scotland's education system performs relatively well in cross-national comparisons. However, there are enduring social inequalities in participation and achievement (OECD, 2007; 2015; Machin, McNally & Wyness, 2013). Raising educational outcomes, especially in disadvantaged communities, requires the alignment of change processes in curriculum development, teacher development and school self-evaluation (Menter et al., 2010, p. 26). *Empowering Scotland* (Scottish Government, 2013, p. 54) recognizes the importance of evidence-informed decision-making in *'closing the opportunity gap'* and has pledged to *'continue to improve the level, focus and frequency of evidence used by education staff to improve standards and drive up attainment'*.

Research has demonstrated that the most effective school improvements are contextualized to fit local needs and often play out in different ways in different settings. Over 40 years ago, House (1974) warned against ignoring the power of context when he wrote that, through the *'primary pursuit of transferable innovation … different innovations will be more or less useful under widely difference specific circumstances'* (p. 245). Research also highlights the importance of local ownership and leadership by teachers and school leaders, often collecting and using data appropriately and working in partnership and collaboration with like-minded professionals and stakeholders, and the value of school-to-school networking, collaborative enquiry and cross-authority partnerships as levers of innovation and education system improvement (Chapman, 2016; Cochran-Smith, 2015; Armstrong, 2015; Wohlstetter, Smith & Gallagher, 2013; Hargreaves & Fullan, 2012; Moolenaar, Sleegers & Daly, 2011; Smith & Wohlstetter, 2001). There is increasing evidence to support investment in the use of collaborative enquiry to support professional learning and teacher leadership in schools in a range of contexts (Ainscow, 2016; Ainscow, Dyson, Goldrick & West, 2012; Chapman, 2008, 2014; Chapman, 2012; Cochran-Smith & Lytle, 2009; Earl & Katz, 2006; Hadfield & Chapman, 2009; Kerr, Aiston, White, Holland & Grayson, 2003).

Taking the lead: teachers collaborating to tackle educational inequity

The Scottish context

Scotland has a population of just under 5.5 million people and its landmass accounts for approximately one-third of the United Kingdom. It has its own Scottish Parliament and Executive who have legislative responsibility for education, health and other areas of public services and tax-raising powers. The Scottish education system has evolved over time, developing its own identity, culture and traditions that are rooted in the eighteenth-century 'Scottish Enlightenment'. Thus, the Scottish education system is different from other parts of the United Kingdom, particularly England. For example, one difference worthy of mention is the role that the 32 local authorities play in delivering education in Scotland, which currently is far greater than in England, where local authorities have become almost moribund as Westminster has pursued the development of an academized system where all schools are funded directly from government as independent state-funded schools (Salokangas & Chapman, 2014). The current Conservative administration in England plans for all schools to become academies by 2020.

The recent OECD report *Improving Schools in Scotland: An OECD Perspective* (2015) concluded that levels of academic achievement in Scotland are above international averages, with greater consistency in outcomes in mathematics for 15-year-olds compared to other OECD countries. However, some measurements indicate a downward trend in mathematics and reading and inspection data indicates '*As many as a third of schools are … performing only just at or even below acceptable standards of provision*' (p. 81). Despite relatively good performance, as with many systems the attainment gap is stark, with children from poorer backgrounds less likely to obtain national qualifications and high tariff scores. For example, the OECD cites Scottish Government (2014) figures:

> in 2012/13 on average 39% of S4 students in Scotland from all areas and not only the least deprived achieved five awards at level 5; the comparable rate for students from the most deprived areas is very nearly half that level (20%).
>
> (OECD, 2015 p. 69)

In March 2013, the then Cabinet Secretary for Education and Lifelong Learning, Mike Russell, announced six new policy priorities:[1]

- School partnerships
- Class sizes and teacher numbers
- Use of data to drive up improvement
- Improving parental involvement
- Leadership
  and
- Innovation.

These policies were designed to support the emergence of a more equitable Scottish education system and therefore form the basis of Scotland's next steps in challenging inequitable outcomes. The Robert Owen Centre for Educational Change at the University of Glasgow was commissioned to design and support a research and development initiative that resonated with this agenda. This initiative became known as the School Improvement Partnership Programme (SIPP).

The School Improvement Partnership Programme: principles and practice

The SIPP is an evidence-based approach to educational change, underpinned by 'joint practice development' (Hargreaves, 2012). The programme involves schools and local authorities working in partnership, drawing on a range of methods or 'tools', including lesson study, collaborative action research and instructional rounds, to provide a set of processes that teachers and others can draw on to implement their change efforts. This approach combines locally initiated and led practitioner collaborative enquiry across classrooms within schools with school-to-school collaborative enquiry that often spans local authority boundaries.

The knowledge that underpins this approach has been generated over decades of development and research activity and is located in a diverse range of systems including Hong Kong, Australia, the USA and Canada and, more recently, South America, Russia and parts of Asia.

There is also a strong tradition of this type of work within the United Kingdom. This includes, for example, *Improving Quality Education for All*, the *Coalition of Research Schools, Schools of Ambition*, the *Networked Learning Communities programme*, the *Best Practice Research Scholarship programme*, the *20:20 Initiative* and *City Challenge*.

So how might this rich vein of experience and evidence inform our thinking? There are a number of useful pointers. For example, the findings from a three-year research project involving schools in England suggested that collaboration between schools is more effective than collaboration that is restricted to within a single school because *'deeply held beliefs within schools prevented the experimentation that is necessary'* (Ainscow et al., 2012, p. 201). Similarly, competing beliefs or priorities were listed as an inhibitor to success in the *Schools of Ambition* 2009 report (Menter et al., 2010). The greater efficacy of teacher collaboration between partnered schools has also been reported by the National College for School Leadership (NCSL) *Networked Learning Communities* programme. Evaluation findings suggested that colleagues, within their own school, might be more likely to take risks, revealing their own weaknesses and gaps in their knowledge, than teachers collaborating within their own school (Earl & Katz, 2005).

Further benefits of school partnerships were found in *City Challenge* when the collaboration extended beyond schools and across local education authorities and schools were grouped as families. Partnerships between schools located at greater distances from each other appeared to benefit from the elimination of competition that exists between schools serving the same neighbourhoods (Ainscow, 2012). Ainscow contends that these long-reaching partnerships allowed a wider range of pupils to benefit from best practices by both transferring and *'generating context specific knowledge'* (Ainscow 2012, p. 296). External support through peers and external Challenge Advisors was also a key component of this approach and Challenge/Attainment Advisors now work with schools in challenging contexts in both Wales and Scotland.

The evaluation of the Extra Mile Programme, a two-year intervention designed to close the gap in performance between pupils eligible for free school meals in England, concluded:

> There was a 20 point difference in favour of the EM [Extra Mile] group, statistically significant at the 5% level. This is equivalent statistically to

compensating for one – but only one and not any combination – of the effect of FSM or 22% adverse deprivation on the IDACI scale or an 8% absence rate.

(Chapman, Mongon, Muijs & Williams, 2011, p. 22)

The evaluation of this programme highlighted the positive characteristics of the design of the Extra Mile as:

- alignment with the values of the local participants;
- providing a framework without imposing prescription;
- raising awareness of a compelling issue for improvement;
- allowing local contexts to determine the design of local activity;
- offering good quality external support and critical friendship and
- promoting but not imposing opportunities for collaboration.

(Chapman et al., 2011, pp. 59–60)

In summary, it would seem that the best examples of collaborative improvement strategies tend to be enquiry-driven and focused on specific issues, work across boundaries, align a so-called 'bottom up' approach with regional/national co-ordination and involve external critical friendship. Where there is a shared commitment to improving outcomes for all children and young people, well-supported partnerships can lead to significant and sustained improvement and raised attainment. Long-term partnerships where schools tackle issues of mutual concern bring mutual success – especially where this forms part of existing improvement planning.

The SIPP is a 'solution-focused approach'[2] to Scotland's attainment issues with an emphasis on supporting innovation and promoting sustainable collaboration across classroom, school and local authority boundaries to tackle educational inequity. The features of this approach align with the education system outcomes identified within Education Scotland's Corporate Plan 2013/16 – specifically, that educational outcomes for all learners must improve and inequity in educational outcomes needs to be eradicated. It also sits with Education Scotland's third strategic objective to build the capacity of education providers to continuously improve their performance, to move from self-evaluation to self-improvement, so changing the focus of organizational change. The SIPP is seen as a natural development of the implementation of the Scottish *Curriculum for Excellence*, with its emphasis on social inclusion and policies and approaches to career-long professional learning outlined in *Teaching Scotland's Future* (Donaldson, 2010).

The SIPP aims to encourage staff to take leadership responsibility for embedding collaborative enquiry to learn from each other, experiment with their practice and monitor and evaluate change. The work of the Partnerships also aims to promote broader leadership opportunities and professional learning at all levels. The Programme seeks to promote focused innovation by fostering a culture of mutual respect, 'co-production' and partnership, rather than replicating traditional hierarchies and ways of working.

Principles of the SIPP approach

The SIPP aligns with and reinforces a number of key national policies, including *Curriculum for Excellence*, *Teaching Scotland's Future*, the *SCEL Fellowship Programme* and *Raising Attainment for All*. All of these are underpinned by the same key concepts of co-production, professional learning and enquiry as part of the broader *Scottish Approach* to public service reform. Informed by the Scottish Approach and combined with evidence and experience outlined above, SIPP is designed around seven core principles:

- *Partnership working* is promoted across schools and local authorities, with a focus on exploring specific issues relating to educational inequity.
- *Action research and evidence* are used to identify key challenges, experiment with innovative practices and monitor developments.
- *Leadership opportunities* are created, alongside the *professional learning* of staff at all levels.
- *Reciprocity and mutual benefit* to all involved underpin planning and implementation.
- *Planning for collaboration* encompasses the development of arrangements to support long-term collaboration and new approaches to capacity building.
- *Strategic improvement planning* in schools and local authorities is explicitly linked to SIPP activity.
- *Partners* are diverse and include schools, local authorities, Education Scotland and other agencies.

Since the SIPP's inception in spring 2013, these key principles have provided an overarching framework that has ensured programme coherence from which systemic lessons can be learned, whilst retaining the flexibility necessary for the development of local, context-specific arrangements to tackle the attainment gap.

Practice: the SIPP in action

The SIPP employed a three-phase implementation strategy. The first phase focused on creating the conditions by building trust and relationships. The second phase worked to embed projects into their context and the final phase focused on issues of sustainability, including strengthening and deepening connections within and between partnerships to create a SIPP network or 'network improvement community'. There are now eight discrete but interconnected projects. Four of the projects involve work across two local authorities while another involves collaboration between schools in three authorities. The remaining three initiatives are located within individual authorities but involve a range of schools and/or partner agencies. Table 1.1 summarizes the eight projects; their aims, partners involved and the scale of the work.

Table 1.1 The eight SIPP projects

Projects	1	2	3	4	5	6	7	8
Aim	To tackle educational inequity							
Approach	Using collaborative action research							
Local authorities	3	1	2	2	2	1	2	1
Schools	3	2	>30	2	12	1 (3)	13	9
School phase	Secondary	Primary	Secondary Primary	Secondary	Secondary	Secondary	Primary	Secondary Primary
Main partners	Teachers and Head Teachers							CLDW, SfL, teachers
Area of focus	• Parental engagement • pupil engagement • monitoring progress	• Maths • CGI • Lesson study	• CPD • Develop LIGs	• Parental engagement • Maths	• CPD	• Pupil mental wellbeing • Attendance • Motivation	• Maths • Literacy	• Literacy

Each of the partnerships used the SIPP's principles to design and develop their own programme of work. The partnerships are supported by a team of university researchers and local authority and Education Scotland (the Scottish school improvement agency) staff who work as critical friends providing challenge, support and guidance as appropriate. In addition to bespoke support for individual projects the university research team facilitates regular 'clinics' for school and local authority staff to meet either virtually or at the university, a 'safe space' in which to problem-solve their concerns, challenges and methodological issues and also discuss their ideas for development. Individual partnership projects are also brought together at regular local and national events. These events provide a forum for sharing ideas and practice and generally making connections across partnerships. This has now evolved to such an extent that we have observed innovative and evidenced-based practice being adapted and moving organically across partnerships without external support, other than the provision of opportunity for the partnerships within the Programme to come together as a whole.

Taking a lead: teachers making a difference

Having outlined the principles and practice and the partners involved we now focus on three areas of *impact*:

- Building effective working relationships
- Understanding of data and its use
  and
- Leadership development and leading learning

and relate these to how teachers have been taking a lead.

Building effective working relationships

The Programme has facilitated greater professional dialogue, collegiality and networking between teachers involved in the partnerships. This has helped drive the work of the partnerships and led to sharing of ideas and practice pertinent to specific project aims as well as to broader teaching and learning, in some cases beyond the scope of the Programme.

Survey evidence indicates that the SIPP's activities were contributing to growing partnership and networking among school staff involved in the initiative. Focusing on the survey results between the first (February 2014) and fourth (June 2015) waves we can see that the following activities tended to increase for the second wave or were maintained at a high level.

- Collaborative working across the Partnership, up from 64 percent in the first survey to 100 percent in the fourth.

- Increased collegiality between colleagues across the Partnership, up from 73 percent to 94 percent.
- More opportunities for teachers to share their ideas and plans with colleagues across the Partnership, up from 73 percent to 92 percent.
- The development of arrangements to support long-term collaboration and new approaches to capacity building, up from 65 percent to 91 percent.
- The involvement of an appropriate range of partners to support the Partnership's activities, up from 51 percent to 80 percent.
- Increased leadership opportunities (91 percent wave 2, 92 percent wave 4).
- Promotion of skills in practitioner enquiry (90 percent wave 2, 91 percent wave 4).
- Increased awareness of sources of support to address our SIPP aims (90 percent wave 2, 91 percent wave 4).

The interview and focus group evidence also revealed the importance of building effective working relationships between teachers from different schools and/or authorities as well as across related professions. Partnership teams stated that this collaborative working was now beginning to demonstrate a positive impact on students' outcomes and aspirations. Most believed that these networks and their impact would be sustainable and reflected in their planning.

Practitioners in Partnership 4 commented, 'It is great to be able to share experiences and work together'. Teachers also commonly noted that being able to observe others' teaching was extremely useful for improving their practice. Teachers saw the increased opportunity for networking as a key benefit of the SIPP:

> Networking with colleagues from other schools and authorities ... has broken down barriers and encouraged excellent opportunities for professional dialogue.
>
> The most successful development in my school is the positive attitude developed towards collaborating with colleagues in other schools within and outwith the authority. This is a terrific foundation for a sustainable partnership and attitude.
>
> Teachers in Partnership 7

> Partnership working has been extremely beneficial as a CLD [Community Learning Development] worker in maximising resources when working with young people.
>
> CLD worker in Partnership 1

The collaborative partnerships meant that teachers were able to engage in professional learning, build confidence and develop leadership capacity.

Comments and evidence from teachers and local authority colleagues regarding positive outcomes as a result of the SIPP indicated that there were benefits from partnership working that were unforeseen at the proposal stage. For example, the opportunities provided by increased collegial working and collaborative networking often led to synergies and new ideas such as new learning and teaching approaches, more critical reflection and new evaluation strategies.

Findings suggest that, from the outset, the Programme promoted leadership opportunities for those involved. It is interesting to note that these remained very high throughout the Programme and the underpinning conditions improved as trust and relationships developed. It may be that these leadership opportunities would not have been sustained if collegiality and opportunities for sharing had not increased.

In addition to positive relationships providing the basis for developing trust and empowering teachers to take a lead, one teacher reported that the Programme has kept them in the teaching profession. They reflected on the importance of ownership and the power of collaborative enquiry, going as far to claim: *'This has inspired me to stay in teaching'* (Partnership 1). This might suggest the emancipatory power of the Programme that helps teachers to understand and take control of their professional work.

Understanding of data and its use

As the Programme has matured there has been growing teacher engagement with the collaborative enquiry process. This is highlighted in the first and fourth surveys.

- We noted a rise from 50 percent of respondents in wave one to 81 percent in wave four who were using systematic enquiry and evidence gathering to inform practice and monitor developments.
- Over the same period, we also witnessed an increase in respondents (from 61 percent to 89 percent) reporting increased teachers' reflective practice and self-evaluation.

Data collected from teachers and local authorities during national and local events, focus groups and interviews highlighted the role of the university team in helping to develop capacity and skills regarding collaborative enquiry. Teachers also learned from one another. It was particularly evident that teachers who had undertaken 'M-level' postgraduate courses were able to lead with confidence and authority. This highlights the important role that 'M-level' learning has in promoting teacher leadership.

In their reports, the partnerships made reference to their improved capacity and expertise regarding the use of data and evaluation approaches and in some cases this went beyond the teaching workforce. For example, Partnership 8 reported that:

The CLD staff 'have increased knowledge in gathering and analysing quantitative and qualitative data to evidence impact, identify themes and address community needs'.

(Partnership 8 final report p. 11).

A Partnership 7 report noted that:

Teachers and head teachers have had the opportunity to lead discussions and evaluations, and learn skills in data collection and analysis.

Practitioners' increased knowledge and experience regarding context-specific methods of assessment and data collection supported the generation and use of a more diverse use of data collection tools and analytical techniques. For example, teachers designed and analysed pupil surveys for secondary pupils to determine key issues regarding attendance; teachers designed and analysed surveys for educational professionals regarding staff knowledge and attitudes; teachers modified pupil attitudinal surveys and this was in addition to accessing and using a number of pre-existing data collection tools and undertaking a range of qualitative methods, including interviews and focus groups with key stakeholders.

One important outcome related to this increased engagement was that, as evaluative approaches became more sophisticated and higher quality data was gathered, capacity was being built within the partnerships. This necessitated further additional support to enable partnerships to undertake more complex analysis and better synthesize this evidence to gain deeper insights. This involved teacher leaders working with a range of professionals including university researchers, inspectors and educational psychologists to draw on a range of analytical expertise from different backgrounds, and then lead local workshops within their partnerships to share the new knowledge and insights gained from external sources. The evidence from the Programme is that the use of collaborative enquiry can be an enabler for teacher leadership in both formal roles, as designated 'research leaders' or 'data leaders', or more informally, working collaboratively as part of a team with colleagues on issues of mutual interest.

Leadership development and leading learning

In the previous two examples of impact we have identified areas where the SIPP has indirectly promoted teacher leadership by building working relationships and through the use and understanding of data. Here we argue that SIPP has explicitly promoted teacher leadership and the leadership of learning.

SIPP has promoted leadership development and provided opportunities for teachers to develop greater responsibility as part of their 'partnership team', leading the work of the partnership across schools. This has included taking responsibility for leading developing interventions/projects, liaising with other professionals within the partnership and beyond and advising on and supporting efforts in other partnerships. For example, one primary teacher worked with local authority, secondary and primary colleagues in another partnership to develop lesson study as an approach to support their work.

Results from the wave one survey indicated that the SIPP initiative had begun to support leadership development opportunities. However, by wave four these figures had risen again to the point where the overwhelming majority of respondents indicated a positive response.

- Eighty-five percent of wave four responses, compared to 76 percent of wave one responses, indicated that involvement with SIPP activity had seen a commitment to developing leadership opportunities.
- Eighty-eight percent of respondents in wave four also indicated that involvement with SIPP had resulted in the creation of leadership opportunities and professional learning of staff at all levels. Two-thirds of respondents (66 percent) reported this at the wave one stage.
- Ninety-one percent of wave four respondents reported an increase in their personal leadership opportunities compared to 92 percent in wave two.

Staff across the partnerships took on a number of diverse and varied leadership roles including: developing project plans, organizing collaborative enquiry, organizing and delivering parent engagement activity, leading and participating in lesson study cycles, writing reports, facilitating and video-recording pupil focus groups, creating pupil assessments, collecting data, analysing data, involving various experts and researching, introducing and instructing staff in new pedagogies, leading a wide range of continuing professional development opportunities for colleagues and presenting at local and national events.

In Partnership 8, teachers commented that they had gained knowledge and leadership opportunities through their involvement. It was not only teachers who benefited from leadership opportunities to take on new roles and responsibilities, but also SfLAs (support for learning assistants) and CLD workers. For example, SfLAs took on teaching roles in this Programme by planning lessons, delivering lessons and participating in shadow observations. SfLAs benefited professionally from these opportunities, but also invested their own time after hours to voluntarily contribute to the lesson planning.

> School D stated that the SfLA was always 'super organised' which saved a lot of time as she ensured that time was used wisely and resources were also prepared for both staff and pupils.
>
> (Partnership 8 final report p. 33).

In this partnership, CLD workers also stated that they benefited from the opportunity to take on new roles and responsibilities. By learning new reading strategies, they were able to share these strategies with parents and with pupils through the homework club. The CLD workers also stated that they gained a better understanding of the issues teachers face in their work. The Partnership 8 report stated that CLD workers 'are more confident in working collaboratively across disciplines and localities' and 'have shared skills and specialisms to enhance family learning and literacy provision' (p. 11).

The opportunities for teacher leaders to work with other educationalists and professionals is a positive and undervalued aspect of teacher leaders' work. The SIPP provided some opportunities for this to occur but more needs to be done if we are to develop a seamless holistic approach to our children's education that moves beyond professional silos to create an inter-professional 'community of inquiry within a community of social practice' where there is a shared language, both literally and figuratively, in terms of values, knowledge and procedures (Argyris, Putnam & Smith, 1985, p. 34).

In Partnership 7, head teachers reported that, through their involvement in the SIPP, their schools were now in position to share innovative approaches and develop leadership in other schools. One head teacher said, 'We felt we had something to give'. Teachers in this partnership also reported benefits from professional learning and leadership opportunities:

> leading our own professional development in order to develop an enhanced understanding of the core curricular area of numeracy, opportunities to lead our core group within the partnership at different times – taking charge of distributing responsibilities, leading CPD activities within home school, leading development at an authority level, opportunities for developing confidence, opportunities to observe in our own and other authorities with a view to sharing our observations with our own partnership group, building a larger network of colleagues.
>
> (Final report Project 2)

In Partnership 1 many teachers were afforded the opportunity to take on leadership roles by leading or participating in the nine development groups and/or the wider partnership group. In addition, a number of staff presented their work and disseminated good practice at a residential conference.

Partnership 5 head teachers and teachers from the participating high schools organized a conference to share good practice. Two hundred and thirty staff participated in the conference's 24 workshops. The leadership of this partnership was shared among a group of head teachers, deputy head teachers and teachers who took on the roles of workshop presenters, conference organizers, working group leaders and personal support programme leaders.

Social Network Analysis has gained popularity in educational settings (Daly, 2010) and our growing interest in this area led us to map the leadership development opportunities for the participants of one of the partnerships. The aspect of school leadership investigated was leading the distribution of ideas and approaches, particularly tried and tested ideas. Within SIPP partnerships various people took on the role of sharing teaching and learning approaches. The following sociogram (Figure 1.1) was constructed by asking teachers, head teachers and local authority officers involved in the SIPP the following question: With whom have you shared tried and tested ideas [relating to effective teaching and learning approaches for the tackling of educational inequity]?

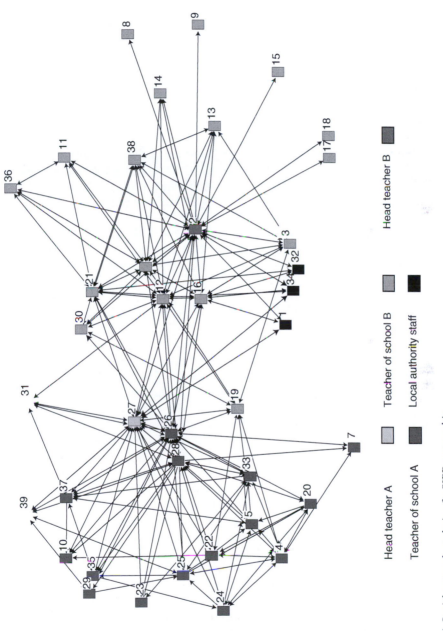

Figure 1.1 Social network analysis of a SIPP partnership

Head teacher A   Head teacher B

Teacher of school A   Teacher of school B

Local authority staff

Participants listed the names of people with whom they had shared tried and tested teaching and learning ideas or approaches. Some of the teachers have multiple lines connecting them to other people. Other teachers have only a single line, suggesting their conversations were limited to a single person. Rather than a single individual occupying a central role in the sharing of ideas, a number of individuals are positioned centrally where they appear to be in leadership roles. Head teacher A and head teacher B have prominent positions, but it is evident that the sharing of ideas is also distributed among other teachers. This was confirmed in focus groups and interviews where teachers reported that the leadership roles were not the preserve of head teachers or local authority staff. One teacher reflected: 'It was kind of just like a big team in terms of who we were, but we were the leaders'.

The sociogram also highlights the involvement of the local authority officers (represented in black) as sources of support to this partnership, but not necessarily taking on leadership roles. This was also mentioned in one of the interviews in which a teacher explained the type of support that had been beneficial:

> So we knew by the end of the first day that we had a focus, but after that the headteachers and the quality improvement managers were very happy to leave us to kind of see where we were going with the next steps.
>
> (Teacher, Partnership 2)

Another teacher reflected:

> People have come in at the right time … At certain times we chose, or through discussion with the head teachers or just in our team we highlighted, the people that we would need or we had a question that we needed support with and that was when we kind of involved more partners.
>
> (Teacher, Partnership 2)

Staff in this partnership took on a number of diverse and varied leadership roles including organizing and delivering parent workshops, writing reports, presenting at SIPP national events, facilitating or video-taping pupil focus groups, creating pupil assessments, collecting data, analysing data, involving various experts, introducing and instructing staff in new approaches, etc. These examples illustrate the diverse range of experiences available to teachers involved with the Programme and the opportunities to take on teacher leadership roles.

Taking the lead: commentary

In this final section we offer a general commentary on the SIPP and then, more specifically, on the relationship between the Programme and teacher leadership.

After three years of development and implementation activity, and the collection of a large volume of data within each of the partnerships and across the Programme, the evidence suggests the SIPP has had a positive impact on many teachers and students in participating schools and in some cases beyond. Furthermore, there is increasing evidence to support claims that the work within partnerships is closing the attainment gap. The range of positive developments and impact demonstrates that the underlying principles for 'disciplined collaborative enquiry' (Hargreaves, 2012) to tackle educational inequity provide a positive way forward. Indeed, progress and impact has been most evident in those partnerships that have been able to adapt and apply the principles and core concepts underpinning the SIPP to their own context. The majority of the partnerships report that lessons learned will be reflected in school and local authority planning to sustain approaches that have been identified as making a difference.

The design of the SIPP deliberately took a phased approach to implementation. This has enabled the Programme to evolve from a set of discrete partnerships to a programme of inter-connected partnerships working as a 'networked improvement community', similar to how Bryk and colleagues (2015) describe their work in the United States. One important distinction is that we view networked improvement communities as more methodologically eclectic. Therefore, rather than relying on improvement science as the only approach, we view it as a useful tool within a toolbox containing a range of approaches including lesson study, instructional rounds and collaborative action research. We argue that the specific tool or approach that is adopted must be fit for purpose. Therefore, the specific approach will be dependent on the aim, the nature of questions to be addressed and the local context. There is no single panacea in this complex and messy work; we need to maximize rather than limit the tools at our disposal.

The complexity and challenge of this type of work is highlighted by the fact that not all partnerships have yet demonstrated impact against their stated aims and they continue to explore how best to configure their approaches and systems. Another key challenge will be ensuring that the positive developments to date are sustained and embedded in practice and continue to impact on students' outcomes.

Feedback from the partnerships reveals that shifting local and national policy priorities and changes in resources and staffing locally can slow or even threaten progress and sustainability. However, on a more positive note, there is also evidence that suggests that the arrangements and ways of working that underpinned the SIPP are now influencing thinking and developmental plans more widely across the participating local authorities, including those involved with the Scottish Attainment Challenge, and in some cases more generally across the wider education system.

The SIPPs' contribution to supporting the development of teacher leadership has also been significant. The new ideas injected by the SIPP have been adopted by a cadre of teachers who have been prepared to rethink their roles and responsibilities. The Programme has tended to have most traction where a group of committed practitioners has been keen to build new working relationships and prepared to take on leadership responsibilities for personal and professional satisfaction rather than monetary reward. Where teacher leaders have been supported by school and local authority leaders, projects have driven forward with pace and focus and have also been able to engage other staff and expand the influence of the Programme to affect behaviours more widely across schools and partnerships.

These teacher leaders have developed a wide repertoire of knowledge and skills, ranging from research methods, data use and understanding to project planning and management and opportunities to practise leadership and management tasks that may not have been possible without involvement in the Programme. In effect this is a small but important step in building leadership capacity within the system which in the past has sometimes been missing.

In addition to developing an expanded repertoire of knowledge and skills teacher leaders received higher levels of exposure to a diverse range of professionals than might ordinarily be expected. The conversations and interactions with researchers, local authority staff, senior education officers and inspectors from Education Scotland, educational psychologists, community development workers and others provided teachers with access to a range of insights and perspectives on a diverse range of issues which enriched teachers' professional experience and their understanding of the complexity of tackling the attainment gap. This highlighted the need for educators to collaborate with a diverse range of public service providers, rather than taking a narrow standards-based perspective of the teaching and learning process or to work in a narrow educational silo.

Perhaps the most significant dimension of teacher leadership development has been the opportunities for teachers to take on leadership roles beyond their own classrooms and schools. This has involved placing quite junior teachers in a position to lead collaborative professional development within and between schools. Put simply, the SIPP has developed a network of early- and mid-career teachers who are leading a range of initiatives at relatively early stages of their careers, in some cases across local authority boundaries, which is relatively uncommon in Scotland and many other systems.

Unlike some other programmes, such as the Learning Partners Programme in New York, those that took on teacher leadership roles within the SIPP did not have a formal designation as a 'Teacher Leader'. Some partnerships assigned titles such as 'Data Lead' but there was no programme-wide designation. This might be something to reflect on and think about for the future in terms of recognizing the role, commitment and contribution of these individuals. A related point is the role that teachers with Master's degrees played in the project and the level of some of the work that the teacher leaders were undertaking which was sophisticated and could, with the appropriate portfolio assessment, have been accredited. This is another consideration for the future.

Finally, in addition to the commentary above it is worthy of mention that, while collaborative enquiry-driven initiatives like the SIPP have an important role to play in delivering specific outcomes and acting as vehicles for meaningful professional learning, their real value may lie in their leverage for handing responsibility, decision-making, ownership and, perhaps most crucially, power over to teachers. Lawrence Stenhouse's words on this issue are just as relevant now as they were over a third of a century ago.

> Only the pursuit of research directly applied to the curriculum and teaching puts the teacher in the power position; for he [*sic*] is in possession of the only valid laboratory, the classroom.
>
> (Stenhouse, 1980, p. 44)

Put simply, Stenhouse reminds us that it is teachers who change classrooms, not policies or protocols. Initiatives such as the SIPP provide a positive context that places teachers at the centre of educational change and empowers them to lead the change at a time when so many policies place them at the margins, with little power or control.

If schools are to play their full role in tackling educational inequities in an authentic way we must place teachers and teacher leadership at the centre of reforms and provide the power and resources to undertake the task in hand within their own schools, in collaboration with other schools and in partnership with the communities and families they serve.

Notes

1   In a speech on raising attainment at the University of Glasgow, Humanities Lecture Theatre.
2   The Solution-Focused model was originally developed in psychological therapy approaches but has since been applied more widely, including in organizational change. It is based on a collaborative, personalized, approach that focuses on positives rather than deficits. It is characterized by enquiry, building on strengths and what is working well to develop action plans that work.

References

Agryris, C., Putnam, R. & Smith, D. (1985). *Action Science: Concepts, methods and skills for research and intervention*. San Francisco, CA: Jossey-Bass.

Ainscow, M. (2012). Moving knowledge around: Strategies for fostering equity within educational systems. *Journal of Educational Change, 13*(3), 289–310.

Ainscow, M. (2016). Collaboration as a strategy for promoting equity in education: Possibilities and barriers. *Journal of Professional Capital and Community, 1*(2), 159–172.

Ainscow, M., Dyson, A., Goldrick, S. & West, M. (2012). Making schools effective for all: Rethinking the task. *School Leadership and Management, 32*(3), 1–17.

Armstrong, P. (2015). *Effective partnerships and collaboration for school improvement: A review of the evidence*. London: DfE.

Bryk, A. S., Gomez, L. M., Grunow, A. & LeMhieu, P. G. (2015). *Learning to improve: How America's schools can get better at getting better*. Boston, MA: Harvard Educational Press.

Chapman, C. (2008). Towards a framework for school-to-school networking in challenging circumstances. *Educational Research, 50*(4), 403–420.

Chapman, C. (2012). School improvement research and practice: A case of back to the future? In C. Chapman, P. Armstrong, A. Harris, D. Muijs, D. Reynolds & P. Sammons (Eds.), *School effectiveness and school improvement research: Challenging the orthodoxy?* Oxford: Routledge.

Chapman, C. (2014). From within- to between- and beyond- school improvement: A case of rethinking roles and relationships? *ICSEI Monograph Series, No. 3.*

Chapman, C. (2016). Networking for educational equity: Rethinking improvement within, between and beyond schools. In A. Harris & M. Jones (Eds.), *Leading futures: Global perspectives on educational leadership.* London: Sage.

Chapman, C., Mongon, D., Muijs, D. & Williams, J. (2011). *A national evaluation of the extra mile.* London: DfE.

Cochran-Smith, M. (2015). Teacher communities for equity. *Kappa Delta Pi Record*, 51, 109–113.

Cochran-Smith, M. & Lytle, S. L. (2009). *Inquiry as stance: Practitioner research for the next generation.* New York: Teachers College Press.

Daly, A. J. (2010). *Social network theory and educational change.* Cambridge, MA: Harvard Educational Press.

Day, C., Sammons, P. & Leithwood, K. (2011). *Successful school leadership: Linking learning with achievement.* Maidenhead, UK: Open University Press.

Donaldson, G. (2010). *Teaching Scotland's future.* Edinburgh: Scottish Government.

Earl, L. & Katz, S. (2005). *Learning from Networked Learning Communities (phase 2) – Key features and inevitable tensions. Phase 2 Report of the Networked Learning Communities External Evaluation.* London: DfES.

Earl, E. & Katz, S. (2006). *Leading schools in a data-rich world: Harnessing data for school improvement.* New York: Corwin.

Gronn, P. (2002). Distributed leadership as a unit of analysis. *The Leadership Quarterly*, *13*(4), 423–451.

Gunter, H., Hall, D. & Bragg, J. (2013). Distributed leadership: A study of knowledge production. *Educational Management Administration and Leadership*, *41*(5), 555–580.

Hadfield, M. & Chapman, C. (2009). *Leading school-based networks.* Oxford, UK: Routledge.

Hargreaves, A. & Fullan, M. (2012). *Professional capital: Transforming teaching in every School.* New York: Teachers College Press.

Hargreaves, D. (2012). *A self improving school system: Towards maturity.* Nottingham: NCSL.

Harris, A. (Ed.). (2010). *Distributed leadership.* Dordrecht, The Netherlands: Springer.

Harris, A. (2013). *Distributed school leadership: Developing tomorrow's leaders.* Oxford: Routledge.

Harris, A. & Muijs, D. (2003). *Teacher leadership-improvement through empowerment? An overview of the literature.* London: General Teaching Council for England.

House, E. R. (1974). *An examination of potential change roles in education.* Berkeley, CA: McCutchan.

Kerr, D., Aiston, S., White, K., Holland, M. & Grayson, H. (2003). *Literature review of networked learning communities.* Nottingham, UK: NCSL.

Lieberman, A. (2000). Networks as learning communities shaping the future of teacher development. *Journal of Teacher Education, 51*(3), 221–227.

Machin, S., McNally, S. & Wyness, G. (2013). Educational attainment across the UK nations: Performance, inequality and evidence. *Educational Research, 55*(2), 139–164.

Menter, I., Elliot, D., Hall, S., Hulme, M., Lowden, K., McQueen, I., … Christie, D. (2010). *Research to support schools of ambition, final report.* Edinburgh: Scottish Government.

Moolenaar, N. M., Sleegers, P. J. C. & Daly, A. J. (2011). Teaming up: Linking collaboration networks, collective efficacy, and student achievement. *Teaching and Teacher Education*, *28*(2), 251–262.

OECD. (2007). *No more failures: Ten steps to equity in education*. Paris: OECD Publishing.

OECD. (2015). *Improving schools in Scotland: An OECD perspective*. Paris: OECD Publishing.

Robinson, V., Hohepa, M. & Lloyd, C. (2009). *School leadership and student outcomes: Identifying what works and why: Best evidence synthesis iteration*. Wellington, NZ: New Zealand Ministry of Education.

Salokangas, M. & Chapman, C. (2014). Exploring governance in two chains of academy schools: A comparative case study. *Educational Management Administration Leadership*, *42*(3), 372–386.

Sammons, P., Mortimore, P. & Hillman, J. (1995). *Key characteristics of effective shools: A review of school effectiveness research*. London: IoE/OfSTED.

Scottish Government. (2013). *Empowering Scotland: The government's programme for Scotland 2013–2014*. Edinburgh: Scottish Government.

Scottish Government. (2014). *Summary statistics for attainment, leaver destinations and healthy living*. Edinburgh: Scottish Government.

Smith, A. K. & Wohlstetter, P. (2001). Reform through school networks: A new kind of authority and accountability. *Educational Policy*, *15*(4), 499–519.

Spillane, J. P. (2015). Leadership and learning: Conceptualizing relations between school administrative practice and instructional practice. *Societies*, *5*(2), 277–294.

Spillane, J. P. & Coldren, A. F. (2015). *Diagnosis and design for school improvement: Using a distributed perspective to lead and manage change*. New York: Teachers College Press.

Spillane, J., Halverson, R. & Diamond, J. B. (2001). Investigating school leadership practice: A distributed perspective. *Educational Researcher, 30*(3). 23–28.

Stenhouse, L. (1980). Curriculum research and the art of the teacher. *Curriculum, 1*(1), Spring.

Stevenson, H. (2012). Teacher leadership as intellectual leadership: Creating spaces for alternative voices in the English school system. *Professional Development in Education*, *38*(2), 345–360.

West-Burnham, J. (2009). *Rethinking educational leadership: From improvement to transformation*. London: Continuum.

Wohlstetter, P., Smith, J. & Gallagher, A. (2013). New York City's Children First Networks: Turning accountability on its head. *Journal of Educational Administration, 51*(4), 528–549.

2 Teachers leading reform through inquiry learning networks

A view from British Columbia

Linda Kaser and Judy Halbert

This book presents the case that teacher-led reform in the form of professional collaboration is a powerful force for change. We agree. For the past 16 years we have been facilitating voluntary networks of schools in British Columbia, Canada. Over this time, we have seen the significant impact that teacher leaders can have when they are linked, supported and engaged in learning communities that use a common framework for disciplined inquiry. From an initial group of 30 schools in 2000, the networks have expanded to include close to one-third of the schools across British Columbia and the Yukon. We have learned a great deal from the work across these schools and international interest in this networked approach to system change is growing. British Columbia was identified as one of the four high performing systems for the 2016 research study *Beyond Professional Development: Teacher Professional Learning in High Performing Systems* (Jenson, 2016). The Whole Education Network in England is using the BC network approach to disciplined inquiry as the framework for a significant initiative focused on closing the gap for underachieving learners. British Columbia was invited to be part of the OECD / CERI Innovative Learning Environment[1] research study and to participate specifically as one of the five international learning labs because of the focus on inquiry networks and the development of teacher leadership as a driver for system change.

In the forthcoming *Innovative Learning Environment Handbook* (2017), David Istance argues that learning leadership is critical for reform and innovation. He further argues that the impetus for innovation comes neither exclusively from top down mandates nor from bottom up pressure. Rather, he suggests that innovation often occurs through rich connections in the meso level:

> [Learning leadership] is exercised through strong visions and corresponding strategies intensely focused on learning. It calls for shared, collaborative activity, not relying only on the principal, in which learners themselves are privileged players. Such leadership may well extend beyond the school in contemporary learning environments embedded in a rich web of networks and partnerships.
>
> (Istance, Draft 2017, p. 29)

In this chapter, we describe the ways in which teacher leadership embedded in rich webs of inquiry learning networks in British Columbia is contributing to system change. We also offer perspectives about sustaining and supporting learning communities both within and across schools. The chapter is organized in five sections:

1   The links and distinctions between professional learning communities and inquiry learning networks;
2   The key conceptual foundations for the BC inquiry learning networks;
3   The importance of a disciplined approach;
4   The evidence of impact;
5   Sustaining teacher led reform through inquiry networks – considerations for other jurisdictions.

Professional learning communities and inquiry learning networks

Much of the early work on professional learning communities (PLCs) focused on the school as the unit of change. For instance, Bolam and his colleagues (Department for Education and Skills [DfES], 2005) defined a PLC as a within school community "with the capacity to promote and sustain the learning of all professionals with the collective purpose of enhancing student learning" (p. 145). The impetus in the early days of professional learning communities was to get PLCs flourishing in schools and then to look for ways to connect across schools. The approach we took in BC was to find, support and connect educators who sometimes were working in cultures that were *not* supportive of collaboration. We wanted to show the difference that could be made when teacher isolation was reduced and inquiry was encouraged. Our hypothesis was that structures – and support – would follow initiatives rather than drive them.

Helen Timperley and her colleagues at the University of Auckland make a distinction between PLCs and teacher inquiry (Timperley, 2011; Timperley, Wilson, Barrar & Fung, 2007). Timperley argues that engaging in rigorous inquiry into teaching and learning practices helps educators to identify the gaps between students' learning and teachers' teaching practices. This then encourages changes in teaching practices that consequently lead to improved outcomes for students. A small but important comparative study of three PLCs (Nelson, 2009) concluded that where the inquiry was sustained (in one of the three schools) both individual and collective learning were evident; in the other two schools such learning failed to materialize. What was evident in this study is that it is not PLCs per se that matter but a collaborative, student-focused teacher inquiry stance that made a positive difference.

In their work, Timperley and Parr (2011) explored the impact of the well-funded and supported Literacy Professional Development Project in New Zealand schools two years after the completion of the initiative. They found that, if teachers applied what they had learned in *systematic* ways during the literacy program, this was enough to support similar gains in achievement for new cohorts of students. However, when teams of teachers engaged in an iterative cycle of inquiry, re-focusing on persistent issues of underachievement, investing in continued knowledge building and establishing coherence in learning and teaching practices across curriculum areas, they dramatically *improved* their achievement gains over time, especially for their most vulnerable learners. When we learned of these findings, our determination to create cultures of inquiry in all network schools was reinforced.

There was an important contextual reason for our decision to focus on developing inquiry learning networks across schools rather than to focus specifically on professional learning communities within schools. In British Columbia, relationships between the formal teachers' association and the government have been difficult for several decades. Job action has been part of the provincial scene with a protracted teacher strike in 2014 adding additional strain to the relationship between teachers and principals. Although there has been encouraging progress recently, these relationships require on-going attention. A culture of mistrust makes top down mandates of any kind especially problematic.

The term "professional" in the context of PLCs has been interpreted in some BC schools and districts to refer only to teachers with the exclusion of principals, support staff, cultural workers and educational assistants. To build a culture of trust and inquiry, and to address the challenges of equity and quality across all schools, an inclusive approach was required. As well, it was important to use language that reflected the emphasis on inquiry, learning and networking. Originally referred to as the Network of Performance Based Schools, the name was changed in 2009 to Networks of Inquiry and Innovation[2] as a broader term to better reflect the work underway.

Key foundations for inquiry learning networks

During our experience with inquiry learning networks as catalysts for system reform, we have actively searched for research studies and practice evidence to inform the work. Over time these ideas have been distilled into a number of foundational elements that have helped to set the direction and to maintain the focus on quality and equity across diverse settings.

1. Intense and shared moral purpose through common goals

Having a sense of shared purpose and a set of common goals for inquiry learning networks is very important. Being clear on why we do what we do in school-to-school networks creates momentum and motivation. The concept of setting ambitious goals that are heartfelt, animated and challenging provides a way of thinking about whether or not the directions established for inquiry learning communities will capture the hearts and imaginations of those involved. Initially the network focus was on assessment for learning as the means to develop learner agency and engagement. Over time this focus has come to be expressed in three goals that have emerged directly from the educators actively involved in inquiry networks. These goals are now reflected in many district and provincial policy statements:

1. Every learner crossing the stage with dignity, purpose and options.

This means that collectively we have agreed to strive for equity and quality through achieving a 100 percent secondary school completion rate. Each learner will experience acceptance and respect for their personal identity. They will each have a sense of direction and purpose – and they will have genuine options for their future learning regardless of the path they choose.

2. Every learner leaving our settings more curious that when they arrived.

Educators we work with have observed that learner curiosity often diminishes over time in school. And, they agree that this is counter to what we hope to achieve through our educational programs. A key goal of system reform is to design learning environments that promote deeper forms of engagement, more opportunities to pursue important questions in depth and a genuine love of learning.

3. Every learner developing an understanding of, and respect for, indigenous ways of knowing.

Developing the capacity for expanded worldviews is important for all citizens in complex and globally connected societies. Within the context of British Columbia, there is a moral imperative for learners of all ages to develop a greater understanding of the perspectives and contributions of indigenous people. The legacy of colonization and of residential schools has contributed to inequitable challenges for Aboriginal learners. Recent efforts to improve outcomes are encouraging[3] – and there is still much to be done.

2. Growth mindset and assessment for learning

Carol Dweck's original research on the importance of mindset in learning and the many subsequent studies examining the impact of a growth mindset on learner outcomes has had a significant influence on network thinking. Enacting the research evidence about the kinds of changes that are possible when learners have access to new strategies and appropriate support – and put forth more effort – has become an essential part of the network approach.

From the outset, one of the key goals across the networks has been the development of learner metacognition and agency. A deep understanding of both the intent and the strategies of assessment for learning provides the bridge from teacher directed learning to student ownership. As educators within the network have gained confidence in making changes to their assessment practices, they have developed resources, conducted workshops, done side-by-side coaching to assist colleagues in shifting their practices and used social media to communicate emerging understandings.[4]

3. A focus on learning and learning principles

The OECD publication *The Nature of Learning* (Dumont, Istance & Benavides, 2010) contains a summary of findings from a number of international researchers about what makes a difference to student learning. The seven transversal principles identified by the editors of this book have become fundamental to the inquiry work in BC. They provide a lens for understanding the learning experiences of our young people and help identify areas that need to be strengthened. The principles also help focus initiatives in areas that have a strong evidence base. With growing enthusiasm for innovation and a desire for system reform, it is easy for policy makers to get distracted by promises of quick fixes. The conclusion by the OECD team that a learning environment cannot be considered innovative unless all seven of the following principles are evident in the experiences of all learners can be very helpful in informing intelligent reform efforts:

1   Learners and their learning are central. Learning is engaging and learners are gaining strength in self-regulation and metacognition.
2   Learning is social and often collaborative through well-organized cooperative strategies.
3   Learning is highly attuned to learners' motivations and the importance of emotions.
4   Learning is sensitive to individual differences including prior knowledge.
5   Learning is demanding for each learner – without excessive overload.
6   Assessments are consistent with learning aims with strong emphasis on formative feedback.
7   Horizontal connectedness is promoted across learning activities and subjects both in and out of school in the broader communities.

In addition to drawing on the OECD learning principles, networked inquiry communities in British Columbia are actively applying the indigenous learning principles developed in our province. From a First People's perspective, learning needs to be focused on connectedness, on reciprocal relationships and a sense of place. An indigenous worldview acknowledges that learning involves recognizing the consequences of one's actions, values the role of patience and the need for time and requires exploration and development of one's personal identity. The practical implications for teachers incorporating the First Peoples' Principle of Learning into their practices include creating greater connections to the broader community and to the wisdom of Elders. It also includes the need for educators to make explicit what is being learned in terms of how this new learning influences the self, the family, the community and the land.[5]

Both these sets of principles are serving to inform system reform in British Columbia. We contend that inquiry floats on a sea of innovation. Having inquiry informed by the best of international research and grounded in the wisdom of indigenous people of the territory assists in generating the kinds of innovations that will genuinely shift the system.

4. Social emotional learning, self-regulation and metacognition

An additional foundation for the inquiry learning networks in BC consists of four key questions that are drawn from research on social emotional learning and self-regulation. All network participants are asked to use these four questions intentionally with their learners as a key part of the inquiry process:

- Can you name two people in this school or learning setting who believe that you will be a success in life? How do they let you know?
- What are you learning and why is it important? Where are you going with your learning?
- How are you doing with your learning?
- What are the next steps in your learning?

These questions sound deceptively simple. When used as a regular routine, however, educators have found that they have a profound effect on shifting practices to increase learner sense of belonging and self-regulation. The first question quickly helps educators identify learners who do not feel connected to adults within the school – and propels them to immediate action. The three cognitive questions help move educator thinking from a preoccupation with content coverage to a focus on what learners actually experience. Student responses provide timely evidence about the extent to which young people are developing greater agency as learners.

5. Teacher professional learning

The final foundational idea for the inquiry networks involves ensuring that designs for teacher professional learning draw on current research and practice evidence. Research into the aspects of teacher professional learning that have an impact on student outcomes has had a significant influence on the approaches taken in BC. Helen Timperley's work on teacher professional learning has been deeply influential. Understanding that teacher professional learning should be based on the identified learning needs of students seems straightforward and yet this does not reflect the reality of many professional development programs – especially those packaged programs that promise dramatic improvements. Professional learning communities that do not incorporate a thorough understanding of the learning needs of their students are doomed to fail.

The previously mentioned research report, *Beyond Professional Development: Teacher Professional Learning in High Performing Systems*, examined teacher professional learning in four high performing systems: Shanghai, Singapore, Hong Kong and British Columbia. Although the cultural context of BC is different from these other jurisdictions, the themes that were identified across systems have provided validation for the approach of the inquiry learning networks. Lead researcher Ben Jensen notes "the strategic approach adopted in these systems requires all professional learning to be developed around an improvement cycle in schools that is always tied to student learning" (2016, p. 4). He further observes that, in isolation, an improvement cycle is not sufficient. To make it effective requires a broad strategy with strong linkages between how leadership roles are structured, how resources are allocated and the focus of accountability measures. With specific reference to BC, the report acknowledged the impact of inquiry networks and a disciplined approach to professional inquiry as contributing to the strength of the BC system.

A disciplined approach to networked inquiry

Right from the outset with the inquiry networks, BC schools agreed to engage in an annual cycle of inquiry to focus their efforts on improving student outcomes. Building on insights from the BC case studies and from the research in New Zealand on teacher professional learning, we collaborated with Helen Timperley to design a new approach to professional inquiry that we describe as a spiral of inquiry. There are several features that distinguish the spiral of inquiry from other action research approaches. It starts with a deep understanding of learning and the experiences of learners. It requires a collaborative approach by teams of educators. It builds in the findings from research on social emotional learning. It is specifically designed to change outcomes for learners. The terminology used respects teacher judgment, their lived experiences and their language. It draws on the school effectiveness and improvement literature while also incorporating frameworks from the emerging understandings about innovation. The approach is built on the best of what we currently know about professional learning. It insists on incorporating indigenous learning perspectives. It is evidence-informed at every stage through an emphasis on ongoing checking about student agency, self-regulation and metacognition.

The spiral of inquiry involves six key stages of scanning, focusing, developing a hunch, engaging in new professional learning, taking new professional action, checking that a big enough difference has been made and then re-engaging to consider what is next. Although the stages in the spiral overlap, paying attention to each aspect is critical in achieving the greatest benefit for all learners. At every stage, inquiry teams ask themselves three important questions: "*What's going on for our learners?*"; "*How do we know?*"; and "*Why does this matter?*"

The first two questions prompt educators to check constantly that learners are at the heart of what they do, and that all decisions are based on thoughtful evidence from direct observations and interviews in addition to more formal

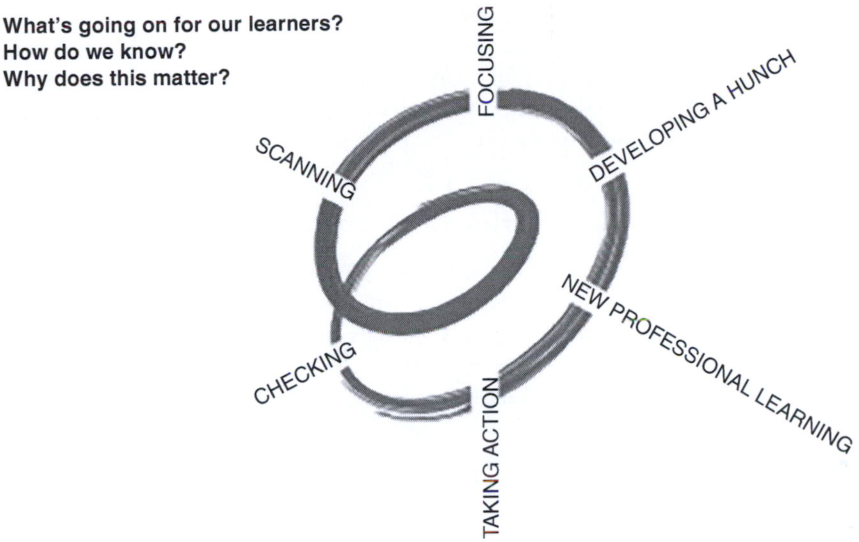

What's going on for our learners?
How do we know?
Why does this matter?

Figure 2.1 The spiral of inquiry, learning and action (Timperley, Kaser & Halbert, 2014)

data sources. The third question helps to ground teams in the importance of the direction they are pursuing. What follows is a short description of the key aspects of each stage.

Scanning: What's going on for our learners?

Just about everyone in a school community has opinions about what is going on for learners. Scanning is about collecting rich evidence about what is *really* taking place. It requires inquiry teams to challenge assumptions and to dig deeper to ensure that they have real evidence to support their beliefs. In a reasonable amount of time – generally no more than two months – inquiry teams gather information in key areas of learning. It is impossible to scan for everything that is important; it is necessary to select some key areas as a starting point. These areas may include personal identity, mathematical confidence, emotional well-being, creativity, scientific understandings, appreciation of other cultures or joy in reading. These initial areas of scanning may emerge from student achievement data, from teacher concerns, teacher curiosity or observations.

A thorough scanning draws on the learning principles from the OECD and the First Peoples' Principles of Learning to determine the extent to which learners' experiences are reflective of what is known and valued about learning. It is impossible to engage in scanning without involving the learners themselves. Understanding the degree to which students feel emotionally connected to adults in their learning environment and the degree to which they fully understand the key learning goals are critically important starting points in scanning. When educators listen to the answers of their learners in response to the four key questions described previously, the impact can be profound. Scanning can reveal a great deal of information that can pique educator curiosity and open up additional possibilities for a closer look. After a reasonable amount of time, initial decisions need to be made about where to focus greater attention.

Focusing: Where are we going to place our attention?

In the focusing phase, inquiry teams ask themselves: *Where are we going to concentrate our professional energies so that we can change the experiences and results for our learners?* Sometimes, the scanning process reveals a somewhat puzzling picture that requires deeper investigation. For example, an initial scan may identify that some learners are deeply engaged in their learning while others are not. Some learners may express a great deal of interest in particular content areas; others say it is totally irrelevant. Some learners are making good progress in developing key competencies; others are stalled. Some learners feel well supported by the adults in their school; others do not. Gaining greater clarity about the situation for learners by hearing from them directly before deciding on a course of action is at the heart of the focus phase. Unlike the scanning process, which requires both a broad perspective and a willingness to listen to the views of learners and their families, the focus stage requires deciding amongst competing priorities. Selecting the one or two areas on which to focus means that inquiry teams will consider the strongest possible new areas of learning – ones that will help learners make big leaps forward.

Developing a hunch: What's leading to this situation and how are we contributing to it?

The phases in the spiral of inquiry framework often overlap; the framework is not a linear process. Evidence from one stage informs the next. Surprises are inevitable and welcomed. They open up the opportunity for reflection and new understandings. The hunch stage asks educators to probe, "what's leading to this situation?" and, even more important, "how are *we* contributing to it?" Everyone generally has hunches about why things are the way they are. Sometimes these views are passionately held. Getting them on the table in a way that they can be discussed and tested is fundamental to moving forward together.

New professional learning: Where and how will we learn more about what to do?

All phases of the inquiry spiral involve learning but at this stage, educators engage with the specific task of carefully designing *new* professional learning. At this point, inquiry teams identify *"how and where can we learn more about what to do?"* The professional learning focus often flows organically from testing out the hunches about what is leading to the situation for learners. Both internal and external expertise may be required depending on the context of the school and the current capacity of the educators in the focus area. New learning also requires attention being paid to research evidence and emerging promising practices. The evidence about professional learning and improved learner outcomes in significant areas indicates that a year of focused effort is required. One year is good; two years are much better and three may be required.

Taking action: What will we do differently?

This is the stage in the inquiry spiral where new learning leads to new practices. Once teams have the evidence and the knowledge about the practices that will help learners, it is time to take action by jumping across the knowing-doing gap. At this stage, the inquiry team makes sure that all those involved are supported to try out the new practices. Teams need to make sure that there are plenty of opportunities for dialogue, observation and reflection. Changing practice can feel risky for many teachers and inquiry teams need to find ways to make the risk-taking less risky. Sometimes second, third and fourth tries are required without fear of judgment or failure.

Checking: Have we made enough of a difference?

The purpose of the inquiry spiral is to make a difference in valued outcomes for learners. Changes in practice do not always lead to substantive improvement and it is in this part of the spiral that inquiry teams ask whether they are making *enough* of a difference. The key is to have general agreement ahead of time about what evidence to look for as well as what constitutes enough of a difference.

What does this look like in practice? During the scanning process, the staff working with a disengaged group of struggling learners in a large urban secondary school noticed that, when the students were involved in hands on learning activities in an outdoor setting, they were far more focused, happy and productive. The staff decided to focus their inquiry on helping students develop more pride and a sense of purpose through goal setting and by exploring a range of career options. Their hunch was that traditional classroom settings did not work for many of their disengaged learners. They decided to provide more learning experiences outside of the school and connected to the community. As part of their professional learning, the staff explored the interests of their struggling learners and reached out to the community to offer job-shadowing opportunities for them. They also learned more about place-based learning and problem-based, hands-on approaches. The changes they made allowed students to develop employability skills and learn from a variety of caring adults sharing stories of their lives in their families, communities and work places.

So what difference did this make? At the beginning of the school year none of the participating students planned to pursue post-secondary education. By the end of the year, there were high levels of intellectual engagement and all the students had plans to continue on to post-secondary study. For these students the potential impact on their life chances was profound.

The impact for their teachers was also significant. Instead of experiencing frustration with the seeming inability of their students to succeed in school, they looked at what was working for their students and then made key changes to build on their strengths and interests rather than focus only on their apparent weaknesses. By publicly sharing the story of their success with this group of learners, this networked team influenced practice in many other schools. The inquiry network and the spiral framework provided both the support to try something new – and the discipline to ensure that their efforts were well informed.

Evidence of impact

From the outset we have focused on impact. What difference is the inquiry work making at the individual student, classroom and school level? What measures do we value? What impact are we seeing at the system level? Is it enough? How do we know? In addition to impact for learners, what impact are we seeing for teachers? How is being part of an inquiry network building capacity for teacher leadership and system change? These questions have driven us for the past 17 years and will continue to drive the networks for the foreseeable future.

The inquiry networks started in 2000 with the challenge of encouraging teachers to use a set of learning progressions[6] in reading, writing, numeracy and social responsibility that had been locally developed and rigorously tested in hundreds of classrooms. These learning progressions provided teachers with measures that they trusted and, as a result, schools and districts were able to avoid the obsession with achievement testing that has been counterproductive in other contexts. We agreed with the warning offered by Andy Hargreaves and Dean Fink (2005) when they argued for creating professional learning communities that make deep and broad learning their priority – rather than a narrow emphasis on particular forms of student achievement and reliance on testing regimes. Initially school teams were asked to report annually on the gains they made for their students in the focus area of their inquiry using the learning progressions. As schools have become more confident in using these progressions and as the focus for their inquiries has broadened, additional measures are being used to determine impact. These include levels of intellectual engagement, learner agency, social emotional connectedness, capacity for self-regulation, resilience, community contributions and overall school success.

Being clear on the purpose for inquiry networks helps provide direction for measuring impact. Initially our goals were to engage teachers in using the learning progressions to improve student outcomes and to shift the power from the teacher to the learner through an emphasis on formative assessment. As the inquiry networks expanded and matured the three key goals described earlier have emerged that reflect, in everyday language, what network educators are striving to accomplish. In short, the goals of system reform from a network perspective in BC are about quality, equity, curiosity, engagement, understanding and respect. So, how are we doing?

Even though the province has high rates of child poverty, a difficult climate of labour-government relationships and a complex and diverse group of learners from all parts of the world, on a range of indicators BC students do very well. The Conference Board of Canada publishes regular reports on Canadian progress towards achieving a high and sustainable quality of life for all citizens. They examine performance in the economy, society, innovation, the environment, health and education and skills. Within the education sector they examine 20 indicators including high school and post-secondary completion rates, achievement levels in reading, math, science, adult literacy levels and adult participation in non-formal job-related education as well as equity measures connected with serving disadvantaged young people. In the most recent report[7] they compared Canada's performance to that of 16 comparable jurisdictions using the size of the population, land mass and income per capita as variables. They also reported on the relative performances of the ten Canadian provinces. On both equity and quality indicators British Columbia was a top performer – in company with Finland and Japan.

We are not claiming that teacher involvement in inquiry networks is solely responsible for the increasingly strong outcomes for BC learners. We were encouraged, however, when a highly regarded policy advisor to a number of systems across the world texted us after the most recent PISA results[8] were released to say "BC leading Canada – that is a network effect." Another way of considering impact is to look at the ways in which network designs and thinking are influencing other provincial initiatives and contributing to a shift in provincial culture.

In 2004, the Ministry of Health and the Ministry of Education launched a joint initiative to focus on healthy living. Representatives from these Ministries were interested in building on the early successes of the inquiry networks in engaging teachers in collaborating around substantive issues of student learning. The question was whether the networked inquiry approach could be applied to health. The Healthy Schools Network[9] now involves over 200 schools across BC and connects health professionals and community members with teachers who are passionate about healthy living.

The next significant expansion of the inquiry networks took place in 2009. School districts and Aboriginal groups had been encouraged by the Ministry of Education to develop formal agreements focused on enhancing the success of indigenous learners. Despite a lot of good intentions, there was limited evidence that these agreements were having an impact on classroom practice. The provincial Director of Aboriginal Education asked whether an inquiry-based network approach could encourage teachers and principals to explore specific ways to make the goals of the enhancement agreements come to life. This led to the formation of the Aboriginal Enhancement Schools Network[10] (AESN) that now includes over 100 schools in BC and the Yukon.

In 2012, the Ministry of Education provided significant funding over a three year period to support an early reading network. This program, titled Changing Results for Young Readers[11] (CR4YR), involved 58 of the 60 school districts with each district having an external facilitator and a designated reading advocate. The majority of the external facilitators and many of the reading advocates were experienced inquiry network educators. CR4YR applied the same disciplined approach to inquiry as had been developed in the inquiry networks and this helped strengthen a sense of coherence across the province.

Network thinking and collaboration is also having an impact at the post-secondary institutional level. The spiral of inquiry as a disciplined approach to teacher collaboration is being introduced in most of the nine pre-service programs. A number of educators who started as classroom teachers in the networks are now on faculties of education and many of them are involved in redesigning teacher education around inquiry mindedness and adaptive expertise. The silos between institutions are being eroded through the personal relationships and respect forged in the networks.

Most teachers we work with do not initially aspire to take on formal leadership roles. They become part of the networks out of a desire to make a bigger difference for their learners and to be part of a professional inquiry community. The practice-focused and evidence-informed graduate leadership programs[12] combined with the on-going community provided by the networks have led to many teachers changing their minds about their career aspirations. Across the province there are also many educators in significant leadership roles – as superintendents, directors, principals, vice principals and senior Ministry staff – who all started out as classroom teachers and whose professional experiences were influenced by their network involvement.

In 2013, the Federal government funded a research study on the impact of teacher involvement in the Aboriginal Enhancement Schools Network. This study, led by Dr Catherine McGregor, titled *Aboriginal Inquiry: Lifting All Learners* (2013), examined several features including the overall impact on the cultures of teachers, school and districts, and the impact on creating leadership for change. The report observed that "the Network is a powerful tool for shared learning among teachers who have a desire to effect change in their schools and to advance the cause of quality, equitable learning" (2013, p. 9). The researchers concluded that there was strong evidence to show sustained, deeply transformative impact in a range of school districts and schools:

> [The network] provides space to develop thinking in diverse and unique ways and doesn't impose a particular model or way of doing things but rather enables the diversity that is the teaching force in BC. It also capitalizes on teachers' deep interest in supporting student learning: this emphasis on putting learning results at the centre of the teachers' efforts to innovate is a spectacularly successful approach. It avoids the pitfalls of top down, systemic efforts at programmatic change because it values the professional knowledge, experiences and capabilities of teachers. It honours their

commitment to teaching and making a difference and then uses that natural energy and passion for the work to invoke deeper thinking about how they can enhance student success. A network that achieves the degree of commitment, passion and dedication we saw throughout this study tells us that it will be sustained even if only by the strength of will shared by its proponents. This is the Network's deepest and most profound area of impact.

(McGregor, 2013, p. 121)

Inquiry learning networks in BC continue to evolve. In 2016, 14 BC school districts agreed to fund a three year research study looking at the impact that a district focus on inquiry was having on student outcomes. The networking that is occurring across these districts as they seek to identify common links and valued measures for determining impact is already changing the nature of dialogue amongst district leadership teams. As well, 14 schools are currently involved in a longitudinal study exploring the impact of their efforts to improve the learning experiences and transition rates for their Aboriginal learners. The links being created across schools, associations, institutions and districts are contributing to a greater sense of coherence in a highly diverse province.

The final section of this chapter includes some perspectives on the ways in which inquiry networks can sustain and support teacher led reform.

Sustaining teacher led reform through inquiry networks

Changing an educational system from a focus on sorting to a focus on learning requires a strong sense of purpose, a deep passion for quality and equity and a great deal of persistence. As we reflect on our experience with inquiry and innovation networks over the past 16 years, five key factors that contribute to system change are emerging:

- Find outlier practices;
- Link the key influencers;
- Infuse intelligence;
- Consistently develop fresh sources of energy to stay flexible; and,
- Persist in pursuing network goals and system change.

1. Find the practices of outliers and make their learning visible

When we looked globally for examples of large scale change in the social sector, we found an impressive example of sustained change in Vietnam.[13] Using a positive deviance model the Vietnamese were able to reduce chronic childhood malnutrition countrywide using a village-by-village peer network strategy. Positive deviants in this case were those families who managed to raise healthier children as a result of small differences in what they were fed – shrimp, crab and sweet potatoes from the rice paddies. Once this practice was identified and understood, it spread quickly to other families and other villages through a grassroots networking process.

We applied this model to learning practices in the inquiry networks in BC. We found many small yet effective outlier practices where co-agency between teachers and students was a matter of course. As an example, one primary teacher developed a practical approach for teaching young children to read by training slightly older students as reading coaches using a set of teacher developed learning progressions. Her work was reflected in a book chapter[14] and also in a video titled "Learners in the Lead."[15] Once other educators could see what this strategy looked like – and the impact it was having – practices shifted rapidly in other parts of the province. On-going searches for innovative practices and on-line publications of case studies,[16] video documentation and regional storytelling events add to the repertoire of promising practices. An annual network symposium where inquiry teams from across the province share their work introduces new thinking, reinforces the sense of common purpose and provides multiple opportunities to make learning visible.

2. Link influencers

In inquiry learning networks the strongest influencers tend to be those who, regardless of their role, have a repertoire of changed practice combined with a mindset of pervasive professional curiosity. In every school, regardless of the culture or context, we have found individuals who are eager to learn, who want to make a contribution and who are seeking a broader community. Establishing formal and informal ways to link the influencers has been key to creating and sustaining momentum for system change. Linking involves the use of social media, discussions at the annual symposium, widespread use of video, focused social events, engaging in research studies, shared readings and face-to-face meetings for groups of cross-role educators. These educators embrace a spirit of generosity and have a drive to influence learning practices more broadly than just in their own settings.

> The network brings together educators of all levels and then puts them all on the same level, making us teaching and learning resources for each other. We are all learners; we are all drivers of change; we are all important in the system.
>
> (Network teacher, 2016)

Cross-role linkages are critically important. Students, support workers, teachers, vice-principals and principals, Elders, university faculty, community members, teacher candidates and their mentors can be linked and strengthened through inquiry networks and coherent frameworks. One of the mantras of the inquiry networks is that, when entering a network meeting, everyone leaves their formal role at the door and enters simply as a learner.

3. Infuse intelligence

Teachers are busy people who do not always have the time to seek out the most current research and practice evidence about what will make a difference for their learners. When they have a chance to learn from the innovative practices of their colleagues – and when they work within the discipline of the spiral of inquiry where new learning is an expected and essential part of the process – promising new practices can spread more quickly.

Provincial network leaders curate and disseminate research evidence in a way that is readily accessible. The partnership with the Center for Innovative Educational Research (CERI: OECD) has provided BC networks with key research insights, useful strategies from other countries, cognitive frameworks and tools and critical friendship. Emphasizing the importance of the learning principles from the OECD has helped to keep an informed and intelligent focus across schools and regions. International researchers who can stimulate and challenge thinking in person through the annual symposium also make valuable contributions. Seeking both strong internal practices and powerful international research evidence has helped keep on-going professional learning central to the work of the inquiry networks:

> The network provided me with new ideas, skills and tools, but more than that, it provided me with a learning community that allowed me to make real changes in my classroom.
>
> (Network teacher, 2016)

4. Develop fresh energy through leadership programs and international connections

Sometimes, inquiry groups operate in cultures where support from the formal district leadership team or the local associations may be weak. It is understandable that even the most determined of educators can become discouraged under such circumstances. In these cultures, we have found that infusing fresh leadership energy at a variety of levels helps to build and sustain momentum. It has been important in our work to create formal graduate level leadership programs[17] where participants systematically acquire and apply knowledge about inquiry, innovation, leadership, Aboriginal worldviews and deeper forms of learning. Graduate students use these concepts to change the experiences of learners in their schools and communities. Their face-to-face and online experiences help to create new communities and networks of support for on-going innovative practices. One of the key findings of an early study of international leadership programs (Huber, 2004) was the importance of sustaining the connections among participants after the formal program had concluded. Creating a space for graduates of BC leadership programs to stay linked and to continue to learn in collaboration with others has been helpful in infusing new energy into inquiry networks.

Strengthening lateral connections across institutional and geographic boundaries also helps to bring fresh energy to the inquiry networks. We are pleased that links with educators in England through the Whole Education Network are opening up new opportunities for teacher learning. New connections that are being forged with educators in Australia and New Zealand are creating opportunities that are mutually beneficial.

5. Persist

Observing the challenges of system change in BC and in other jurisdictions has led us to a deeper understanding of the necessity for persistence. There are few, if any, quick fixes. We have seen centralized efforts to mandate change through school-to-school networks flounder and fade away. To create learning systems with high quality, high equity and deep forms of intellectual engagement requires a willingness to persevere over time. As Steven Johnson points out in *Where Good Ideas Come From* (2011, pp. 77–78):

> Most hunches that turn into important innovations unfold over much longer time frames. They start with a vague, hard-to-describe sense that there's an interesting solution to a problem that hasn't yet been proposed, and they linger in the shadows of the mind, sometimes for decades, assembling new connections and gaining strength. And then one day they are transformed into something more substantial. Sustaining the slow hunch is less a matter of perspiration than of cultivation. You give the hunch enough nourishment to keep it growing, and plant it in fertile soil, where its roots can make new connections. And then you give it time to bloom.

Developing more innovative learning environments requires active cultivation. Successful cultivation of any kind requires persistence and attention to the soil conditions. Inquiry learning networks that tackle difficult goals *must* be prepared to persevere often amidst shifting policy and political environments. Having key network leaders in a variety of roles can help accelerate the pace of change and sustain the momentum. Provincial policy makers who minimize mandates and create space for inquiry and innovation to thrive are helping to support new and stronger educational practices. Persistence matters in the building of networks and it matters in sustaining effort and momentum.

> The network as a learning community and support system creates the conditions for educators to make real and lasting changes in practice. As a teacher, the network gave me the support I needed to make changes within my classroom and with my colleagues. As an administrator, the network gives me a vehicle to connect with my staff and school to help influence change on a larger scale. With the network, I can work alongside teachers in a way that is non-threatening and non-hierarchical. It is not top

down or inauthentic. There is rigor and accountability but it is built on true collaboration with a true purpose.

(Network educator, 2016)

Financial support matters and persistence matters more. The inquiry networks in BC have benefited from on-going financial support from the Ministry of Education over the past 17 years. Compared to the investments made in some other jurisdictions, the overall amount of the provincial contribution is modest.[18] We have taken a micro credit approach to supporting schools in the network by providing a small grant[19] at the completion of a year's focused inquiry. Schools are not incentivized to join a network – rather they are thanked for their contribution.

In conclusion, we believe teachers involved in inquiry learning networks in British Columbia are making a significant contribution to system reform. By finding the emerging practices, linking the influencers, continuously infusing new knowledge, developing new leaders at all levels of the system and persisting over time, the BC inquiry networks are helping to change the learning lives of young people in our province and in the Yukon. We are convinced that inquiry networks create and cultivate spaces for professional curiosity and collaboration. As teachers participate in networks of disciplined, collaborative inquiry, they become the leaders of change.

Notes

1 www.oecd.org/edu/ceri/Canada-BC-Monitoring-Note-2.pdf
2 http://noii.ca
3 www.bced.gov.bc.ca/abed/performance.htm
4 See for example Brooke Moore's wiki http://ownlearning.wikispaces.com and Jacob Martens' blog http://renomyclass.com
5 For background information and suggestions on how to incorporate First Peoples Principles of Learning into all learning settings please see this blog created by JoAnne Chrona: https://firstpeoplesprinciplesoflearning.wordpress.com
6 www.bced.gov.bc.ca/perf_stands/
7 www.conferenceboard.ca/hcp/details/education.aspx
8 www.oecd.org/pisa/keyfindings/pisa-2012-results.htm
9 http://dashbc.ca/what-we-do/programs-initiatives/healthy-schools-network/
10 http://noii.ca/aesn/
11 http://youngreaders.ca
12 See for example www2.viu.ca/education/programs/masters/medl/distance/MEDL_brochure_distance.pdf
13 The evolution of this approach is described in *The Power of Positive Deviance: How Unlikely Innovators Solve the World's Toughest Problems* (2010) by Pascal, Sternin and Sternin.
14 See Earl and Timperley's (2008) *Professional Learning Conversations: Challenges in Using Evidence for Improvement,* Chapter 5, pp. 534–68 (Dordrecht, NL: Springer).
15 www.youtube.com/watch?v=FYqE98VP-QA
16 http://noii.ca/case-studies/ and http://noii.ca/aesn/case-studies/
17 www2.viu.ca/calendar/Education/mastereducation.asp#distance; http://telp.educ.ubc.ca

18 In 2015–2016 the Province contributed $70,000 to the networks of inquiry and innovation.
19 $500 CDN was provided to each school in 2016.

Bibliography

Department for Education and Skills (DfES). (2005). *Creating and Sustaining Effective Professional Learning Communities, Research Report RR 637*. London: Bolam, R., McMahon, A., Stoll, L., Thomas, S., Wallace, M., Greenwood, A., … Smith, R. Retrieved on 4 June 2016 from http://dera.ioe.ac.uk/5622/1/RR637.pdf

Dumont, H., Istance, D. & Benavides, F (Eds.). (2010). *The Nature of Learning: Using Research to Inspire Practice*. Paris: OECD.

Earl, L. & Timperley, H. (2008). *Professional Learning Conversations: Challenges in Using Evidence for Improvement*. Dordrecht, NL: Springer.

Halbert, J. & Kaser, L. (2013). *Spirals of Inquiry for Equity and Quality*. Vancouver, Canada: BCPVPA Press.

Hargreaves, A. & Fink, D. (2005). *Sustainable Leadership*. San Francisco: Jossey-Bass.

Huber, S. G. (2004). *Preparing School Leaders for the 21st Century: An International Comparison of Development Programs in 15 Countries*. London: Taylor and Francis Group.

Istance, D. (2017). *Innovative Learning Environments Handbook*. Paris: OECD Publications.

Jensen, B. (2016). *Beyond Professional Development: Teacher Professional Learning in High Performing Systems*. Retrieved on 22 May 2016 from www.ncee.org/beyondpd/

Johnson, S. (2011). *Where Good Ideas Come From: The Natural History of Innovation*. New York: Riverhead Books.

McGregor, C. (2013). *Aboriginal Inquiry: Lifting All Learners. An Impact Assessment of the Aboriginal Enhancement Schools Network (AESN). Report to the BC Ministry of Education and The Office of the Federal Interlocutor, Aboriginal and External Relations Branch, Aboriginal Affairs and Northern Development Canada*. Retrieved on 22 May 2016 from http://inquiry.noii.ca

Nelson, T. H. (2009). Teachers' collaborative inquiry and professional growth: Should we be optimistic? *Science Education, 93*(3), 548–580. doi:10.1002/sce.20302

Pascal, R., Sternin, J. & Sternin, M. (2010). *The Power of Positive Deviance: How Unlikely Innovators Solve the World's Toughest Problems*. Boston, MA: Harvard Business Press.

Timperley, H. (2011). *Realizing the Power of Professional Learning*. London: Open University Press.

Timperley, H., Kaser, L. & Halbert, J. (2014). *A Framework for Transforming Learning in Schools: Innovation and the Spiral of Inquiry. Center for Strategic Education Seminar Series, Paper No. 234*. Melbourne, Australia: Center for Strategic Education.

Timperley, H. & Parr, J. (2011). *Coherence and Inquiry as Key Dimensions for Sustainability of Professional Learning. Improving Learning For All: Learning from the Literacy Professional Development Project*. Retrieved on 22 May 2016 from www.literacyonline.tki.org.nz

Timperley, H., Wilson, A., Barrar, H. & Fung, I. (2007). *Teacher Professional Learning and Development: Best Evidence Synthesis Iteration*. Wellington, New Zealand: New Zealand Ministry of Education. Retrieved on 3 June 2016 from www.educationcounts.govt.nz/publications/series/2515/15341

3 Teacher leadership within and across professional learning communities

Louise Stoll, Chris Brown, Karen Spence-Thomas and Carol Taylor

Collaboration is now the name of the game. Increasing complexity and the pace of change facing education systems have led to increased demands around teachers' practice and professionalism. A call from the OECD argues that education today necessitates "high-level knowledge workers who constantly advance their own professional knowledge as well as that of their profession" (Istance, Vincent-Lancran et al., 2012, p. 36). In line with this, a growing number of countries now expect that their teachers will draw on and generate evidence as they develop their practice. But an expectation of collective responsibility also underlies the quote.

Knowledge work has a collegial element – its purpose is not just for individual gain; it must enhance the profession as a whole. Teachers in "21st century schools" have to be confident and innovative. Collaboration is viewed as integral to this (Schleicher, 2015), through the orientation of professional development towards developing professional learning communities in schools (OECD, 2013), and peer networks now being viewed by the OECD as a core feature of teacher professionalism (OECD, 2016).

Developing professional learning communities (PLCs) or networks does not happen by itself; it needs the energy and influence of leadership. If PLCs are to be sustainable and impactful, leadership cannot only be the domain of one person or a few people "at the top"; it has to ripple throughout schools; in short, teacher leadership needs to be harnessed. In England this particularly means ensuring that those teachers designated "middle leaders" have the knowledge, skills, and attributes that enable them to draw, use, and develop evidence to promote PLC activity within and across schools that makes a difference to colleagues' practice and students' learning experiences and outcomes.

In this chapter, we first explore the context for middle leadership within and across professional learning communities within England. We then describe three relevant national projects led by team members, offering some findings. Finally, we conclude with cross-cutting messages from the projects about impactful evidence-informed teacher leadership of change and improvement within and across professional learning communities.

England's policy context for professional learning communities

The landscape of England's school system has shifted quickly over the last few years. Collaboration can be found in a policy focus on partnership working between schools to develop what has been described as a "self-improving school system" (Hargreaves, 2010) – schools supporting each other's improvement. While this goes back to earlier policy initiatives, this is increasingly intertwined with increased autonomy of schools (Department for Education [DfE], 2010, 2016). There is a fast-growing autonomous system where over 60 percent of secondary schools and 15 percent of primary schools are now academies or free schools, out of local authority (district) control and directly responsible to national government, with the intention that this number will increase significantly (DfE, 2016). Aligned policy promotes increasing collaboration between schools through academy chains and multi-school trusts and federations, with an emphasis on ensuring that collaboration between schools will drive up standards (DfE, 2016). Many schools are connecting with others, whether through formal or informal partnerships and networks. School-to-school support and peer-to-peer learning are viewed as important strategies to raise standards and improve the quality of teachers and school leadership, and Ofsted's[1] framework inspects how effectively schools work in partnership.

In England, strong school leaders and schools who support other schools' development are also a core feature of the self-improving school system. Among several examples is a national network of teaching schools. Outstanding schools apply to become teaching schools, supported by an alliance of other schools and partners.[2] In October 2015, there were 692 designated teaching schools across 538 teaching school alliances, with 32 percent of schools known to be part of a teaching school alliance (TSA) as of October 2014 (Gu et al., 2015). Teaching schools initially had six leadership responsibilities, one of which was research and development (R&D).[3]

Schools in England also have a designated "middle leader" role. This person may have responsibility for a subject, for a cross-curricular aspect of teaching and learning, for pastoral care of students, for a particular stage, or for a phase of schooling.

Developing teaching as an evidence-informed profession

Alongside the emphasis on collaboration, a thrust has been towards developing teaching as an evidence-based[4] profession. England's National College for Teaching and Leadership suggests that this will exist when:

> All teaching practice reflects both individual teaching expertise and the best and most up-to-date external evidence from systematic research.
> (Hammersley-Fletcher & Lewin, 2015, p. 9).

Schools are increasingly expected to use evidence when selecting, implementing, and evaluating improvement efforts.[5] Many schools draw on research to identify reliable and good value interventions with demonstrable impact, and some schools encourage teachers to use evidence in the classroom (Nelson & O'Beirne, 2014). If a self-improving system underpinned by evidence-informed teaching is to become a reality, leadership needs to spread beyond senior leaders and involve middle leaders who become champions for change, evidence use and evaluation of impact, and act as catalysts in helping to change the system (Stoll, 2015a). Professional learning communities (PLCs) offer a potentially powerful vehicle for this kind of change where teachers use evidence to create knowledge and collaborate within and across schools to share this knowledge, as well as develop and deepen their practice.

Professional learning communities in England

Unlike some jurisdictions where PLCs refer to small groups of teachers who come together at mandated times, the national research which introduced "professional learning communities" in England (Department for Education and Skills [DfES], 2005a) explored whole-school, collaborative, open, reflective, and growth-oriented cultures. The term is used in England in several ways:

- an entire school staff can be described as a PLC – some schools advertise themselves as such;
- smaller groups of teachers within a school are sometimes referred to as a PLC (Harris & Jones, 2010) although other terms are also used, e.g. teacher learning communities (Wiliam & Leahy, 2015);
- cross-school PLCs also exist; for example, the Ealing Professional Learning Community (Stoll, Halbert, & Kaser, 2011), although learning communities spanning colleagues from more than one school frequently go by other names, including network, partnership or alliance.

Despite these differences in interpretation, we would expect to see familiar characteristics of PLCs as identified in the literature (e.g. Stoll et al., 2006), but also characteristics that fit the greater emphasis on knowledge work. For example:

- members are purposeful; their common goal is to make a positive difference to all students' learning experiences and outcomes now and for the future – with a focus on having an impact. In TALIS's (OECD, 2013, p. 3) terms, professional learning communities in England, as elsewhere, are "developing the values, norms, and shared expectations";
- they are inclusive, trusting, mutually supportive, and collectively responsible for the learning of students and each other;
- they are endlessly curious, investigating and learning more about their practice together through inquiry, collaborative forms of learning, and

joint practice development (DfES, 2005b; Sebba, Kent, & Tregenza, 2012). Crucially, they deprivatize practice (Louis, Kruse, & Associates, 1995) through reciprocal scrutiny and critical friendship;

- they have the necessary structural architecture, within (DfES, 2005a) and between schools (e.g. Hadfield & Chapman, 2009);
- to be evidence-informed as knowledge workers, they also need to create, exchange, and circulate knowledge, including through stimulating learning conversations, and supported by external facilitators where necessary (Stoll, 2015a; Brown, Daly, & Liou, 2016).

In England, while collaborative activity is increasingly common, unless this is underpinned by deep collegiality (Little, 1982) focused on enhancing learning and teaching, we would argue that the term "professional learning communities" is inappropriate.

Leadership is essential to PLCs' success (Hipp, 2006). Effective leadership strengthens professional community which, in turn, strongly predicts the teaching and learning practices strongly associated with student achievement (Louis & Wahlstrom, 2012). Creating, developing, and sustaining PLCs is a major strategic leadership task. While the contribution of the head teacher (principal) and senior staff are crucial, distributed leadership also has a positive influence on student learning outcomes when it occurs in "planful ways" (Harris, 2009). Middle leaders – teacher leaders such as heads of subject departments or subject coordinators – can be fundamental to successful school improvement and improved teacher practice in leading teaching and learning. Through their commitment to supporting peers' development and the learning of students beyond those they teach, they demonstrate collective responsibility, a core characteristic of PLCs.

Three projects

Our involvement in three national R&D projects has enabled us to investigate middle leadership within and across professional learning communities in England. Our emphasis is on how middle leaders can become change catalysts within and across schools to have an impact. In this respect, common features of all three projects are the involvement of members of the team as facilitators, at least at early stages, and the use of evidence to inform collaborative inquiry processes. Two projects – a middle leader knowledge exchange project with Challenge Partners, a national voluntary network of schools, and a national teaching schools network inquiry project – are completed at the time of writing. The third – Research Learning Communities, a research use randomized control trial project – was nearing completion at the time of writing and provided the opportunity to further examine methodologies and test out findings in a pilot with potential for national scale up. The three projects took different stances on the conceptualization of PLCs, but all participants were introduced to the underpinning research.

Middle leaders as catalysts for improving teacher practice

This one-year applied research project, funded through the Economic and Social Research Council's Knowledge Exchange Scheme,[6] was designed, co-facilitated, and jointly evaluated by a partnership involving the London Centre for Leadership in Learning at the UCL Institute of Education (IOE) and Challenge Partners. The UCL IOE team was led by Louise Stoll and included the other authors. Challenge Partners is a collaborative group of 350+ schools across England, focused on improving the quality of teaching and leadership in pursuit of better outcomes for its students. It provides a vehicle for schools that wish to learn from the best of their peers via effective networking, with "hubs" (networks) established across the entire partnership.[7]

We worked with a group of leading Challenge Partners schools' middle leaders to explore and develop teacher leaders' capacity throughout the partnership to share expert knowledge with other middle leaders and teachers, especially in other schools. This also included tracking their interventions' impact through to changes in teachers' practice and, ultimately, student learning, progress, and development (Stoll & Brown, 2015). By the project's end the group of 16 "catalyst" middle leaders were extending this learning to their hub school partners, and some were sharing the outcomes more widely to benefit a broader range of educators.

The middle leaders acted as a PLC, supporting and challenging each other as they worked with or developed smaller PLCs within their own spheres of influence within their school (e.g. a secondary school mathematics department, a primary school key stage) or with other schools (e.g. a group of middle leaders in their hub partner schools). They also learnt more about developing whole-school PLC conditions to support their efforts.

Our project questions were:

1   What do we know about effective middle leadership within and across schools that changes teachers' practice?
2   What are powerful ways to share knowledge about excellent middle leadership practice within and across schools?
3   What evidence-based tools can be designed collaboratively between Challenge Partners middle leaders and academic partners to track changes in teachers' practice as a result of middle leaders' interventions?
4   What leadership conditions in schools help develop and embed cultures of shared outstanding practice?

Combining research findings with their own practice knowledge, the middle leaders created and refined processes and tools to help them lead more effectively and track their impact, testing ideas and trialling tools in their own and other schools through face-to-face and social networking activities. They evaluated these experiences and impact on themselves and colleagues, using self-evaluation tools to analyze changes over time, and jointly developed processes to embed the notion of sharing high-quality research-informed practice between schools in their networks and for practitioners elsewhere.

An iterative co-construction process combining research-based and practice-based knowledge generated answers to the research questions (Stoll, Brown, Spence-Thomas, & Taylor, 2015). Seven messages (answers) were derived for each question and verified against data gathered. Final "key messages" were then validated with Challenge Partners' colleagues who had attended workshops.[8] Drawing on workshop and evaluation data, these "soundbite" messages were expanded and used to develop professional (leadership) learning resource cards (Stoll, 2015c).

Middle leaders as change catalysts

We concluded that middle leaders within and across schools are more likely to change teachers' practice when they understand how to lead change, read and develop their knowledge of relevant research, use this and other data to identify issues, inform changes, improve practice, and evaluate progress. This gives them further confidence to take initiative. The most successful middle leaders had drive and energy, stimulated meaningful, informal conversations to connect and support development, and were outward-facing, networking and seeking great practice elsewhere. They role-modelled, championed improvement, were constructive critics, involved others, and kept morale up. They were clear about their vision of great teaching and learning and understood the importance of strategically planning ahead, but adapted plans to fit different colleagues' needs. They also supported and coached colleagues to experiment and develop new practice, developing a trusting, collaborative culture within their smaller professional learning teams in which colleagues felt valued.

Tracking impact

Middle leaders learnt research-informed approaches to tracking impact (e.g. Guskey, 2000; Timperley, 2011; Halbert & Kaser, 2013) – an essential feature of professional learning communities – and enabled others to do the same. They designed tools that they found powerful in helping stimulate and track changes in colleagues' practice and which were focused on improvements in students' learning. Impact measures were contextualized to specific situations and issues, but inquiry processes always included a baseline against which impact could be judged (Taylor & Spence-Thomas, 2015). They crafted questions to open up conversations between them and colleagues, shifting the emphasis from accountability of colleagues to their professional development. Catalysts described changes in colleagues' practice and greater openness to change because the process helped build ownership. Follow up interviews highlighted how tools were being used in different situations, and that some catalysts had influenced senior leaders to embed them within school development plans.

Seven messages the middle leaders generated about tracking impact were that in supporting and challenging colleagues to track impact they need to:

1   *Start with the end in mind* – Ensure shared understanding about the difference they want to make, by focusing on the benefit to learners and listening to their voice up front, whether this is a student or a teacher. Well-designed questions help to elicit issues.
2   *Know what they're measuring* – The ultimate impact is always improvements in student learning. Collecting a baseline enables tracking of progress and comparisons to be made at the end. Colleagues then can explore what has had the desired impact using different methodologies – gathering both "hard" and "soft" data.
3   *Plan clear action* – Informal conversations, supported by understanding great practice and knowledge of research findings, help identify appropriate interventions. Professional learning opportunities, time, and space are arranged to help put plans into action. Progress is monitored.
4   *Share ownership* – Collaboration between middle leaders and practitioners is important, as they share the same experience. Engaging in positive, supportive, and challenging dialogue, questioning and coaching, helps build a culture of trust.
5   *Plan for sustainability* – The process is part of whole-school development. Big picture thinking ensures that it's not just superficial change, but is something that lasts. Attention is paid to checking that it's working and using feedback to improve the process.
6   *Provide opportunities for reflection* – Knowing what made the impact is central. Middle leaders and teachers need to ask themselves "have I made a difference?" and need time and space to reflect on this.
7   *Treat it as an ongoing cycle* – The whole process of auditing, training, developing capacity, and measuring impact repeats itself.

Figure 3.1 presents an impact-tracking cycle based on middle leaders' presentations of their collaboratively designed tools and interview data highlighting successful elements in stimulating changed behaviour of colleagues.

The process is intended to be collaborative and sustainable. The ongoing learning conversations help stimulate reflection and encourage co-ownership of the learning process. Introducing relevant external research helps to inform decisions about interventions or strategies to try out. A check-in conversation identifies barriers and enables refinements to be made for greater impact. A further conversation then explores the evidence of change, further data collected, and then impact on student learning experiences and outcomes is assessed. The cycle then continues.

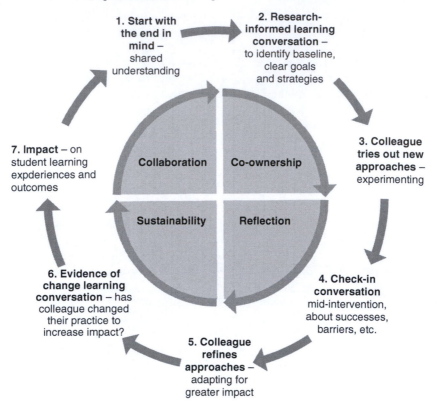

Figure 3.1 Middle leaders' impact-tracking cycle focused on colleague's practice change and student learning

Knowledge sharing within and across schools

Most middle leaders' initial knowledge about tracking impact was superficial and tacit – this wasn't something they discussed in school meetings or informally with colleagues. Their understanding of the theory underpinning impact tracking deepened throughout the project and they had used it with colleagues. Most were now sharing this knowledge within their schools and some also with other schools, for example through an early years' network and in a secondary school network using research lesson study (Dudley, 2014).

We found that sharing knowledge about excellent middle leadership and other practice within and across schools is enhanced when middle (teacher) leaders create a culture for learning with openness to dialogue, where people can speak their minds in a safe environment, issues are explored, and experimentation and acceptable risk taking is encouraged. They also need to understand others' contexts and realities through observing practices and meetings in different contexts, and careful listening so they can tailor support approaches and bring back ideas to their own school. The most successful middle leaders created opportunities to share successes and innovation, using professional learning forums, meetings, newsletters, and social media to help build shared objectives around knowledge exchange, and were supported by time and resources. They also devoted attention to finding common interests and goals, involving participants in the change, and distributing leadership.

Teaching Schools Research and Development Themes project

Over two-and-a-half years from 2012–2014, teaching school alliances (TSAs) across England involved in the National College for Teaching and Leadership's (NCTL) research and development (R&D) network engaged in collaborative R&D projects investigating three themes:

- Theme one: what makes great pedagogy?
- Theme two: what makes great professional development which leads to consistently great pedagogy?
- Theme three: how can leaders lead successful TSAs which enable the development of consistently great pedagogy?

The NCTL funded 98 teaching schools to undertake collaborative R&D in their alliances within one theme, with one-third focusing on each theme.

The project aimed to:

- support teaching schools to engage in and build their capacity for R&D activities using evidence;
- provide opportunities for training and forums for networking and sharing expertise between teaching school leaders and teachers so that they could learn from each other;
- produce robust evidence to disseminate more widely.

External facilitators from UCL IOE and Sheffield Hallam University were commissioned as the national research partner for themes one and two (Nelson, Spence-Thomas, & Taylor, 2015a). Karen Spence-Thomas and Carol Taylor led the team, and Louise Stoll was involved, also writing an overarching report across the three themes at the project's completion (Stoll, 2015b). This chapter mainly focuses on the 66 alliances involved in themes one and two. To provide structure and direction, we convened regional inquiry clusters once each school term. These inquiry clusters were themselves professional learning communities, although the bulk of their work was carried out with the participating teachers, leaders, and schools in their alliances – their own professional learning communities.

These clusters aimed to support them to develop and embed a sustainable model for deep professional learning through a rigorous and supported R&D methodology (Harris & Jones, 2012) elaborated with the UCL IOE's own impact framework (Earley & Porritt, 2014), based on Guskey's (2000) work on evaluating impact of professional development. The TSAs were focused on making a difference. Ultimate goals were enhanced student learning and social outcomes and many projects targeted these directly. Others focused on creating and evaluating conditions necessary to ensure the great teaching and learning experiences that would lead to that impact. Ensuring the early involvement and engagement of middle leaders was particularly relevant.

It was important to find ways to connect teachers with the research base. Schools were encouraged to engage in innovative and creative ways with bespoke literature reviews produced for each theme (Husbands & Pearce, 2012; Stoll, Harris, & Handscomb, 2012). Each review proposed "claims" from the literature which schools used to reflect on their practices and to determine focus areas for inquiry and joint practice development. TSAs and schools also chose to draw on a range of other research sources and/or Higher Education Institute (HEI) support.

These findings are based on analysis of final reports, case studies, and impact reports written by project leaders. Case studies (Nelson, Spence-Thomas, & Taylor, 2015b) were written to a common structure and describe activity and findings under the R&D methodology phases of *implementation, innovation,* and *impact.* Evidence from the final reports and case studies were compared with claims from the literature reviews which formed part of the framework for the research.

Impact on students and teachers

Many of the cross-school PLC projects, which targeted student learning both directly and indirectly, showed a range of impact on these students. Project evaluations identified positive effects in a range of curriculum outcomes, e.g. literacy skills, mathematical problem solving, attitudes to reading, etc. Improved engagement and confidence, increased independent working, managing self-behaviour, mindfulness, and improved orientation to learning were other positive outcomes. For example, one TSA focused on using higher-order thinking skills through exploratory talk. Outcomes included more evidence of children questioning each other and engaging in dialogue which involved cause and effect, predicting, seeking, and verbalizing patterns. Cross-school networking also had positive effects on many involved teachers and other staff, including enhanced classroom practice, increased confidence, better planning for effective assessment, and increased subject and pedagogic knowledge, with the ability to articulate this clearly. Teachers reflected more and used a wider range of strategies, with greater inclusion of students in designing resources. Staff now worked more closely with colleagues, readily seeking and sharing pedagogies, engaging in improved professional conversations, and being more involved in and enjoying R&D. Examples also exist of improved staff morale and self-esteem.

There were also significant shifts at school level with the growth of new research, coaching, or lesson study cultures. Growth in leadership capacity resulted from opportunities offered to teachers engaged in leading and working with small groups of colleagues, and positive impacts on students led to more widespread staff confidence. One TSA's focus had been coaching to raise attainment and address transition issues. Outcomes included teacher leadership competences developed as a direct result of involvement, with success evidenced in 70 percent of coaches gaining senior leadership positions and 50 percent of coachees promoted into middle leadership following their project involvement.

Teacher leaders and their roles in tracking impact

As TSAs joined the project in three waves over the two and a half years, so the roles of those participating changed. For the first group of schools the majority of staff attending regional clusters were TSA heads or principals. By wave two, several head teachers had distributed project leadership to a senior colleague with designated responsibility for R&D. By wave three, middle leaders and more recently qualified teachers, often loosely defined as "research champions", were brought on board to drive collaborative investigations within and across schools. This suggests a strategic move by schools over time to create capacity for R&D by shifting its leadership from senior level through to the middle tier and even directly and more widely to classroom teachers. This distribution of leadership within and across schools as part of a collaborative inquiry process appears to be important for sustainability and capacity building. Where collaborative activity was most productive, senior leaders created a clear and compelling shared vision for the difference it would make for student learning. They then operationalized this by creating the PLC structural conditions of time and space for middle and teacher leaders to engage positively with each other over time. Enabling teachers to centre their enquiries in their classrooms within a common, overarching, cross–alliance theme or focus was highly motivating and effective, ensuring that teacher engagement was more likely to be sustained over time (Nelson et al., 2015a).

Teacher leaders can play a powerful role in tracking impact. Impact depends on teacher leaders having the commitment and the skills to know what difference their interventions make. Facilitators worked with their teachers to flesh out the desired impact of the investigations on student learning and outcomes. Teams then gathered baseline evidence of practice and learning against which the impact of changed practices could be evaluated. This process of individual, classroom-centred visioning proved empowering for teacher leaders, providing them with a rigorous framework with which to think deeply about and articulate their students' needs. Inquiry facilitators – who were frequently middle or teacher leaders in phase three – supported inquiry teams of teachers to analyse data and determine whether changes in teacher practices had brought about improvements in student learning. Collaborative approaches, for example research lesson study (Dudley, 2014), enabled teachers to grow in confidence and develop the criticality necessary to critique and scrutinize each other's practices.

TSAs combined "external" knowledge from the literature reviews with their experiential, practice-based knowledge to create insights and capabilities in ways which were new for them (Nelson et al., 2015a). They rarely focused exclusively on one claim. In one TSA, blending five different research claims about effective pedagogies in projects helped deepen participants' insights and enrich their learning. Analysis following each of two cycles of lesson study showed that the process had "opened some teachers' eyes to how many children were learning to calculate without necessarily understanding the structure behind what they were doing. Using manipulatives had enabled teachers to get an insight into the pupils' understanding" (Nelson et al., 2015a, pp. 37–8).

Research Learning Communities project

This Education Endowment Foundation (EEF)-funded project's aim was to test a pilot designed to increase research use and improve learning outcomes among primary (elementary) school teachers at scale. Led by Chris Brown and involving two other authors, we have been developing then exploring the efficacy of an approach that has involved researchers working intensely with small groups of practitioners, many of whom are teacher leaders. These practitioners, in turn, have been charged with engaging in peer-to-peer support with a much greater number of colleagues. As in the other projects, therefore, we have different forms of professional learning communities operating within one project.

The EEF has a mandate to invest in proven initiatives and stipulated the necessity for an independent evaluation of the pilot, including a randomized control trial to assess its impacts effectively.[9] This includes effectiveness in terms of increasing research use (the process evaluation) as well as the ability to raise outcomes for pupils in national assessments at Key Stage 2.[10] In line with this, we recruited 110 primary schools across England, with half forming Research Learning Communities (RLCs) (made up of ten groups of 5–6 schools), and half forming the control group.

Teacher leadership is fundamental to RLCs

Teacher leadership is fundamental to RLCs. Each school engaged in RLC activity provided two leaders: a senior leader and an informal opinion leader (teacher leader). Formal leadership buy-in to research use is vital. School leaders promote the vision for and develop the culture of a research-engaged school. They also provide necessary resources and structures for sustained and meaningful research use (DfES, 2006). Their first-hand participation ensures that such activity is more likely to remain a priority. In addition, they can "walk the talk": in demonstrating commitment and engaging in leadership for learning (Southworth, 2009), they are more likely to ensure wider school buy-in.

At the same time, if leadership is a process of influence, leadership activity can be undertaken by more than those possessing formal responsibility. Informal leaders frequently determine the fate of change initiatives, and implementing initiatives must attend to the informal day-to-day aspects of an organization (Spillane, Healey, & Kim, 2010). Drawing on our existing experience about the importance of catalysts, in designing the project, we knew it was essential to have the right people in the room. Social network analysis was used to identify and map informal structures and understand the roles of social actors within these structures. Specifically, we were interested in how potential central actors – teacher leaders – in favour of the idea of research-informed practice might act as research "champions", circulating research knowledge within their schools. Based on this rationale, each participating primary school is represented by a senior leader (sometimes the head teacher) and a teacher leader evidence champion.

Research Learning Communities extends the concept of professional learning communities

Research Learning Communities (RLCs) have evolved from the literature on professional learning communities (PLCs) and networked learning communities (NLCs). RLCs, however, were designed with the specific purpose of increasing research use in schools at scale. So their networked approach explicitly focuses on learning from and building upon existing academic knowledge to tackle key teaching and learning issues. As a result, knowledge creation activity within them necessarily has to centre on learning conversations (Earl & Timperley, 2008) between explicated practitioner knowledge and academic knowledge, with experience and external knowledge/theory brought to the fore and made equal partner with practitioner knowledge (Brown & Rogers, 2015; Stoll & Brown, 2015). In addition, to achieve expertise in evidence use among large numbers of practitioners, RLC activity takes place within a double helix of activity. This ensures that first, newly-created knowledge and solutions that build on such knowledge can be engaged with practically and so help RLC participants build an understanding as to when and how it is appropriate to use them (i.e. to develop their expertise). Second, RLC leaders have the opportunity to build capacity to engage with and share their expertise with others, who can then also begin to practise what they have learned through a subsequent structured series of activities within their individual schools. This has the added benefit of RLC participants, those who are "one step ahead" in terms of their understanding and ideas, being able to gain further understanding through modelling and for others to be able to learn through interaction with their peers (Penuel, Sun, Frank, & Gallagher, 2012).

The process draws on and extends the methods and findings of the two previous projects. We work with the pairs of leaders in their ten RLCs, who came together for a one-day workshop four times a year in the first year supported by UCL Institute of Education researcher-facilitators (Coburn, Penuel, & Geil, 2013), team members conversant with using evidence and able to engage participants in learning conversations. Workshops focus on a specific issue of importance identified by schools and agreed on in advance and introduce research evidence that investigates "what seems to work" in relation to these issues. Researcher-facilitators engage in learning conversation exercises to enable participants to:

• engage interactively with both research and their own and colleagues' tacit practice-based knowledge;
• conceive of specific enquiries (in terms of issues) that apply to their school and develop, trial, and embed evidence-informed solutions to tackle these; and
• evaluate the impact of these approaches employing a variety of perspectives.

Cycles of inquiry are central to RLCs' activity. After analysing approaches to developing cycles of inquiry (e.g. Halbert & Kaser, 2013; Timperley, 2011; Harris & Jones, 2012; Schildkamp & Ehren, 2013; Coburn et al., 2013), and considering RLC project requirements to increase dissemination and research use within schools, the RLC's cycle of inquiry principles were developed.

1   The inquiry has to be grounded within the RLC's overall focus area.
2   It has to be data informed: it needs to address a real issue faced by the school, not one based on perception.
3   Because the inquiry is data informed, baseline data can and should be gathered so that progress can be ascertained later.
4   Expected outcomes/the resulting transformative vision should be determined so that participants (and those in their "home" school) understand what is expected of them.
5   Research evidence needs to be employed as part of solutions developed to address the issue of inquiry.
6   All activity within the inquiry cycle must involve meaningful interaction between those participating in the RLC and members of their "home" school.
7   Impact of evidence-informed solutions must be evaluated to ascertain their use value.
8   Results of the evaluation should be shared (with other RLC participants and back in their "home" schools).
9   Following evaluation and sharing, solutions should be collaboratively refined, radically changed, or removed, as appropriate.

Sharing with RLC colleagues in other schools has been important, although the first-year emphasis was on within-school inquiry. In year two,[11] RLC leaders took the main role in workshops, taking it in turns to facilitate the learning of their peers in other schools with leading researcher-facilitators offering bespoke resources and support around networked inquiry.

Impactful teacher leadership within and across professional learning communities

Through the opportunity to collaboratively develop, lead, and analyse these projects and their impacts thus far, our thinking is evolving. The RLCs project enabled us to continue testing these ideas and trialling others for better understanding and increased impact. Meanwhile, we conclude with messages about impactful teacher leadership within and across professional learning communities.

Teacher leaders are more likely to have an impact within and across PLCs when supported by evidence-informed collaborative inquiry that stimulates powerful conversations

Our experience suggests that blending data and external research evidence within an impact-oriented inquiry framework helps middle leaders to ensure they make a difference for students and for teachers' practice. We are continuing to refine and extend our inquiry cycle principles, but our evidence (including emerging experiences from RLC initiatives) is that when provided with compelling and accessible research findings on relevant teaching and learning issues, teacher leaders can quickly become conversant with and interested in deepening their knowledge about their practice. They engage in deep conversations about how best to test out interventions, the benefits, drawbacks, and ethics of using control groups, and how to track impact, as well as the importance of not over-claiming impact. It is also necessary to remember that teacher leaders are not academics and that using research, inquiry processes, and tracking impact does not, nor should it, require them to have doctorates.

Our evidence also demonstrates that these rich, evidence-informed conversations don't stop with the teacher leaders. As they become excited about the inquiry projects they generate, and the impact that they can see, they are sharing their experiences increasingly widely and involving more colleagues.

Teacher leaders are more likely to have an impact within and across PLCs within a culture of trusting relationships

In line with other work on professional learning communities (e.g. Louis, 2008), our projects highlight the need for trusting relationships as a basis for impactful action. In using impact tracking tools, knowledge exchange project participants concluded that stimulating meaningful conversations helped to build the kind of relationship that enabled them to work successfully with colleagues in other schools:

> With somebody you don't know they may not trust you but you have the opportunity to build that trust through the conversation you have. Trust

does need to be built with the person you're working with in order for it to succeed.

(Middle leader reporting on tool use)

The RLCs project social network analysis survey found that higher levels of trust are likely to lead to more frequent ties that result in a variety of reciprocal efforts, including collaboration, learning, complex information sharing and problem solving, shared decision making, and coordinated action – actions essential to development of new and effective practice informed by research and evidence. Consequently, high trust levels appear to lead to teachers perceiving that they are encouraged to use research and that their school's improvement is being driven by research.

Given that these projects include school-to-school relationships, as well as within-school relationships, developing trust with less well-known colleagues is likely to be even more challenging, even if social media is changing the nature of some relationships. Further work is needed on how social networking analysis can support school-to-school learning communities as well as those within schools.

Teacher leaders need the support of senior leaders

Our evidence supports teacher-led reform as a powerful force for change, but it also highlights that senior leaders play a significant role in teacher leaders' ability to develop knowledge and skills around using evidence to increase impact across professional learning communities. In particular, head teachers' commitment to evidence-informed practice is essential. This includes creating a culture in which this is valued and expected, modelling this in their practice, and ensuring that necessary structures provide time, space, resources, and other support. The national R&D project and RLCs project both involved senior leaders as active participants, while the knowledge exchange project was sponsored by head teachers. All projects, however, included examples where teacher leaders did not receive necessary support and backing. Schools are beset by competing priorities, and there are senior leaders who do not appear to see wider benefits of research and data-informed inquiry and other forms of joint practice development. This was a key reason for involving both a senior leader and an opinion former in the RLCs project. Nonetheless, even if head teachers (principals) are convinced about the benefits of evidence-informed practice, persuading them to make changes when other interventions are in full swing can be difficult. While encouraging teacher-led reform in and with PLCs, it is essential that principals understand potential benefits and are given their own opportunities to learn about, experience, and model such forms of evidence-enriched inquiry and joint practice development.

Teacher leaders benefit from external support in their own professional learning
communities to deepen evidence-informed practice and knowledge exchange

Our evidence demonstrates that it isn't sufficient to model excellent classroom practice. Teacher leaders need to understand how to work alongside others within their school and elsewhere over time to articulate and share their knowledge about what makes great pedagogy in systematic ways. They need to learn powerful forms of inquiry. This was not included in many teachers' initial teacher training or they were trained sufficiently long ago that this is not part of their everyday repertoire. Within and across schools, teacher leaders need to be able to: facilitate professional learning; access, critique, and share the external knowledge base; trial new strategies and evaluate their impact; bring colleagues into investigations and build teams; evaluate the impact of changed practice on student learning and achievement; and share findings in accessible and sustainable ways.

Our experience is that it cannot be left to chance that teachers will be able to learn such skills without the support of colleagues and external input. These skills need systematic and structured development from skilled facilitators in supportive PLCs with opportunities to apply and reflect on learning between sessions. Teacher leaders gained considerably from participating in a group of colleagues focused on the same goals. Significant parts of workshops were devoted to colleagues acting as each other's critical friends, supporting and challenging, asking probing questions. Through this, they learnt about each other's successes, difficulties, and how to deal with blockages.

Middle leaders were able to participate in all three projects because of external opportunities and incentives – funding secured or offered to encourage them and their schools to join initiatives that would help them grow aspects of PLC leadership. Each project contained an imperative around building capacity for sustainability of the approach to ensure that middle leaders and their schools can continue to use evidence effectively over time in their PLCs and track impact through to enhanced student learning experiences and outcomes. Time will tell how successful this has been.

Teacher leadership has great potential for strengthening sustainability of
professional learning communities but it can't be left to chance

Reflecting on the national R&D themes project, Nelson et al. (2015a, p. 59) caution: "Mobilising learning from school-led collaborative inquiry to influence wider staff across a school or alliance is challenging and often neglected". Leaders used various strategies to share project outcomes and learning with colleagues within their schools and in other schools. Many approaches focused on raising awareness, but did not always sufficiently engage colleagues to "jump on board" and try out project strategies themselves. Some, however, showed a strong learning orientation in their approach to mobilizing new knowledge. In particular, those using a form of collaborative professional learning or development of inquiry skills within or as their project focus took this forward as a mechanism to engage more colleagues. Teacher leaders played a significant role in this.

The RLCs project highlights how sustainability can be planned through a staged reduction in support process and the other two projects show how existing networks between schools can help extend teacher leaders' impact across a wider canvas, thereby spreading their influence.

Notes

1 England's external inspection agency.
2 www.gov.uk/government/policies/improving-the-quality-of-teaching-and-leadership/supporting-pages/teaching-schools gov.uk website
3 The six responsibilities have now been woven into three: initial teacher training, professional development, and supporting school improvement (DfE, 2016).
4 The terms evidence-based and evidence-informed are used interchangeably in policy documents, although they have different connotations.
5 Two of us have also been involved in a project for the Department of Education evaluating progress towards an evidence-based teaching system – a collaborative project between colleagues at Sheffield Hallam University, the UCL Institute of Education, and Durham University.
6 ESRC Knowledge Exchange Opportunities Scheme R&D project – Grant: ES/l002043/1.
7 See http://challengepartners.org
8 www.lcll.org.uk/uploads/2/1/4/7/21470046/ml_change_catalyst.pdf
9 Full detail on the evaluation including its methodology can be found via https://educationendowmentfoundation.org.uk/projects/research-learning-communities/ and results will be available in 2017.
10 Key Stage 1 refers to 5–7 year olds, Key Stage 2 to 7–11 year olds (KS1 and KS2 are primary stages), Key Stage 3 to 11–14 year olds, Key Stage 4 to preparation for GCSE examinations, and KS5 to preparation for A levels.
11 This was nearing completion at the time of writing.

References

Brown, C., Daly, A., & Liou, Y-H. (2016). Improving trust, improving schools: findings from a social network analysis of 43 primary schools in England. *Journal of Professional Capital and Community, 1*(1), 69–91.
Brown, C., & Rogers, S. (2015). Knowledge creation as an approach to facilitating evidence-informed practice: examining ways to measure the success of using this method with early years' practitioners in Camden (London). *Journal of Educational Change, 16*(1), 79–99.
Coburn, C., Penuel, W., & Geil, K. (2013). *Research-Practice Partnerships: A Strategy for Leveraging Research for Educational Improvement in School Districts*. New York: William T. Grant Foundation.
Department for Education (DfE). (2010). *The Importance of Teaching White Paper*. London: Department for Education.
Department for Education (DfE). (2016). *Educational Excellence Everywhere*. Crown Copyright.

Department for Education and Skills (DfES). (2005a). *Creating and Sustaining Effective Professional Learning Communities, Research Report RR 637.* London: Bolam, R., McMahon, A., Stoll, L., Thomas, S., & Wallace, M.

Department for Education and Skills (DfES). (2005b). *Factors Influencing the Transfer of Good Practice, Research Report RR 615.* Falmer, UK: Fielding, M., Bragg, S., Craig, J., Cunningham, I., Eraut, M., Gillinson, S., Horne, M., Robinson, C., & Thorp, J.

Department for Education and Skills (DfES). (2006). *Successful School Leadership: What It Is and How It Influences Student Learning. Research Report 800.* London: Leithwood, K., Day, C., Sammons, P., Harris, A., & Hopkins, D.

Dudley, P. (2014). *Lesson Study: Professional Learning for Our Time.* London: Routledge.

Earl, L., & Timperley, H. (2008). *Professional Learning Conversations: Challenges in Using Evidence for Improvement.* Dordrecht, NL: Springer.

Earley, P., & Porritt, V. (2014). Evaluating the impact of professional development: the need for a student-focused approach. *Professional Development in Education, 40*(1), 112–129.

Gu, Q., Rae, S., Smethem, L., Dunford, J., Varley, M., & Sammons, P. (2015). *Teaching Schools Evaluation: Final Report December 2015.* Nottingham: NCTL, The University of Nottingham.

Guskey, T. (2000). *Evaluating Professional Development.* Thousand Oaks, CA: Corwin.

Hadfield, M., & Chapman, C. (2009). *Leading School-based Networks.* London: Routledge.

Halbert, J., & Kaser, L. (2013). *Spirals of Inquiry for Equity and Quality.* Vancouver, Canada: BCPVPA.

Hammersley-Fletcher, L., & Lewin, C. (2015). *Evidence-based Teaching: Advancing Capability and Capacity for Inquiry in Schools. Interim Report. Autumn 2015.* NCTL.

Hargeaves, D. H. (2010). *Creating a Self-improving School System.* Nottingham, UK: National College for Leadership of Schools and Children's Services.

Harris, A. (2009). Distributed leadership: what we know. In A. Harris (Ed.), *Distributed Leadership: Different Perspectives.* Dordrecht, NL: Springer.

Harris, A., & Jones, M. (2010). Professional learning communities and system improvement. *Improving Schools, 13*(2), 172–181.

Harris, A., & Jones, M. (2012). Connect to learn: learn to connect. *Professional Development Today, 14*(4), 13–19.

Hattie, J. (2012). *Visible Learning for Teachers: Maximizing Impact on Learning.* London: Routledge.

Hipp, K. (Ed.). (2006). Leadership and student learning in professional learning communities. *Journal of School Leadership, 16*(Special issue), 5.

Husbands, C., & Pearce, J. (2012). *What Makes Great Pedagogy? Nine Claims from Research.* Nottingham, UK: NCSL.

Istance, D. and Vincent-Lancran, S. with Van Damme, D., Schleicher, A., & Weatherby, K. (2012). Teacher development, support, employment conditions and careers. In A. Schleicher (Ed.), *Preparing Teachers and Developing School Leaders for the 21st Century: Lessons from Around the World.* Paris, OECD.

Little, J. W. (1982). Norms of collegiality and experimentation: workplace conditions of school success. *American Educational Research Journal, 19*(3), 325–340.

Louis, K. S. (2008). Trust and improvement in schools. *Journal of Educational Change, 8*(1), 1–24.

Louis, K. S., Kruse, S. D., & Associates. (1995). *Professionalism and Community: Perspectives on Reforming Urban Schools.* Thousand Oaks, CA: Corwin.

Louis, K. S., & Wahlstrom, K. (2012). Shared and instructional leadership: when principals and teachers successfully lead together. In K. Leithwood and K. S. Louis (Eds.), *Linking Leadership to Student Learning*. San Francisco: Jossey-Bass.

Nelson, J., & O'Beirne, C. (2014). *Using Evidence in the Classroom: What Works and Why*. Slough, UK: NFER.

Nelson, R., Spence-Thomas, K., & Taylor, C. (2015a). *What Makes Great Pedagogy and Great Professional Development: Final Report*. Nottingham, UK: NCTL.

Nelson, R., Spence-Thomas, K., & Taylor, C. (2015b). *What Makes Great Pedagogy and Great Professional Development: Case Studies*. Nottingham, UK: NCTL.

OECD. (2013). *Fostering Learning Communities among Teachers. Teaching in Focus. O4 (June)*. Paris: OECD.

OECD. (2016). *Supporting Teacher Professionalism: Insights from TALIS 2013*. Paris: OECD Publishing.

Penuel, W., Sun, M., Frank, K., & Gallagher, A. (2012). Using social network analysis to study how interactions can augment teacher learning from external professional development. *American Journal of Education, 119*(1), 103–136.

Schildkamp, K., & Ehren, M. C. M. (2013). *From "intuition"- to "data"-driven decision making in Dutch secondary schools?* In K. Schildkamp, M. K. Lai, & L. Earl (Eds.), *Data-based Decision Making in Education: Challenges and Opportunities*. Dordrecht, NL: Springer.

Schleicher, A. (2015). *Schools for 21st-Century Learners: Strong Leaders, Confident Teachers, Innovative Approaches*. Paris: OECD Publishing.

Sebba, J., Kent, P., & Tregenza, J. (2012). *Joint Practice Development (JPD): What Does the Evidence Suggest are Effective Approaches*. Nottingham, UK: National College for School Leadership and University of Sussex.

Southworth, G. (2009). Learning centred leadership. In B. Davies (Ed.), *The Essentials of School Leadership (2nd edition)*. London: Sage.

Spillane, J., Healey, K., & Kim, C. (2010). Leading and managing instruction: formal and informal aspects of elementary school organization. In A. Daly (Ed.), *Social Network Theory and Educational Change*. Cambridge, USA: Harvard Education Press.

Stoll, L. (2015a). Using evidence, learning and the role of professional learning communities. In C. Brown (Ed.), *Leading the Use of Research and Evidence in Schools*. London: IOE Press.

Stoll, L. (2015b). *Three Greats for a Self-improving School System – Pedagogy, Professional Development and Leadership: Teaching Schools R&D Network National Themes Project 2012–14*. Nottingham, UK: NCTL.

Stoll, L. (2015c). How do we create and exchange knowledge for systemic change? *ICSEI Monograph Series, Issue 6*.

Stoll, L., Bolam, R., McMahon, A., Wallace, M., & Thomas, S. (2006). Professional learning communities: a review of the literature. *Journal of Educational Change, 7*(4): 221–258.

Stoll, L., & Brown, C. (2015). Middle leaders as catalysts for evidence-informed change. In C. Brown (Ed.), *Leading the Use of Research and Evidence in Schools*. London: IOE Press.

Stoll, L., Brown, C., Spence-Thomas, K., & Taylor, C. (2015). Perspectives on teacher leadership for evidence-informed improvement in England. *Leading and Managing, 21*(2), 76–91.

Stoll, L., Halbert, J., & Kaser, L. (2011). Deepening learning in school-to-school networks. In C. Day (Ed.), *International Handbook on Teacher and School Development*. London: Routledge.

Stoll, L., Harris, A., & Handscomb, G. (2012). *Great Professional Development which Leads to Great Pedagogy: Nine Claims from Research*. Nottingham, UK: NCSL.

Taylor, C., & Spence-Thomas, K. (2015). Understanding impact and the cycle of inquiry. In C. Brown (Ed.), *Leading the Use of Research and Evidence in Schools*. London: IOE Press.

Timperley, H. (2011). *Realizing the Power of Professional Learning*. Maidenhead, UK: Open University Press.

Wiliam, D., & Leahy, S. (2015). *Embedding Formative Assessment: Practical Techniques for K-12 Classrooms*. West Palm Beach, Florida, USA: Learning Sciences International.

4 Teacher–led professional collaboration and systemic capacity building

Developing communities of professional learners in Ontario

Carol Campbell, Ann Lieberman and Anna Yashkina

Introduction

The concept and application of professional learning communities has become widespread in approaches to large-scale system and school improvement. What are less common, however, are teacher-led collaborative communities of professional learners, compared to "professional learning communities" being a whole-school improvement approach or a system-supported strategy for educational change. In practice, you need a combination of these approaches – teacher-led, principal-supported and system-enabled. However, what needs to be considered most are the intended purpose and outcomes of developing communities of and for professional learning. In this chapter, we focus particularly on an example of a teacher-led approach to developing a community of professional learners in order to explore what teachers do, and how they choose to do it, when they have the opportunity and support to develop their own and their peers' professional learning.

Developing a professional community of learners

DuFour and Eaker (1998, pp. xi–xii) explain:

> Each word of the phrase "professional learning community" has been chosen purposefully. A "professional" is someone with expertise in a specialized field, an individual who has not only pursued advanced training to enter the field, but who is also expected to remain current in its evolving knowledge base.
>
> "Learning" suggests ongoing action and perpetual curiosity ... The school that operates as a professional *learning* community recognizes that its

members must engage in the ongoing study and constant practice that characterize an organization committed to continuous improvement.

Much has been written about learning organizations, but we prefer the term "community". An organization has been defined both as an "administrative and functional structure" (Webster's Dictionary) and as "a systematic arrangement for a definite purpose" (Oxford Dictionary). In each case, the emphasis is on structure and efficiency. In contrast, however, the term "community" suggests a group linked by common interests ... In a professional learning *community* ... educators create an environment that fosters mutual cooperation, emotional support, and personal growth as they work together to achieve what they cannot accomplish alone.

Yet, while the emphasis is on community, the intended purpose and outcome is *school* improvement:

> The most promising strategy for sustained, substantive school improvement is developing the ability of school personnel to function as professional learning communities.
>
> (DuFour & Eaker, 1998, p. xi).

Indeed, the concept and practice of professional learning communities originates in a concern for effective approaches to school restructuring (Hord, 1997) and school improvement (Department for Education and Skills [DfES], 2005). As the focus of educational change has become larger – extending to entire education systems (Campbell, 2015; Fullan, 2009; 2010) – strategies to establish and develop professional learning communities within and across schools have also become a common approach (OECD, 2016).

When the content and processes of professional learning communities are effective (DfES, 2005; Stoll, Bolam, McMahon, Wallace & Thomas, 2006), there can be benefits for school improvement, for teachers' self-efficacy and practices, and for students' learning. However, when professional learning communities become something that system or school leaders require all school staff (Hord, 1997) to participate in with externally defined purpose and goals and with prescribed processes, the dangers of "contrived collegiality" (Hargreaves, 1991) emerge:

> Contrived collegiality is characterized by formal, specific bureaucratic procedures to increase the attention being given to joint teacher planning and other forms of working together.
>
> (Hargreaves & Fullan, 2012, p. 118).

As Hargreaves and Fullan (2012) continue to suggest,

> Contrived collegiality is double-edged, though. It has positive and negative possibilities depending on how it is used. At its best, it is a useful way to

kick-start collaborative relationships between teachers where few had existed before. It is a way of putting teachers in touch. Principals can then build on those elements of recognition, trust, and support to focus conversations and activity more tightly around teaching and learning. To avoid confusion here, we prefer to call this *arranged collegiality* – a stepping stone to deeper forms of working together.

[...]

At its worst, though, when arranged collegiality turns into contrived collegiality, it can become a slick administrative surrogate for collaborative teacher cultures.

(pp. 118–19).

The original goals and continuing development of professional learning communities is not intended to be "contrived"; in essence, professional learning communities are – or should be – about engaging, developing and supporting teachers in order to improve schools and benefit students' learning. This is consistent with the key characteristics of professional learning communities identified in research reviews. For example, the DfES (2005) concludes the importance of the following features:

- Shared values and vision.
- Collective responsibility for pupils' learning.
- Collaboration focused on learning.
- Individual and collective professional learning.
- Reflective professional enquiry.
- Openness, networks, and partnerships.
- Inclusive membership.
- Mutual trust, respect and support.

Such approaches can engage teachers authentically and may involve forms of "shared and collegial leadership" (Hord, 1997, pp. 7–8). However, such school-wide professional learning communities are not primarily or exclusively teacher-led. Indeed, while cautioning against omnipotent approaches by school leaders, Hord (1997, p. 6) proposes, "It seems clear that transforming the school organization into a learning community can be done only with the leaders' sanction and active nurturing of the entire staff's development as a community." In the origins and in some forms of the continuing development of professional learning communities, while community is proposed to be inclusive and democratic, the primary leadership is from senior administrators and the focus is on organizational goals and outcomes. Such approaches are important for school improvement, but they differ from emerging understandings of teacher leadership and developing teachers' collaborative professional learning for informed professional knowledge, judgement and practices (Lieberman, Campbell & Yashkina, 2016).

What then, if instead of starting with formal leadership and organizations, the originating purpose was primarily to cultivate teachers as leaders of a community of professional learners? This may appear semantic, but it is significant in changing the intent and the approach to the purpose and implementation of learning communities. In this chapter, I discuss one approach to teacher-led professional learning – Ontario's Teacher Learning and Leadership Program – which may have relevance to rethinking and developing communities of professional learners.

Introducing the Ontario Teacher Learning and Leadership Program (TLLP)

The TLLP began in 2007 as a joint initiative between the Ontario Ministry of Education (Ministry) and the Ontario Teachers' Federation (OTF) with shared goals to:

- support experienced teachers to undertake self-directed advanced professional development;
- develop teachers' leadership skills for sharing their professional learning and exemplary practices; and
- facilitate knowledge exchange for spread and sustainability of effective and innovative practices.

In response to an annual call for TLLP proposals from the Ministry and OTF, experienced teachers can submit a TLLP project proposal. The proposal is to include a description of the proposed project, how the project will contribute to student learning and Ontario's priorities for educational excellence, equity, well-being and public confidence, and a rationale for the proposed TLLP team's professional learning objectives. A plan including specific goals, activities, measures and budget for each of the teachers' professional learning and for sharing is to be submitted. School district committees review applications and submit their priority choices to a provincial committee comprised of teacher union and government representatives, who select projects for funding. In 2016, the tenth cohort of TLLP began.

Successful teacher applicants receive training, support and funding for their TLLP projects. TLLP projects vary considerably in size (from a team of 1 to 60) and budget; however, the average TLLP project has a core team of 2–4 members and budget of $14,000 (CDN). In the May prior to the school year in which they will embark on their TLLP projects, teacher leaders attend a *Leadership Skills for Classroom Teachers* training to support their preparation to take on the professional learning, project management and leadership expectations of a TLLP. TLLP teacher leaders are expected to develop and implement their projects throughout the following school year. Participants become part of *Mentoring Moments*, an online community, and are required to share at least two artefacts from their TLLP. More recently a further online platform, *TeachOntario*, has been created and is becoming widely used by teachers to share resources. In the November of the next school year, following their TLLP projects ending, TLLP teams attend the *Sharing the Learning Summit* to showcase completed projects and to further spread their practices. Typically, a TLLP project spans 18 months from initial training, through implementation and then the culminating Summit. TLLP project leaders are required to submit a Final Report, including information regarding project goals and successes, professional learning, project sharing, challenges and project learning and impact beyond the TLLP funding. In addition, to further spread learning from completed TLLP projects, school districts can apply for Provincial Knowledge Exchange (PKE) funding to provide resources for release time and travel to enable former TLLP teacher leaders to share their knowledge and practices with other schools and school districts across Ontario (and potentially beyond).

We have been funded by the OTF to research the TLLP since 2012 (Campbell, Lieberman & Yashkina, 2013; Campbell et al., 2014; Campbell, Lieberman, Yashkina, Hauseman & Rodway, 2015; Lieberman et al., 2016) and draw on our research in the sections below.

Teachers leading the what and how of their professional learning

Through the TLLP, teachers can propose what particular topic, focus, knowledge and/or practice they wish to explore and develop over the 18 months of a TLLP project. In our analysis of approved proposals for Cohorts 1–6, a wide variety of project foci exist (see Table 4.1). Mainly, the projects connected in some way with provincial, school district and/or school priorities. However, the fact that teachers had *choice* over the focus of their professional learning and they could identify a topic that they were passionate about investigating – for example to innovate a new approach, to examine an area they felt was not currently being well addressed in their school, or to deepen and spread existing knowledge – was extremely important to the teachers involved:

> The fact that the program itself seemed to be designed to empower … instead of the teachers being told what to do by perhaps other research or other consultants or whatever, that this project empowered me and my team to drive what we were doing; we had control of it. I think that was huge … In the 21st century, professional development needs to be customized and driven by the people who want to learn … rather than sitting in a room and being directed to or being instructed at. So, I think that this program was able to customize our leadership, customize our learning as we went along.
>
> (Interview quote from TLLP teacher leader)

Teachers choose also what the intended goals of their TLLP projects will be connected to professional learning and knowledge exchange. Based on analyses

Table 4.1 Cohorts 1–6: Total approved projects by project theme (rank order)

Theme	Cohort 1	Cohort 2	Cohort 3	Cohort 4	Cohort 5	Cohort 6	Total
Differentiated instruction	26	17	34	33	42	38	190
Technology	22	19	29	23	37	41	171
Literacy	38	22	21	15	26	26	148
Professional learning community	27	25	20	16	23	22	133
Student assessment	18	14	20	13	14	19	98
Math literacy	11	15	11	14	19	17	87
Student with special needs	10	9	9	7	13	13	61
Transition years	5	6	13	10	10	7	51
Media literacy	4	5	2	5	10	5	31
French	3	7	5	2	8	3	28
Arts	1	5	6	6	5	3	26
Gender-based learning	4	5	5	7	2	2	25

(Campbell et al., 2014, p. 8)

of recent cohorts of TLLP proposals, the top three goals for the majority of TLLP projects were to develop and improve knowledge (79 percent), strategies (67 percent) and skills (48 percent), mainly with a focus on improving teaching and learning (Campbell et al., 2014, p. 16). Developing professional collaborations within and across divisions and panels within and/or across schools was a goal of almost half of the projects. Projects also planned to develop resources for use in classrooms, professional training sessions or by parents. Other projects aimed to raise awareness of issues such as mental health or Aboriginal education among staff, students and local community. Still others wanted to establish community relationships by connecting with Aboriginal communities, engaging parents or developing school–community projects.

As well as the importance of teacher voice and choice in identifying what the focus and goals of their professional learning would be (Lieberman et al., 2016), the TLLP also enables teachers to lead *how* professional learning will occur for themselves and, vitally, in leading professional learning for other teachers. The majority of TLLP projects involve a core group of two to four teachers working together. Over time, proposals for groups of teachers rather than an individual teacher leading a TLLP have increased and our evidence suggests that group projects spread and sustain professional knowledge and practices further. So the first element of building a community of professional learners is *working together as a group* to lead professional learning. The second element is considering *what approaches to professional learning this group will engage in* to develop their own knowledge, skills and practices. Based on a survey of TLLP teacher leaders in Cohorts 1–7, Table 4.2 indicates that forms of collaborative learning, dialogue and joint work are important.

Participation in such teacher-led professional learning appears to be highly beneficial for teachers' learning and practice. All of the TLLP teacher leaders responding to our survey reported improvements in their knowledge, skills and/or practice. As indicated in Table 4.3, over three-quarters (78 percent) of the respondents reported improvements in their knowledge and understanding, and three-quarters (75 percent) of respondents reported improvements in their instructional practices. Almost three-quarters (73 percent) of the respondents reported improvements in communication and collaboration between teachers. Over half of the TLLP members felt more inspired to teach and try new things

Table 4.2 Professional learning activities (rank order)

What activities/strategies did you/your TLLP team engage in to improve your knowledge/skills/practice?	#	%
Teacher collaborative learning group	167	68.7%
Professional dialogue	164	67.5%
Self-reflection	155	63.8%
Analysis of student data/work	141	58.0%
Literature/research review	138	56.8%
Planning	131	53.9%
Action research	118	48.6%
Workshops/courses	113	46.5%
Networking (including online)	102	42.0%
Co-teaching	95	39.1%
Conferences/seminars	83	34.2%
Working with a specialist/expert	68	28.0%
Working with the community/service organizations	19	7.8%
Other	16	6.6%

(Campbell et al., 2015, p. 7)

Table 4.3 Teacher learning benefits (rank order)

How did your learning and practice improve as a result of your engagement in the TLLP project?	#	%
New knowledge/improved understanding	189	77.8%
Improved instructional practice	182	74.9%
Improved communication/collaboration between teachers	177	72.8%
Greater energy/inspiration	140	57.6%
Increased self-efficacy	132	54.3%
Improved technological skills	121	49.8%
Improved assessment skills	117	48.1%
Improved classroom management skills/practice	79	32.5%
Improved research skills	56	23.0%
Other	19	7.8%

(Campbell et al., 2015, p. 8)

and more self-confident about their practice. Half of the respondents reported improvements in their technological and assessment skills. A third of the respondents also improved their classroom management skills, and a quarter became better researchers as a result of participating in a TLLP project. "Other" benefits included improved relationships with students, parents, community and other teachers.

Teachers leading and developing a community of professional learners

In addition to supporting the TLLP teacher leaders' own learning, a goal of the TLLP is for teachers to lead the professional learning of other teachers, as well as school and system leaders, to develop, share and spread their professional knowledge and practices. In our research (Campbell et al., 2015), over three-quarters (77 percent) of the TLLP projects shared their learning within their own school(s), and 88 percent of those projects shared outside their schools as well, including with other schools, local communities, their own or other school districts and across Ontario. Ten percent of projects shared their knowledge, practices and/or resources nationally and/or internationally. This has involved TLLP teacher leaders developing and expanding professional networks to collaborate, communicate and co-develop professional knowledge and practices.

The most common professional learning activity initiated and undertaken by TLLP participants was teacher collaborative learning. In about 70 percent of the TLLP projects, professional learning communities were created among TLLP members and some others to learn together by analyzing student data, reflecting on practice, creating resources, discussing strategies and teaching together; and almost half of the projects developed learning communities or groups to spread the knowledge and practice beyond the TLLP team (Lieberman et al., 2016). For example, one project on teaching measurement in the elementary panel involved a 15-person TLLP team and undertook a range of activities to develop learning communities:

> We created a PLC [professional learning community] for teachers on different levels: Full staff – big ideas, three part lesson, student data, strengths and needs in teaching measurement; Division – identified areas of learning difficulty for the students, … used measurement continuum based on Ministry expectations for each grade; Teacher Math Quest Planning Teams – work with teachers from other divisions to develop rich tasks designed for the whole school …; Teacher Math Buddies – teachers had an opportunity to observe and work with students at different grade levels. We also created a PLC for students. We paired Junior classes with Primary classes. Students had the opportunity to experience and investigate a wide variety of activities with a peer. They had the opportunity to work with each other, either as a student expert, articulating their thinking, or

as the less experienced learner, observing and learning from their buddies
in a variety of ways.

TLLP Teacher Leader cited in Lieberman,
Campbell and Yashkina (2016, p. 39)

In this example, the professional learning and collaboration moves from the
core TLLP group to a series of professional learning communities engaging
teachers and students.

Almost all TLLP projects (94 percent) used more than one method to share
their learning and/or practices. Broadly speaking, two main strategies were
prevalent. First, the provision of events and opportunities for professional
learning collaborations to occur including workshops and professional
development sessions, teacher learning communities/groups, modeling
practices and classroom visits, and mentoring teachers. Second, TLLP teachers
engaged in communication to share knowledge: in person within their school
(for example, staff meetings) or with a wider audience (for example, conference
presentations); through online communication and collaboration (for example,
websites, blogs and Twitter); and in print forms of communication within
school (newsletters), locally (such as newspapers) or more widely (including
journals and books).

The substance of sharing mattered also; TLLP projects (co)developed and
shared professional resources for use in classrooms, schools and/or communities.
By developing and sharing professional knowledge, practices and resources,
TLLP teachers expand their own learning and become leaders and collaborators
with other teachers for their peers' professional learning also.

The challenges and benefits of leading a community of professional learners of, by and for teachers

While research about teacher leaders encourages teachers to support learning
through professional networks and contribute to school improvement
(Hargreaves & Fullan, 2012; Little, 1990; Rosenholz, 1989), few large-scale
approaches to professional development have tried putting teachers in positions
where they organize the development of ideas, lead, implement and share their
findings and get money and support to organize the development of the work.
In the TLLP, teacher leadership is not about formalized organizational authority
and responsibilities; rather teacher leadership is about influencing, co-developing
and sharing professional knowledge and practices.

In order to understand the process involved in teachers' learning leadership
by doing leadership through the TLLP, we invited TLLP teachers to write
vignettes describing their leadership experiences, successes and challenges while
working on a TLLP project (Campbell et al., 2015; Lieberman et al., 2016).
Nineteen teachers wrote vignettes and from these we discovered that, for
teachers, learning to collaborate was new and challenging, but important in
developing their leadership skills and practices and, ultimately, rewarding.

Moving from working alone to working with others in the development of a project was a huge part of the participants' leadership learning. All vignette writers who worked with someone else wrote that part of their learning was gaining an ability to work with others and keeping everyone involved in contributing (as well as learning). Teachers needed to learn how to keep people involved, how to use other people's strengths and how to build ideas together so that people would stay interested and committed and stick with the project for the year and more. But at the same time, they needed to feel trusted and respected for their contributions. Most of them had never had this kind of experience before; this was a new idea for the majority of teachers who wrote vignettes and it was complicated. Indeed, teachers had to learn how to collaborate in order to develop a community of professional learners. This was challenging for most teachers in our vignettes:

> Sometimes it is difficult to make connections without dictating or overstepping from "facilitating" to "directing."

> Sometimes it is hard to remember that people need to feel heard.

These quotes from TLLP vignette writers begin to show the tensions of organizing teachers (by teachers). Teachers struggled with the right tone and way of moving the work forward and had to learn the nuances of what it means to deepen the work, give peers a way into the group and still get the work accomplished. For the TLLP teachers, learning to lead and participate in professional collaborative communities became powerful.

The TLLP enabled teachers to come to understand that they were gaining leadership experiences in the process of helping organize professional development. Through these experiences, they were given the opportunity to change the culture of their schools as well as the content and pedagogy of their and their colleagues' teaching:

> As team leader, I learned a great deal about leadership and working with other adults. I learned the value of collaborative goal setting and planning and the importance of ensuring that all team members feel like valued contributors.

Half of the teacher vignette writers wrote about how they had to learn to let go of the controls so they could build a team. Many wrote about how they reached out to colleagues and sometimes other groups outside the school to do the work involved in their TLLP projects. Learning to share with others and encouraging them to help shape the ideas was an important part of their leadership experience:

> The team is significant. By enlisting team members who know their input is valued, one creates the great potential for ideas to grow exponentially. This is what happened in our team. A brilliant idea grew brighter and brighter. Team members were acknowledged for their individual strengths.

In terms of leadership, we needed to look inside the project and outside. We developed a shared responsibility. We found that at times one of us would take the lead, and then others who may have essential expertise would assume a leadership role.

In our survey of TLLP teachers (Campbell et al., 2015), 97 percent identified that the TLLP had developed their leadership skills, including facilitation/ presentation skills (74 percent of respondents), project management skills (70 percent of respondents), communication/listening skills (54 percent of respondents), interpersonal skills/relationship building for 53 percent of respondents and troubleshooting/problem solving (47 percent of respondents). Furthermore, the benefits of TLLP projects extend to other adults engaged beyond the core TLLP team. For example, in our analyses of a sample of TLLP Final Reports, 94 percent of adults beyond the core team who were engaged in the TLLP were reported to have improved their knowledge and understanding (see Table 4.4). Vitally, in our survey of TLLP teacher leaders, the majority reported benefits for their students' engagement, learning environments, achievement and/or motivation (see Table 4.5).

Table 4.4 Sample projects: Benefits of shared learning (rank order)

Benefits of shared learning	Projects	
	#	%
Improved knowledge and understanding	31	94%
Inspired to make a change	10	30%
Change in practice	10	30%
Increased self-efficacy	6	18%
Stronger community	3	9%

(Campbell et al., 2014, p. 28)

Table 4.5 Student benefits (rank order)

How have your students benefited as a result of your involvement in the TLLP project?	#	%
Improved engagement	177	72.8%
Enhanced learning experience	164	67.5%
Improved achievement	136	56.0%
Improved motivation	127	52.3%
Improved attitude and behaviour	104	42.8%
Improved technological skills	93	38.3%
Improved learning and innovation skills	78	32.1%
Character development	49	20.2%
Student leadership	45	18.5%
Other	18	7.4%

(Campbell et al., 2015, p. 13)

Teacher-led collaboration and systemic capacity building: developing communities of professional learners

In contrast to some forms of professional learning communities where the membership and purpose are mandated or required by formal district or school leaders, TLLP teams are teacher-initiated, teacher-formed and teacher-developed. Furthermore, generally concepts of "professional learning communities" or "communities of practice" involve a defined set of individual members working *within* a group and usually within one school. The TLLP involved working *between* and *across*, as well as within, groups to further knowledge exchange and sharing of practices. Teachers' knowledge and sharing of practices flow through networks of relationships and interactions, rather than being constrained or restricted to formally-established organizational boundaries. As Warren Little (2010) commented,

> With the introduction of social network theory, we find a shift in gaze from formal organization to the networks of actors engaged with one another in various ways and degrees. Social network theorists suspend or challenge assumptions about the meaningfulness of organizational boundaries and forms, asking instead how patterns of stability and change might be explained by the web of relations through which ideas, information, resources, and influence flow.
>
> (p. xi).

However, while the TLLP is teacher-led, it is not about isolated or individualized teacher autonomy. The TLLP is part of a wider system for teachers' collective and collaborative professional development.

TLLP teachers benefit from the support (or are challenged when there is lack of support) from school principals and district leaders. TLLP teachers also benefit from a system of support in preparation for, in the implementation of and for the spreading and sustaining of their TLLP projects and the knowledge and skills developed. The Ministry and OTF work together to provide a *Leadership Skills for Classroom Teachers* training prior to the start of the TLLP project, provide funding to support the teachers' projects, provide online networking and sharing platforms, troubleshoot to offer advice and support throughout the TLLP project and host a *Sharing the Learning Summit* to bring together all the TLLP projects after their completion. The TLLP is teacher-led, but it is not about individualized or isolated activity.

Furthermore, the TLLP is only one part – albeit a very important part – of the wider development of the human, social and decisional capital involved in "professional capital" (Hargreaves & Fullan, 2012) of teachers in Ontario. Attending to the human capital of the individual capacity and career development of teachers, there is a range of teacher policies and standards, including initial teacher education, a New Teacher Induction Program (NTIP), and Annual Learning Plans (ALP) and performance appraisals (Campbell,

Osmond-Johnson, Lieberman & Sohn, 2017). The TLLP offers an important aspect of social capital – opportunities for professionals to collaborate. In addition, there are also collaborative professional learning opportunities which are principal-led connected to school improvement plans and priorities and also system-wide initiatives connected to provincial priorities, for example in literacy and mathematics. School-wide professional learning communities and system-wide initiatives are important for supporting large-scale changes in practice connected to school and system goals. Teacher-led professional learning communities alone cannot fully replace these needs; however, the essence of teacher-led communities must be the decisional capital (Hargreaves & Fullan, 2012) of valuing, enabling and prioritizing teachers as leaders of their own learning and their peers' learning to develop informed professional knowledge, judgement and practices. In our research, we have evidence of strong benefits of teacher-led communities of professional learners for teachers. Importantly, our evidence indicates benefits also for other adults' knowledge, skills and practices, including school principals, affected by the TLLP projects and also for students' engagement, attitudes and learning (Campbell et al., 2015; Lieberman et al., 2016). We propose that the combination of teacher-led, principal-supported and system-enabled communities of professional learners benefiting students' learning are vital to realizing the intention of a truly professional learning community.

References

Campbell, C. (2015). Leading system-wide educational improvement in Ontario. In A. Harris & M. Jones (Eds.), *Leading Futures: Global Perspectives on Educational Leadership*. London: Sage.

Campbell, C., Lieberman, A. & Yashkina, A. (2013). *The Teacher Leadership and Learning Program: A Research Report*. Toronto, Canada: Ontario Teachers' Federation. Retrieved from www.otffeo.on.ca/en/wp-content/uploads/sites/2/2013/09/tllp_full_report-.pdf

Campbell, C., Lieberman, A., Yashkina, A., Carrier, N., Malik, S. & Sohn, J. (2014). *The Teacher Leadership and Learning Program: Research Report 2013–14*. Toronto, Canada: Ontario Teachers' Federation. Retrieved from www.otffeo.on.ca/en/wp-content/uploads/sites/2/2014/08/TLLP-Executive-Summary-April-2014.pdf

Campbell, C., Lieberman, A., Yashkina, A., Hauseman, C. & Rodway, J. (2015). *The Teacher Learning and Leadership Program: Research Report 2014–15*. Toronto, Canada: Ontario Teachers' Federation. Retrieved from www.otffeo.on.ca/en/wp-content/uploads/sites/2/2015/11/TLLP-Report-2015.pdf

Campbell, C., Osmond-Johnson, P., Lieberman, A. & Sohn, J. (2017). Teacher policies and practices in Ontario. In C. Campbell, K. Zeichner, P. Osmond-Johnson & A. Lieberman (Eds.), *Developing Teachers and Teaching in Canada: Policies and Practices in Alberta and Ontario*. San Francisco, CA: Jossey-Bass.

Department for Education and Skills (DfES). (2005). *Creating and Sustaining Effective Professional Learning Communities, Research Report RR 637*. London: Bolam, R., McMahon, A., Stoll, L., Thomas, S., Wallace, M., Greenwood, A., … Smith, R.

DuFour, R. & Eaker, R. (1998). *Professional Learning Communities at Work: Best Practices for Enhancing Student Achievement*. Bloomington, IN: Solution Tree.

Fullan, M. (2009). Large scale reform comes of age. *Journal of Educational Change, 10*(2–3), 101–13.

Fullan, M. (2010). *All Systems Go: The Change Imperative for Whole System Reform*. Thousand Oaks, CA: Corwin Press.

Hargreaves, A. (1991). Contrived collegiality: The micropolitics of teacher collaboration. In J. Blasé (Ed.), *The Politics of Life in Schools: Power, Conflict and Cooperation*. London: Sage publications.

Hargreaves, A. & Fullan, M. (2012). *Professional Capital: Transforming Teaching in Every School*. New York: Teachers College Press and Toronto, Canada: Ontario Principals' Council.

Hord, S. M. (1997). *Professional Learning Communities: Communities of Continuous Inquiry and Improvement*. Austin, Texas, USA: Southwest Educational Development Laboratory.

Lieberman, A., Campbell, C. & Yashkina, A. (2016). *Teacher Learning and Leadership: Of, By and For Teachers*. London, UK: Routledge/Taylor & Francis.

Little, J. W. (1990). Teachers as colleagues. In A. Lieberman (Ed.), *Schools as Collaborative Cultures* (165–193). London: Falmer Press.

OECD. (2016). *Supporting Teacher Professionalism: Insights from TALIS*. Paris: OECD Publishing. Retrieved from: www.keepeek.com/Digital-Asset-Management/oecd/education/supporting-teacher-professionalism_9789264248601-en#page1

Rosenholtz, S. (1989). *Teachers' Workplace: The Social Organization of Schools*. London: Longman Publishers.

Stoll, L., Bolam, R., McMahon, A., Wallace, M. & Thomas, S. (2006). Professional learning communities: A review of the literature. *Journal of Educational Change, 7*, 221–58.

Warren Little, J. (2010). Foreword. In A. Daly (Ed.), *Social Network Theory and Educational Change*. Cambridge, USA: Harvard Education Press.

5 Teacher leaders in professional learning communities in Singapore

Challenges and opportunities

Salleh Hairon and Jonathan W.P. Goh

Introduction

This chapter considers the possibilities and challenges of developing teacher leadership, at scale, through the system-wide implementation of PLCs in Singapore. The idea of a professional learning community (PLC) has been given a formal status in centralized Singapore education. After a pilot with 51 schools in 2009, using a PLC model which the Ministry of Education (MOE) has produced, along with a tool kit containing relevant frameworks, tools, and templates, about two-thirds of Singapore schools have indicated that they are on board the PLC journey (Hairon & Dimmock, 2012).

By 2010, the MOE formally made PLCs a system-wide and state-led initiative with three main aims: ensuring students learn; building a culture of collaboration; and focusing on student learning outcomes (Training and Development Division [TDD], 2010). The MOE PLC model espouses the use of four critical questions, which were adapted from DuFour et al. (2010): (1) What is it we expect students to learn? (2) How will we know when they have learned? (3) How will we respond when they do not learn? and (4) How will we respond when they already know it? Teacher groups, comprising a handful of teachers sharing either the same grade-level students or content subject, called 'Professional Learning Teams' (PLTs), play the role of deepening pedagogical understanding and competencies using learning tools such as action research and lesson study. PLTs are supported by a Coalition Team, comprising key people in the management team such as the principal, vice-principal, and school staff developer, who provide appropriate structures and culture to support the school's PLC framework (Lee & Lee, 2013).

Although the Singapore education system is highly centralized (Hairon & Dimmock, 2012; Dimmock & Tan, 2013), the implementation of PLCs has a tight-loose combination (Lee & Lee, 2013). While school leaders are strongly encouraged and expected to implement PLCs, the nitty-gritty details are to be decided by school leaders and teachers. The setting aside of weekly 1-hour timetable time for PLCs and using the four critical questions to guide PLC discussion are examples of tightness in implementation. The choice of learning tools (e.g. action research or lesson study) for PLC discussions is an example of looseness in implementation. The tight-loose combination is understandable bearing in mind the need to maintain standards across schools, yet being cognizant that teacher-led professional learning such as PLCs requires a fair degree of autonomy by the schools that implement it.

The motivation behind the state-wide and state-led PLC initiative is mainly to do with satisfying the MOE's primary goal of providing school curricula that are sensitive to the needs and challenges of the 21st century – that is, reconstructed curricular models that support diverse learning needs of students yet are consistent with 21st century competencies. The prevailing force pushing for these reconstructed curricular models is the *Teach Less, Learn More* (TLLM) policy initiative, which was announced in 2004 and commenced in 2005 (Ministry of Education [MOE], 2005). At the heart of this policy initiative is the emphasis on school-based curriculum development that essentially requires the extension of school autonomy and enhancement of teacher competency – all of these are inter-related. In order to make school-based curriculum development happen, schools do need to be given greater autonomy to make the necessary changes to the curriculum. Furthermore, this autonomy must go beyond school senior (e.g. principal) and middle (e.g. heads of department) leadership positions, and to include teachers making appropriate changes to their teaching pedagogies. In this regard, the MOE has even crafted the slogan 'Bottom-Up Initiative, Top-Down Support' to emphasize the importance of teachers trying out curricular innovations along with the support to be given by school leaders and the MOE within the ambit of the schools' niche areas (e.g. Learning for Life Programme and Applied Learning Programmes). All these, however, imply that teachers' teaching competency must be enhanced in order to make school-based curriculum development work successfully.

The growth in the interest of PLCs has been brought about by not only school leaders' support to the MOE, but also the intuitive rationale that PLCs can enhance teacher learning and student learning. This coupled with the centralized support structure provided by the MOE such as the mandatory 1-hour timetabled time for PLCs and training for PLC team leaders has helped to sustain the continued momentum of PLCs in Singapore schools. However, the implementation of PLCs is not devoid of real challenges. These include the following: ambiguities in what PLCs look like in practice; time and workload constraints; lack of teacher belief in the effectiveness of PLCs; lack of common interest and goals among PLC members; weak facilitation skills; tension between the need for ground-up, teacher-led PLC initiative and hierarchical work culture; lack of strong leadership support; and insufficient leveraging of PLCs in achieving school objectives (Hairon & Dimmock, 2012; Hairon, Goh & Diwi, 2014). Even though resolving these challenges in a comprehensive and coherent manner is needed, schools are compelled to strategically use limited resources to address these challenges.

One promising way of resolving these challenges is to build the capacity and competency of teacher leaders leading PLCs. In their PLC study investigating the impact of PLCs on student learning outcomes, Hairon, Goh, Chua and

Wang (2015) identified the crucial role of PLC team leaders in building collaborative culture, developing teacher competencies, and ensuring improvements in classroom teaching. As PLCs tend to favour ground-up change in teaching and learning, teacher leaders are inadvertently involved with working and leading other teacher colleagues in PLC contexts. They are in ideal positions and situations to impact the way teachers collaborate with one another to collaboratively implement changes in teaching practices so as to impact on student learning outcomes. Once the link between teacher learning and student learning is achieved, PLCs become sustainable insofar as it motivates teachers to participate in PLCs. However, the task of leading PLCs has its own challenges too.

In this chapter, we seek to give further insights into the challenges that teacher leaders might face in PLCs drawn from Rasch analysis on questionnaire data. We will first present key challenges pertaining to PLC enactment followed by the rationale for investing in teacher leadership to support PLCs, albeit focusing on participation in PLCs. We will then present the findings of the Rasch analysis, followed by a discussion on the findings.

Challenges in implementing PLCs

The challenges to PLCs in school settings have been fairly well documented. One of the most common challenges is to do with time, or the lack of it. The lack of time has been cited as the biggest hindrance for professional learning communities (Flogaitis, Nomikou, Naoum & Katsenou, 2012; Chou, 2011; Jaipal & Figg, 2011; Schechter, 2012; Slick, 2002; Parks, 2009). Finding time within school days to implement new practices is often difficult for teachers. It is indeed difficult to find the appropriate time for teachers to meet in groups (Flogaitis et al., 2012). Furthermore, not all teachers are able to commit to all meetings due to their job demands (Maloney & Konza, 2011). In such a given situation, teachers may regard engagement in collaboration and communal discourse as an encroachment of their valuable time. Furthermore, Slick (2002) contends that teachers will likely require more than 20 percent of their work time for learning and collaboration if they are to be successful in implementing ambitious reform initiatives.

Besides the practical challenge of time, Schecter (2012) highlighted several obstacles inhibiting teachers' participation in learning communities. These include fear of exposure resulting from invasion of privacy and fear of criticism. There seems to exist in learning communities a tacit agreement to expose one's vulnerability to others, which triggers tension that comes from having to reveal to others some of their uncertainties in relation to practice (Savoie-Zajc & Descamps-Bednarz, 2007). Therefore, without appropriate in-school culture, teachers could view learning as a criticism of their work, and perhaps as undermining their authority. Gough (2005) attributed this difficulty as being largely associated with the lack of participants' familiarization with participative and self-critical processes and with their difficulty in showing trust in this different quality of communication offered by the community of practice.

Also many schools are not accustomed to participative and collaborative processes. Jeffers (2006) asserts that learning communities are generally teacher-driven without a clear-cut, pre-determined structure and are dependent on the group to agree each new stage, which interestingly can generate much uncertainty in teachers. Hence, some teachers would prefer a more defined structure and clearer directions rather than the more participative type of relationship. Carroll, Rosson, Dunlap, and Isenhour (2005) highlighted their findings that in many organizations, collaborating with peers, sharing resources, and codifying know-how are not typical facets of work activity. Collaboration therefore can be even more difficult in schools than in other organizations because of the structure and culture of schools (Seo & Han, 2012). The assumption here is that the more hierarchically structured an organization or institution is, the less the chances are of forming a community of practice. Since the functioning of a school is based on specific and institutionally-defined structures, it is more difficult to break free from its existing culture and to put aside or overturn well-established attitudes and habits (Flogaitis et al., 2102; Seo & Han, 2012).

Finally, the lack of leadership supporting learning communities has been identified as a challenge (Harris & Jones, 2010). Leadership plays an important role for the creation of supportive conditions that would encourage the function of learning communities in school organizations. Shifting traditional patterns of interaction, building networks of trust, and opening up students' work for all to examine requires appropriate leadership support (Nelson, 2008). In this regard, it is not sufficient to merely create opportunities within a school day or in addition to teachers' traditional work for teachers to come together as a PLC. Teachers need support in the processes of inquiry and the creation of an environment that models, nurtures, and embeds an inquiry stance (Slick, 2002). School leaders are essentially members of a learning community and are entitled to engage in its most important enterprise (Levine, 2010). Hence, the enactment of PLCs will be hindered without appropriate leadership support.

These challenges have been observed in the Singapore education setting (Hairon & Dimmock, 2012; Hairon, Goh, & Diwi, 2014). These include ambiguities in what PLCs look like in practice, time and workload constraints, lack of teacher belief in the effectiveness of PLCs, lack of common interest and goals among PLC members, weak facilitation skills, tension between the need for ground-up teacher-led PLC initiatives and hierarchical work culture, lack of strong leadership support, and insufficient leveraging of PLCs in achieving school objectives. Notwithstanding these multi-faceted and inter-related challenges, and the temptation to resolve them in a comprehensive way, we argue that focusing on building the capacity and competency of facilitation and thus teacher leadership in PLCs is one significant way to produce positive outcomes.

Teacher leadership in support of PLCs

The term teacher leadership is not a new concept and has been around for more than two decades largely emanating from the professionalization discourse in the USA in the 1980s and 1990s (Frost, 2012). Since then it has gained a footing in the educational reform discourse to varying extents but predominantly in Western Anglophone countries. Notwithstanding the lack of agreement on the definition and conceptualization of the term for the last 20 years (Leonard, Petta, & Porter 2012), the definition given by York-Barr and Duke (2004) seems to be most compelling – that is, 'the process by which teachers, individually or collectively, influence their colleagues, principals, and other members of school communities to improve teaching and learning practices with the aim of increased student learning and achievement' (pp. 287–288). This conceptualization was derived from their literature review on teacher leadership resulting in an overarching conceptual framework. The framework consists of seven components: 1) characteristics of teacher leaders; 2) type of leadership work engaged in by teacher leaders; 3) conditions that support the work of teacher leaders; 4) means by which teachers lead; 5) targets of their leadership influence; 6) intermediary outcomes of changes in teaching and learning practices; and 7) student learning.

York-Barr and Duke (2004) were not alone in attempting to come up with a conceptual framework for teacher leadership. Muijs and Harris (2003) framed teacher leadership as containing four aspects: 1) brokering role of teacher leaders to ensure that links within and across schools are in place and that opportunities for meaningful development among teachers are maximized; 2) participative leadership role of teacher leaders where they work collegially with other teachers to encourage the examination of instructional practices; 3) mediating role of teacher leaders where they become sources of instructional expertise and information; and 4) teacher leaders' role in forging close relationships with individual teachers through mutual learning. Extending this conceptualization, Harris (2005) highlighted four aspects in the definition of teacher leadership: 1) creation of collegial norms; 2) opportunities to lead; 3) working as instructional leaders; and 4) re-culturing schools.

In their work, Leonard, Petta, and Porter (2012) claimed that numerous studies over the last 20 years have wrestled with the definition and conceptualization of teacher leadership. In their analysis of selected studies that directly or indirectly pertain to teacher leadership, they concur with the definition of teacher leadership outlined by Katzenmeyer and Moller (2001) – that is, 'Teacher leaders lead within and beyond the classroom; identify with and contribute to a community of teacher learners and leaders; influence others toward improved educational practice; and accept responsibility for achieving the outcomes of that leadership' (p. 6).

The close relationship between teacher leadership and teacher learning in communities (e.g. PLCs) has been sufficiently highlighted in the literature (e.g. Lieberman & Mace, 2009; Mindich & Lieberman, 2012). Harris (2003) claimed that the optimal function of teacher leadership is in the direct establishment of PLCs within and between schools. Harris (2005) asserts that PLCs embrace the notion of teacher leadership insofar as they assume teachers to be catalysts for change and development towards a commitment to shared collaborative learning in a community. Teacher leadership understandably provides the means for open communications, trust and rapport, and continuous inquiry and improvement of work, which are characteristics of PLCs (Childs-Bowen, Moller, & Scriver, 2000). Some researchers argue that teacher leadership is centrally embedded in communities – that is, it 'contributes to long-term, enhanced quality of community life' (Crowther, Kaagen, Ferguson, & Hann, 2002, p. xvii).

In the Singapore education context, we argue that teacher leadership is the next phase of leadership development supporting school improvement. As contemporary education reforms demand greater substantive transformation in curriculum and pedagogy, the greater the need for school leaders to distribute decision-making power and leadership (Harris, 2016), especially on curriculum and pedagogy, to staff members beyond middle leaders such as Heads of Department (HODs), Subject Heads (SHs), and Level Heads (LHs) to teacher leaders such as Senior Teachers (STs), Lead Teachers (LTs), Subject Reps, and Level Reps or Coordinators. The need to distribute decision-making on curriculum and pedagogy is further compounded by the rise of accountability mechanisms that are put in place by not only policymakers, but also parents and the general public, and the rise in the use of popular social media platforms.

Understanding the enactment and the difficulties that teacher leaders face in PLCs is therefore critical to ensure their effectiveness when such difficulties are appropriately attended to and resolved. Consistent with this argument, three key practices of teacher leaders have been found to have significant impact on PLCs (Hairon, Goh & Chua, 2015). They are (1) building collegial and collaborative relations, (2) promoting teacher development and learning, and (3) enabling change in teachers' teaching practices. The findings and discussions presented in the remainder of this chapter will focus on how teacher leaders lead participation in PLCs.

The findings presented in this chapter were drawn from a Rasch analysis of questionnaire data collected from 56 Singapore teachers from 11 primary schools (refer to Hairon & Goh, 2015, for details on Rasch analysis). The questionnaire contained eight items measuring the construct on teacher leadership practices supporting participation in PLCs. Teacher respondents were asked to rate their respective schools' PLC teacher leaders' practices supporting participation in PLCs using a 5-point Likert scale.

Findings

Based on the Wright Map (Figure 5.1), the mean person's ability, or specifically the strength of perception of teacher leadership to support participation in PLCs, is 1.88 (SD 2.94) logits away from the mean item's difficulty, which is set at 0. This suggests that teacher respondents generally are highly agreeable that their teacher leaders support participation in PLCs. Furthermore, the mean person's ability is slightly more than 2 standard deviations from the mean item's difficulty suggesting that the cohort sample for this study generally finds the items easy to agree to. In total, 36 out of 56 teacher respondents or two-thirds of the teacher respondents (64.3 percent) found all eight items easy to agree to. Further, about a third of teacher respondents (20 out of 56) found difficulty in agreeing to Items 4 and 2. Both of these items suggest the difficulty teacher leaders faced in getting every member to contribute to discussions without imposing on members. With regard to Item 2, although two-thirds of teacher respondents consider that teacher leaders do not compel members to speak during discussions, this poses the problem of non-participation in discussions. Conversely, although one-third of teacher respondents consider that teacher leaders do compel members to speak up during discussions, this poses the problem of forced participation in discussion. Both ways, it attests to the difficulty of teacher leaders in getting every member to contribute to discussions without coercion.

In terms of items analysis, Table 5.1 summarizes the degree of difficulty in agreement by respondents in descending order.

Table 5.1 Note: SD 0.86

Logit	Qn No.	Item
1.97	2	My facilitator does not impose on members to speak up during discussions.
0.51	4	My facilitator makes sure that every member contributes to the discussion.
−0.01	1	My facilitator provides clear direction to the group.
−0.19	6	My facilitator encourages members to have common values while working together in the group.
−0.19	7	My facilitator helps members complement one another's strengths.
−0.37	3	My facilitator ensures the well-being of individual group members.
−0.76	5	My facilitator encourages members to reach agreement on decisions.
−0.96	8	My facilitator ensures that the PLC environment is non-threatening to new members.

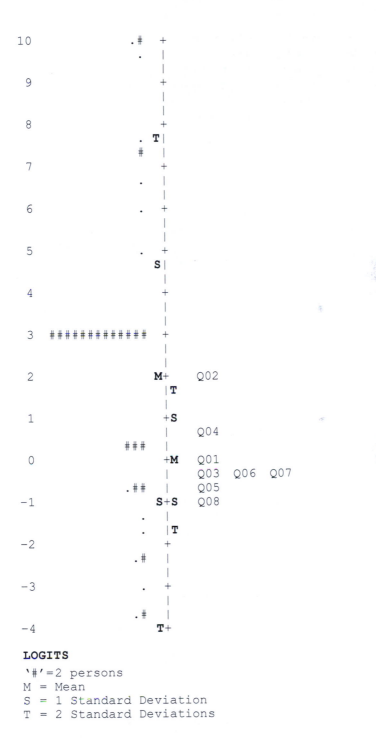

```
  10            .#   +
               .    |
                    |
   9                +
                    |
                    |
   8                +
               .  T|
              #     |
   7                +
               .    |
                    |
   6           .    +
                    |
                    |
   5           .    +
                  S|
                    |
   4                +
                    |
                    |
   3  ############  +
                    |
                    |
   2              M+   Q02
                  |T
                    |
   1              +S
                  |   Q04
            ###   |
   0              +M   Q01
                  |    Q03  Q06  Q07
              .## |    Q05
  -1            S+S   Q08
               .  |
               .  |T
  -2              +
              .#  |
                  |
  -3           .  +
                  |
              .#  |
  -4            T+
```

LOGITS

'#' = 2 persons
M = Mean
S = 1 Standard Deviation
T = 2 Standard Deviations

Figure 5.1 Person map of items

The item's difficulty analysis suggests that teacher leaders found least difficulty in building collegial relations in PLCs in relation to all other items as evidenced from Items 8, 5, and 3 insofar as they are able to support new members joining in, help members reach agreement on decisions, and safeguard the well-being of individual members. The analysis further suggests that teacher leaders found relative ease in supporting how members work collaboratively in relation to the rest of the items in terms of complementing one another's strength and having common values as evidenced from Items 7 and 6. However, the analysis suggests that teacher leaders found providing clear direction to groups as neither a strength or weakness as evidenced from Item 1.

The analysis also suggests that teacher leaders found relative difficulty in relation to the rest of the items in optimizing individual members to contribute to group discussions. Although in terms of person's ability analysis only about a third of teacher respondents (35.7 percent) found difficulty in agreeing to Item 4, the items' difficulty analysis shows that the task of optimizing individual members to contribute to group discussions in PLCs is considered hard in relation to the rest of the tasks. Finally, the analysis shows that leading others without imposing on others to participate in a PLC is the hardest as evidenced in Item 2, which is about three times harder than Item 4 in terms of logits – 1.97 and 0.51 logits correspondingly.

Discussion

The findings suggest there is a spread of difficulties or challenges that teacher leaders are confronted with when engaging in PLCs. From the Wright map analysis, the spread of difficulties or challenges that teacher leaders leading PLCs faced can be grouped into five types – in order of difficulty. The first and the easiest in terms of leading members to participate in PLCs is the building of collegial relations among PLC members. In essence, teacher leaders need to have the necessary skills to create a safe and trusting environment for members to learn and work with one another. In this regard, the importance of trust in PLCs has been well established (Hipp, Huffman, Pankake & Olivier, 2008; Lieberman & Miller, 2011). It is all too apparent that without trust no relationship can survive or thrive, and that all solid relationships need to be built on trust. Although the importance of trust is so apparent, it can become too obvious to be missed out in the equation in leading others to form successful PLCs.

The next area of difficulty is ensuring teachers can collaborate with one another. Teacher leaders need to be aware therefore that members of the PLC, who are generally teachers, share the same overarching goal of optimizing student learning, and thus to direct members' resources towards improving student learning.

The third area of difficulty or challenge that teacher leaders faced in supporting participation in PLCs is clarity of direction to members. This type of teacher leadership enactment can be considered fundamental insofar as leadership is essentially influencing others towards shared goals (Bush & Glover, 2003). While members of PLCs may share common values in the collaboration with one another, they still require clarity in the intended outcomes resulting from them coming together and collaborating with one another. Although there is the universal goal of enhancing student learning, members need to know the specifics of the goal and the means to reaching the goal. The need to influence others on shared goals and shared values among group members – a feature of consensual power relations (Haugaard, 2002) – would thus become a key defining feature in leading PLCs.

The fourth area of difficulty teacher leaders faced in supporting participation in PLCs was ensuring that every member contributes to discussions. A PLC cannot work fully if one, a few, or a majority of the PLC members are not willing to share their knowledge with the group. Getting the participation of every member is crucial bearing in mind that the strength of a community rests on how every member contributes their individual views to discussions. The task of teacher leaders to support participation by ensuring every member contributes his or her individual knowledge to the PLC can therefore understandably be a daunting task taking into consideration that every individual is uniquely different one to another.

The fifth area of difficulty that teacher leaders faced in supporting participation in PLCs is leading without imposing on others – that is, without coercion. This task is challenging when teacher leaders need to ensure that the individual members contribute to the discussion out of their own free will instead of being coerced into participation in discussions. The dilemma thus becomes one where teacher leaders have to ensure that every member contributes to discussions, but doing so without coercion. We are all too familiar with the notion and problem of 'contrived collegiality' (Hargreaves, 1994). The 'shared decision' aspect of distributed leadership (Hairon & Goh, 2015; Harris, 2013) or 'participative leadership' (Muijs & Harris, 2003) thus becomes more apparent in teacher leadership than leadership enacted by school leaders. The need to respect the individual members' decision to participate is also consistent with Tönnies' (1887) conception of *Gemeinschaft* (community) in contrast to *Gesellschaft* (society or association), arguing that *Gemeinschaft* is a more cohesive social entity than *Gesellschaft* because of the 'unity of will' – that is, unity of motives or intentions. Teacher leaders thus have to first allow assertions of individual members' will, but then to congeal all individual members' wills to become one.

The central difficulty that teacher leaders faced in supporting participation in PLCs is closely related to the ambiguity surrounding the concept of community. There is currently a lack of substantive grounding in the theory of community in the education (Bolam et al., 2005; Hairon et al., 2017; Grossman, Wineburg & Woolworth, 2001; Watson, 2014). This explains why ambiguities in what PLCs mean and how PLCs look is one key challenge identified in the literature. Likewise, it explains why members in PLCs are themselves uncertain about participating in PLCs (Jeffers, 2006). If teacher leaders do not fully understand the concept of community well enough, they are going to be unable to lead a community successfully. In this regard, the work of McMillan and Chavis (1986) on 'sense of community' can be instructive in aiding our understanding of the concept of community. McMillan (1996) identifies four dimensions of community: 1) spirit – feeling that there is a community, membership, sense of belonging, acceptance; 2) trust – feeling that the community can be trusted, influence, order, group norms; 3) trade – feeling that mutual benefit comes from community, reinforcement, shared values; and 4) art – shared emotional connection in time and space.

In addition, some of the key ideas presented by McMillan and Chavis (1986) and McMillan (1996; 2011) on the concept of community can be found in the four types of teacher leadership practices supporting participation in PLCs. The first type on building collegiality as part of participation in PLCs is consistent with the idea of *membership* where members feel that there is a sense of acceptance and emotional safety with one another. The second type on collaboration as part of participation in PLCs is consistent with the idea of *influence* where there is inter-dependence between members and the community, and the community and members through the presence of group norms. The third type on clarity of direction is consistent with the idea on *trade* – that is, the feeling that mutual benefit comes from community, reinforcement, and shared values. The main benefit that the members of the PLCs share is positive gains in student learning.

Conclusion

The underlying premise of this chapter is that teacher leadership can have a multiplier effect in terms of resolving many of the challenges that pertain to the implementation of PLCs in schools. The central argument which we propose is that teacher leadership in PLCs can bring about the translation of teacher learning in PLCs to gains in student learning – and the latter will sustain the former. When the connection between teacher learning in PLCs and student learning gains is sustained, school leaders will provide appropriate support for PLCs and teachers will prioritize energy and time in engaging in PLCs.

The findings from the Rasch analysis also suggest that schools have to strategically invest in the development of teacher leadership to support PLCs, and empirical studies do need to look further into the micro level operationalization of teacher leaders in supporting and sustaining participation in PLCs, which is at the heart of a community. The findings of the study suggest the need do this at the system level. Hence, the MOE, through the Academy of Singapore Teachers (AST), will need to not only continue investing in the development of teacher leadership to support PLCs, but being cognizant of the different levels of growth required in the development of PLC teacher leaders.

Since its introduction in 2010, the AST has continued the work of its predecessors – specifically, the Teachers Network (TN) – in developing team leaders facilitating teacher learning in communities through its regular workshops for PLC team leaders (refer to Hairon & Dimmock, 2012, for more details on AST and TN). The Singapore education system has long been known for its ability to provide quality teaching *nationally*. Singapore school leaders are likewise strongly encouraged to lead *nationally*. The effort at developing teacher leaders leading PLCs must likewise be done *nationally*. Setting aside time for PLCs does not automatically translate to positive impact on teaching and learning. PLCs require strong leadership from within the system and across the system in order to develop and sustain collegial interactions among team members so as to impact classroom practices and student learning outcomes.

References

Bolam, R., McMahon, A., Stoll, L., Thomas, S., Wallace, M., Greenwood, A., ... Smith, R. (2005). *Creating and Sustaining Effective Professional Learning Communities, Research Report RR 637*. London: Department for Education and Skills (DfES).

Bush, T., & Glover, D. (2003). *School leadership: Concepts and evidence*. Nottingham, UK: National College for School Leadership.

Carroll, J. M., Rosson, M. B., Dunlap, D., & Isenhour, O. (2005). Frameworks for sharing teaching practices. *Educational Technology and Society, 8*(3), 162–175.

Childs-Bowen, D., Moller, G., & Scriver, J. (2000). Principals: Teachers of leaders. *NASSP Bulletin, 84*(616), 27–34.

Chou, C. H. (2011). Teachers' professional development: Investigating teachers' learning to do action research in a professional learning community. *The Asia Pacific Education Researcher, 20*(3), 421–437.

Crowther, F., Kaagen, S. S., Ferguson, M., & Hann, L. (2002). *Developing teacher leaders: How teacher leadership enhances school Success*. Thousand Oaks, CA: Corwin Press.

Dimmock, C., & Tan, C. Y. (2013). Educational leadership in Singapore: Tight coupling, sustainability, scalability, and succession. *Journal of Educational Administration, 51*(3), 320–340.

DuFour, R., DuFour, R., Eaker, E., & Many, T. (2010). *Learning by doing: A handbook for professional learning communities at work* (2nd ed). Bloomington, IN: Solution Tree Press.

Flogaitis, E., Nomikou, C., Naoum, E., & Katsenou, C. (2012). Investigating the possibilities of creating a community of practice. Action Research in three educational institutions. *Journal for Critical Education Policy Studies, 10*(1), 217–233.

Frost, D. (2012). From professional development to system change: Teacher leadership and innovation. *Professional Development in Education, 38*(2), 205–227.

Gough, A. (2005). Sustainable schools: Renovating educational processes. *Applied Environmental Education and Communication, 4*, 339–341.

Grossman, P., Wineburg, S., & Woolworth, S. (2001). Toward a theory of teacher community. *Teachers College Record, 103*(6), 942–1012.

Hairon, S., & Dimmock, C. (2012). Singapore schools and professional learning communities: Teacher professional development and school leadership in an Asian hierarchical system. *Educational Review, 64*(4), 405–424.

Hairon, S., & Goh, J. W. P. (2015). Pursuing the elusive construct of distributed leadership: Is the search over? *Educational Management Administration and Leadership, 43*(5), 693–718.

Hairon, S., Goh, J. W. P., & Chua, C. S. K. (2015). Teacher leadership enactment in PLC contexts: Towards a better understanding of the phenomenon. *School Leadership and Management, 35*(2), 163–182.

Hairon, S., Goh, J. W. P., Chua, S. K., & Wang, L. Y. (2015). *The impact of community-based teacher learning on student learning outcomes. NIE Research Brief Series, No. 15–001.* Singapore: National Institute of Education, Nanyang Technological University.

Hairon, S., Goh, J. W. P., Chua, C. S. K., & Wang, L. Y. (2017). A research agenda for professional learning communities: Moving forward. *Professional Development in Education, 43*(1), 72–86. http://dx.doi.org/10.1080/19415257.2015.1055861

Hairon, S., Goh, J. W. P., & Diwi, A. (2014). Challenges to PLC enactment in Singapore hierarchical school system. *Speaking Back through Research 2014 AARE/NZARE Conference Proceedings* (1–17). Brisbane, Australia: Australian Association for Research in Education.

Hargreaves, A. (1994). *Changing teachers, changing times. Teachers' work and culture in the Postmodern Age.* London: Cassell.

Harris, A. (2003). Teacher leadership as distributed leadership: Heresy, fantasy or possibility? *School Leadership and Management, 23*(3), 313–324.

Harris, A. (2005). Teacher leadership: More than just a feel-good factor? *Leadership and Policy in Schools, 4*(3), 201–219.

Harris, A. (2013). Distributed leadership: Friend or foe? *Educational Management Administration & Leadership, 41*(5), 545–554.

Harris, A. (2016). Distributed leadership in practice: Evidence, misconceptions and possibilities. *Management in Education, 30*(4), 141–146.

Harris, A., & Jones, M. (2010). Professional learning communities and system improvement. *Improving Schools, 13*(2), 172–181.

Haugaard, M. (2002). *Power: A reader.* Manchester, UK: Manchester University Press.

Hipp, K. K., Huffman, J. B., Pankake, A. M., & Olivier, D. F. (2008). Sustaining professional learning communities: Case studies. *Journal of Educational Change, 9*(2), 173–195.

Jaipal, K., & Figg, C. (2011). Collaborative action research approached promoting professional development for elementary school teachers. *Educational Action Research, 19*(1), 59–72.

Jeffers, G. (2006). Talking about teaching in non-crisis situations: Learning from a teacher support project. *Irish International Studies, 25*(2), 187–206.

Katzenmeyer, M., & Moller, G. (2001). *Awakening the sleeping giant: Helping teachers develop as leaders,* 2nd ed. Thousand Oaks, CA: Corwin Press.

Lee, D., & Lee, W. O. (2013). A professional learning community for the new teacher professionalism: The case of a state-led initiative in Singapore schools. *British Journal of Educational Studies, 61*(4), 435–451.

Leonard, J., Petta, K., & Porter, C. (2012). A fresh look at graduate programs in teacher leadership in the United States. *Professional Development in Education, 38*(2), 189–204.

Levine, T. H. (2010). Tools for the study and design of collaborative teacher learning: The affordances of different conceptions of teacher community and activity theory. *Teacher Education Quarterly, 37*(1), 109–130.

Lieberman, A., & Mace, D. H. P. (2009). The role of 'Accomplished Teachers' in professional learning communities: Uncovering practice and enabling leadership. *Teachers and Teaching: Theory and Practice, 15*(4), 459–470.

Lieberman, A., & Miller, L. (2011). The starting point for professional learning is in schools and classrooms. *Journal of Staff Development, 32*(4), 16–20.

Maloney, C., & Konza, K. (2011). A case study of teachers' professional learning: Becoming a community of professional learning or not? *Issues in Educational Research, 21*(1), 75–87.

McMillan, D. W. (1996). Sense of community. *Journal of Community Psychology, 24*(4), 315–325.

McMillan, D. W. (2011). Sense of community, a theory not a value: A response to Nowell and Boyd. *Journal of Community Psychology, 39*(5), 507–519.

McMillan, D. W., & Chavis, D. M. (1986). Sense of community: A definition and theory. *Journal of Community Psychology, 14*(1), 6–23.

Mindich, D., & Lieberman, A. (2012). *Building a learning community: A tale of two schools.* Stanford, USA: Stanford Center for Opportunity Policy in Education.

Ministry of Education (MOE). (2005). *Speech by Mr Tharman Shanmugaratnam, Minister for Education, at the MOE Work Plan Seminar 2004,* Ngee Ann Polytechnic Convention Centre, Thursday 22 September at 10:00 a.m. Retrieved on 30 September 2006 from www.moe.gov.sg/media/speeches/2005/sp20050922.htm

Muijs, D., & Harris, A. (2003). Teacher leadership – improvement through empowerment. *Educational Management Administration and Leadership, 31*(4), 437–448.

Nelson, T. H. (2008). Teachers' collaborative inquiry and professional growth: Should we be optimistic? *Science Teacher Education, 93*(3), 548–580.

Parks, A. N. (2009). Collaborating about what? An instructor's look at preservice lesson study. *Teacher Education Quarterly, 36*(4), 81–97.

Savoie-Zajc, L., & Descamps-Bednarz, N., (2007). Action research and collaborative research: Their specific contributions to professional development. *Educational Action Research, 15*(4), 577–596.

Schechter, C. (2012). The professional learning community as perceived by Israeli school superintendents, principals and teachers. *International Review of Education, 58*(6), 717–734.

Seo, K, & Han, Y. K. (2012). The vision and the reality of professional learning communities in Korean schools. *KEDI Journal of Educational Policy, 9*(2), 281–298.

Slick, S. (2002). Teachers are enthusiastic participants in a learning community. *The Clearing House, 75*(4), 198–201.

Tönnies, F. (1887). *Community and society (translated by Charles P. Loomis).* New York: Harper.

Training and Development Division (TDD). (2010). *Schools as professional learning communities.* Singapore: Training and Development Division, Ministry of Education.

Watson, C. (2014). Effective professional learning communities? The possibilities for teachers as agents of change in schools. *British Educational Research Journal, 40*(1), 18–29.

York-Barr, J., & Duke, K. (2004). What do we know about teacher leadership? Findings from two decades of scholarship. *Review of Educational Research, 74*(3), 255–316.

Section 2

Teachers leading educational reform within and across districts and schools

Section 2 takes a close look at the meso-layer, largely but not exclusively focusing upon the district or local level. For many large education systems, it is the sub-system at the district, municipal or local authority level that is a catalyst for school change and system innovation. This layer been called the 'middle tier' by some writers and this section offers evidence linking system-wide improvement to professional learning communities *within and across* districts or localities and schools.

Chapters 6 to 9 in this section report on multi-year, mixed method research that identified leadership practices and processes, and thus enabled and supported the implementation of the professional learning community framework at a district level. It is proposed that, as the PLC process becomes embedded, within schools in the United States, the level and extent of district support has a direct impact on schools' ability to re-culture and sustain highly effective collaborative practices.

The first chapter in this section by Hipp and Brazouski explores the process of building a district wide culture of professional learning in the context of the USA. The chapter outlines the findings from an in-depth case study of a single K12 District, over a three-year period, to describe the leadership practices and processes that enabled and supported the implementation of an effective district-wide professional learning community. The chapter emphasizes the norms of shared vision, leadership and collaboration that exist and permeate the district as part of the road to sustaining a professional learning culture.

The next chapter by Olivier et al. similarly focuses on one district in the USA and shares findings from a qualitative research study that explored the process of developing and sustaining the professional learning community process within and across all schools. The chapter also focuses upon issues of implementation and impact by drawing upon the empirical evidence in the study. A number of key conditions for success are outlined in the chapter, particularly the importance of transparency and trust in maintaining a positive professional learning community. The chapter concludes by highlighting how professional learning communities have the potential to be catalysts for cultural change and system transformation at the district level.

The chapter by Huffman, Wilson and Mattingly follows on with the theme of district transformation in their account of the process of implementing a PLC framework. Drawing heavily on the idea that 'isolation is the enemy of improvement' (Schmoker, 2006), the chapter charts the development and progress of district wide transformation through an investment in supporting professional learning community schools. The chapter focuses specifically on the role of the school board in building the individual and collective capacity for change as well as the transformation of learning over time. It highlights that the PLC framework is an ongoing process rather than an event and that district wide support is a crucial part of success.

The chapter by Chen leaves the context of the USA to describe the emergence of networked professional learning communities in the city of Taipei in Taiwan. In 2012 the city government launched networked learning communities as a way of fostering professional collaboration and school improvement. The chapter describes the progress to date and the challenges of networking with colleagues from other schools in a meaningful way. It outlines how 17 school-to-school professional learning communities formed a citywide network that has become a large epistemic community. The chapter concludes that lasting impact of NLCs is dependent on 'disciplined innovation' (Harris & Jones, 2013a; 2013b) where the prime focus is upon improving learning and teaching.

Overall, the chapters in this section provide an important reminder that: first, creating PLC networks across schools is no guarantee of authentic and effective professional collaboration; second, that deep, embedded collaboration takes time and effort; and third, that sustaining the PLC work is dependent upon appropriate challenge and timely, ongoing support. The chapters in this section also highlight that the PLC work across schools is a process of cultural transformation where teachers' practice changes and improves through reciprocal learning and mutual trust.

References

Harris, A., Jones, M., Sharma, S. & Kannan, S. (2013a). Leading educational transformation in Asia: Sustaining the knowledge society. *Asia Pacific Journal of Education, 33*(2), 212–221.

Harris, A., Jones, M. & Baba, S. (2013b). Distributed leadership and digital collaborative learning: A synergistic relationship? *British Journal of Educational Technology, 44*(6), 926–939.

Schmoker, M. (2006). *Results now: How we can achieve unprecedented improvements in teaching and learning.* Boston, MA: Houghton Mifflin Harcourt.

6 Teachers at the forefront

A comprehensive, systematic process for creating and sustaining a district-wide culture of learning

Kristine Kiefer Hipp and Anthony E. Brazouski

Introduction

The concept of *professional learning communities (PLCs)* continues to elicit varying responses in educators. Some teachers and administrators argue that they are already "doing *IT*" in their schools and districts despite a lack of basic understanding of what *IT* is or what it takes to become an authentic culture of learning. Others, particularly teachers, are highly skeptical of PLCs, perceiving them as just another add-on to an already overwhelming list of district-level initiatives that never take hold over time in the name of school reform. Rarely do educators embrace the concept from the start and collectively and wholeheartedly engage in a comprehensive process that predictably takes years to embed in a culture that advances teacher learning and, in turn, student achievement.

Success will depend on how PLCs are first introduced and what visions, plans, actions, and resources will follow. It is common for a handful of teachers and administrators to attend an all-day session in some venue on PLCs, get highly motivated, and feel compelled to initiate the concept in their schools and districts. Unfortunately, their excitement about the power of PLCs to ultimately increase student achievement is rarely matched when they return to their home schools. Over 30 years ago, Guskey (1986) provided insight into the temporal sequence that characterizes the actual process of teacher change with regard to staff development. His model is relevant today and can clearly be adapted for PLCs, revealing that only after teachers change their practices and witness change in student learning outcomes will they actually change their beliefs and attitudes.

PLCs are very complex and with skill are developed and guided gradually, slowly building and deepening knowledge, skills, and applications that move people to create and sustain a culture of learning. This process demands constant attention, stick-with-it-ness, and an undeviating focus on adult and student learning. School leaders must understand the current culture, distribute and nurture teacher leadership, and build a pervasive sense of ownership, commitment, and capacity in human capital over time. Their message regarding motives, support, and promise of resources needs to be transparent as to how the entire school community will work and learn together to assume collective responsibility for student learning. Further, school leaders need to be willing to engage the community in creating a vision that reflects a collective image of excellence and describes what the community might become. At the onset, the challenge is to create an infrastructure that supports and sustains such a vision in which teachers and administrators collectively foster deep learning, where teacher leadership is pervasive, and inclusive and meaningful participation is evident across the school community.

The purpose of this chapter is to share an account of how one mid-size district utilized a PLC Framework (Hipp & Huffman, 2010; Hord, 1997; Huffman & Hipp, 2003) to develop a comprehensive, systematic process for creating and sustaining a district-wide culture of learning. Hipp and Huffman (2010) define a professional learning community as "Professional educators working collectively and purposefully to create and sustain a culture of learning for all students and adults" (p. 12). Furthermore, the intent is to re-culture the district by growing and nurturing teacher leadership, commitment, authority, and responsibility to guide PLC efforts district-wide. "When given opportunities to lead, teachers can influence school reform efforts. Waking this sleeping giant of teacher leadership has unlimited potential in making a real difference in the pace and depth of school change" (Katzenmeyer & Moller, 2001, p. 102).

Theoretical framework

The theoretical framework for this study centers upon the five dimensions of professional learning communities (Hord, 1997), further developed by Hipp and Huffman (2003; 2010), and Fullan's (1985; 1995; 2001) organizational change theory. Currently, the framework identifies six dimensions of a professional learning community: Shared and Supportive Leadership; Shared Vision and Values; Collective Learning and Application; Shared Personal Practice; Supportive Conditions – Relationships; and Supportive Conditions – Structures. The developmental critical attributes that further define these dimensions are correlated with Fullan's stages of change as presented in Figure 6.1, the Professional Learning Community Organizer (PLCO) (Hipp & Huffman, 2010). The six dimensions are further defined in the "Quantitative Measures" section of this chapter. Underlying this framework is the need to develop leadership capacity to nurture the professional learning community resulting in increased student learning. It is the responsibility of leaders at the district, site, and classroom levels to study, develop, support, and sustain the professional learning community in partnership with stakeholders.

Fullan (1985; 2001) identifies three main change stages – initiation, implementation, and institutionalization (sustainability) – and suggests that effective leadership enables permanent or sustainable change. Such change, however, must be meaningful to its members; organizational leaders cannot simply mandate what matters. Instead, leaders, as agents of the change, facilitate, support, and actively participate with members as they collaboratively explore

EXTERNAL SUPPORT SYSTEMS

ADMINISTRATOR AND TEACHER ACTIONS

CENTRAL OFFICE, PARENTS AND FAMILIES, COMMUNITY MEMBERS

STUDENT LEARNING AND SCHOOL IMPROVEMENT

	SCHOOL PHASES OF DEVELOPMENT		
	INITIATING	IMPLEMENTING	SUSTAINING
SHARED AND SUPPORTIVE LEADERSHIP	• Nurturing leadership among staff • Sharing information	• Sharing power, authority, and responsibility	• Broad-based decision making for commitment and accountability
SHARED VALUES AND VISION	• Espoused values and norms	• Focus on students • High expectations	• Shared vision guides teaching and learning
COLLECTIVE LEARNING AND APPLICATION	• Sharing student data • Dialogue	• Collaboration using data related to students needs • Planning • Problem solving	• Application of knowledge, skills, and strategies based on data
SHARED PERSONAL PRACTICE	• Observation and encouragement	• Sharing outcomes of practice • Offer feedback • Mentoring and coaching	• Analaysis of student work and related practices
SUPPORTIVE CONDITIONS Structures	• Assessment and identification of the need for systems and resources	• Appropriate use of systems and resources	• Maximum utilization of systems and resources
SUPPORTIVE CONDITIONS Relationships	• Caring relationships	• Trust and respect • Recognition and celebration	• Risk taking • Unified effort to embed change

Figure 6.1 Professional Learning Community Organizer (PLCO), from Hipp, K. K. & Huffman, J. B. (2010). *Demystifying professional learning communities: School leadership at its best.* Lanham, MD, USA: Rowman and Littlefield.

the needs of the organization and grapple with their own core values. "Effective change agents neither embrace nor ignore mandates. They use them as catalysts to re-examine what they are doing" (Fullan, 1995, p. 24). The basis of this study forms at the intersection of these two frameworks.

A delicate balance between individual engagement and collective efforts needs to be maintained in order to affect sustainable change. While individuals wrestle with internal shifts in core values, diverse groups within the organization ask questions, generate answers, and problem solve with the intent to apply and test newly-founded ideas and hypotheses. Therefore, sustainable change requires a "codependent and dynamic two-way relationship of pressure, support, and continuous negotiation" (Fullan, 2007, p. 33). In order to support this continuum of change, leaders and the organization's members understand the systemic functions and results of such relationships and "promote contextual or job-embedded learning in which working and learning together is the norm and leadership permeates throughout the organization" (Olivier & Hipp, 2006, p. 507). The culture of the organization is built upon the concept that sustainable change is only possible through purposeful collaboration, the empowerment of all stakeholders to affect change, and meaningful engagement of teachers and leaders in professional dialogue.

A third underlying concept of the study's theoretical framework suggests the development and sustainability of a professional learning culture is heavily dependent upon catalytic leadership at multiple levels – district (administrators), site (principals), and classroom (teachers) (Brazouski, 2015) as depicted in Figure 6.2. In order to systematize or sustain change, leaders strategically support their learning organizations through three distinct stages of change similar to Fullan's (1985; 1995; 2001) sustainable change theory.

Specifically, leadership is actively involved in supporting and advancing each stage of change, as the model illustrates, across three levels – district (administrators), site (building administrators), and classroom (teachers). The level of leadership's role or influence at each stage of change varies, enabling successful transition to the next stage and eventual systematization of the change. The change only moves toward sustainability (systemization) once the learning culture centers on meaningful and purposeful collaboration driven by shared responsibility among site (principals) leaders and teacher (classroom) leaders. While district leadership plays a more significant role early in the initiation phase, school principals assume greater responsibility throughout implementation, and, ultimately, equally share leadership and responsibility with teacher leaders toward systemization.

Methodology

The findings reported resulted from an in-depth case study of a single, K–12, public school district, Whitnall School District, from August 2012 through January 2016. The purpose of the study was to identify and describe the leadership practices and processes that enabled and supported the implementation

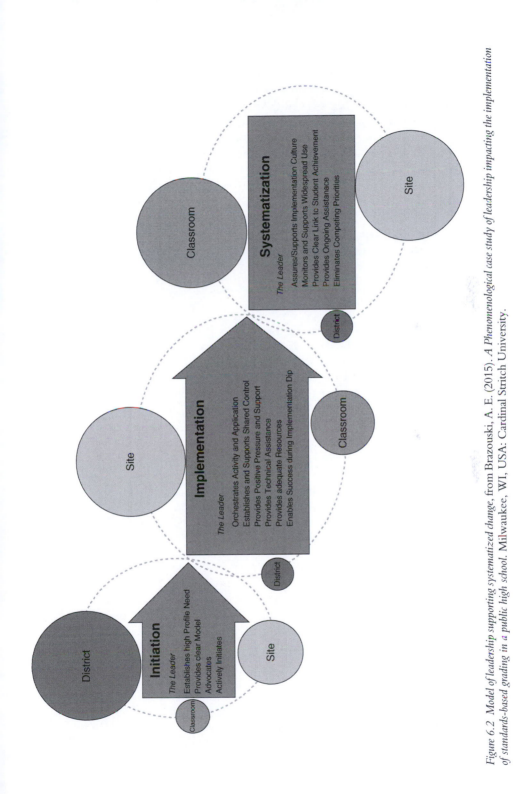

Figure 6.2 Model of leadership supporting systematized change, from Brazouski, A. E. (2015). *A Phenomenological case study of leadership impacting the implementation of standards-based grading in a public high school.* Milwaukee, WI, USA: Cardinal Stritch University.

Initiation

The Leader

Establishes high Profile Need
Provides clear Model
Advocates
Actively Initiates

Implementation

The Leader

Orchestrates Activity and Application
Establishes and Supports Shared Control
Provides Positive Pressure and Support
Provides Technical Assistance
Provides adequate Resources
Enables Success during Implementation Dip

Systematization

The Leader

Assures/Supports Implementation Culture
Monitors and Supports Widespread Use
Provides Clear Link to Student Achievement
Provides Ongoing Assistance
Eliminates Competing Priorities

District

Classroom

Site

Site

Classroom

District

Classroom

Site

District

of an effective district-wide professional learning community. Data were derived from both qualitative and quantitative measures designed to assess district- and school-level leadership capacities and professional learning cultures. Additionally, data were triangulated through individual and group interviews, informal observations, and document reviews.

As the researchers, and authors of this chapter, were directly engaged with the school district throughout the change, the qualitative methodology supports Denzin and Lincoln's (2011) suggestion to "locate the observer in the world so as to study things in their natural settings, attempting to make sense of, or interpret, phenomena in terms of the meanings people bring to them" (p. 3). The intent of this chapter is to reveal the specific and continuing leadership practices and processes that nurture the professional learning culture of the Whitnall School District, resulting in the implementation of a maturing, district-wide professional learning community.

Quantitative measures

The *Professional Learning Community Assessment – Revised (PLCA-R)*, developed by Olivier, Hipp, and Huffman (2010), was the primary measure used in this effort and guided other means of assessment. Specifically, this 52-item descriptive tool was used annually over the past three years (November 2012 – January 2015) as a diagnostic tool that measures teacher perceptions about the school's principal, colleagues, and central office personnel regarding their practices toward becoming a PLC. The PLCA-R is based on the six dimensions of a PLC and related critical attributes (Hipp & Huffman, 2010; Huffman & Hipp, 2003) as depicted below:

Shared and supportive leadership
○   Nurture leadership among staff
○   Shared power, authority, and responsibility
○   Broad-based decision-making that reflects commitment and accountability
○   Sharing information

Shared values and vision
○   Espoused values and norms
○   Focus on student learning
○   High expectations
○   Shared vision guides teaching and learning

Collective learning and application
○   Sharing information
○   Seeking new knowledge, skills, and strategies
○   Working collaboratively to plan, solve problems, and improve learning opportunities

Shared personal practice
- Peer observations to offer knowledge, skills, and encouragement
- Feedback to improve instructional practices
- Sharing outcomes of instructional practices
- Coaching and mentoring

Supportive conditions
Structures
- Resources (time, money, materials, people)
- Facilities
- Communication systems

Relationships
- Caring relationships
- Trust and respect
- Recognition and celebration
- Risk-taking
- Unified effort to embed change

The items of this instrument are comprised of practices observed at the school level using a 1–4 Likert scale of strongly disagree – disagree – agree – strongly agree. Due to the small sample of teachers, approximating 200 each over the past three years, results were reported and compared qualitatively to enhance the meaning of data analyses, and identified strengths, challenges, and themes per dimension.

Each year, once data were analyzed by the out-of-district expert facilitator, data analysis work sessions occurred by school to engage teachers actively in further analyzing the data by determining perceived strengths, areas of challenge, priorities, and plans to move their schools forward. Two different processes were used through Year 3 involving the PLC dimensions:

a   Year 1 – Teachers were distributed the school's results and worked in dimension teams to determine what they should *Stop* – What is hindering our progress? – and what they should *Start* – What do we do to get this going? Next, teachers identified themes and patterns, which prioritized next step actions.

b   Years 2 and 3 – Teachers were given the mean scores of each item compared to scores from the previous year. Items with means were listed subjectively under Strengths (3.0 or greater), Mid-Range (2.76–2.99), and Challenges (2.75 or less). Teachers then provided key take-aways based on their analyses.

In the latter part of Year 2, Professional Learning Community Teams, comprised of the principal and nine teachers from each school, were initiated. In Year 3, a district-wide team, composed of the principals, a teacher representative in each school, and the Executive Director of Academic Achievement, was formed. Work sessions, in which teams analyzed PLCA-R data and developed action plans, were led by the expert facilitator and researcher contracted by the District. The purpose of these teams was three-fold: 1) to continually assess their schools as PLCs to develop PLC plans related to strengths and challenges; 2) to deepen understanding of the underlying culture of PLCs, so as to guide efforts and gradually assume the roles and responsibilities of the out-of-district facilitator and the Executive Director of Academic Achievement; and 3) to share and discuss actions, needs, and resources with the intent of nurturing a district-wide culture of professional learning.

Qualitative measures

On-site interviews of district administrators, including the Executive Director of Academic Achievement (EDAA), the Superintendent, and site principals, were utilized to establish a baseline understanding of the quantitative data and generate themes based upon expressed perceptions. The entire teaching staff at all four sites engaged in PLC data workshops aligned to principal interviews to add meaning and contextualize quantitative survey results. Additionally, the researchers conducted observations of site and district PLC team meetings and document analyses of site and district PLC teams including meeting agendas and minutes, key take-away worksheets, goals, action plans, strategic actions, and documentation of goal achievement.

As Seidman (2006) suggested, the interview protocols were designed with open-ended questions and meetings were held repetitiously over time; therefore, participants were afforded multiple opportunities to establish trustworthiness and accuracy of responses. Building principals were provided the questions prior to the interview in order to best prepare thoughtful and complete responses. Interviews were recorded, transcribed, and analyzed.

Additionally, the researchers facilitated workshops in which teachers responded, in writing and within small groups targeting specific dimensions, to questions two, five, and six of Interview Protocol 2, as Miles, Huberman, and Saldana (2014) suggest "findings are more dependable when they can be buttressed from several independent sources. Their validity was enhanced when they are confirmed by more than one data collection instrument measuring the same thing" (p. 307). Responses were transcribed and utilized by principals and PLC teams for planning.

Overall district performance, as measured by the Wisconsin Department of Public Instruction, was tracked prior to (2011–2012) and during (2012–2015) the study, showing both growth and sustainability of high student achievement (see Table 6.1). All schools are required to achieve a minimum rating of "Meets Expectations" with a cut-off score of 63.0.

Table 6.1 Performance scores for Whitnall School District

Year	2011−12	2012−13	2013−14	2015−16
Report Card	72.8 − Meets	78.1 − Exceeds	74.1 − Exceeds★	79.0 − Exceeds

★ Due to a change in proficiency ratings for National Assessment of Educational Progress (NAEP) realignment, Department of Public Instruction (DPI) calculations resulted in lowered scores at all schools state-wide.

The results indicate that, despite many changes in state accountability measures, calculations, and the state tests themselves, the Whitnall School District has sustained progress while continuing to strive for increased teacher quality and student achievement.

Stories from the field: The Whitnall School District

The Whitnall School District is located in a southwest suburb of Milwaukee, Wisconsin and serves the City of Greenfield, and Villages of Hales Corners and Franklin. The district has a history of academic performance within the mid- to upper-eightieth percentile of the state, and consists of one 4K charter school, two elementary schools, one middle school, and one high school. The district serves approximately 2,553 students (4K through 12th grade), 74.5 percent white, 13 percent Hispanic, 4.5 percent Asian, 2.6 percent Black, less than 1.0 percent Native American and Pacific Isle, and 5.0 percent reporting two or more ethnicities.

Approximately 2.5 percent of the district's population is English Language Learners with over 28 languages/dialects spoken at home. Socio-economically, three of the Whitnall School District's schools receive Title I support with a district 33.7 percent categorized free and reduced lunch population (eligibility rates are higher). Approximately 13 percent are identified as students with disabilities. The Whitnall School District is governed by a seven-member board and consists of five district administrators, five site administrators, one district technology coordinator, four instructional technology leaders, four instructional coaches, 178 teachers, and seven guidance counselors. Uniquely, the Whitnall School District's professional development, curriculum, and instruction efforts are directed by a 24-member academic achievement team, consisting of the district's Executive Director of Academic Achievement, Technology Director, school principals, and 18 teacher leaders serving as K–12 curriculum coordinators, instructional technology leaders, or instructional coaches.

The following quantitative and qualitative findings are discussed according to three major phases and transfers of leadership related to PLC efforts thus far:

- Phase I: Acquisition of knowledge, deepening understanding, and leadership transfer from district to site administrators;

- Phase II: Application of and deepened understanding and leadership transfer from site administrators to teacher leaders;
- Phase III: Analysis of application, strategic action, and equalization of leadership among site administrators and teacher leaders.

These three phases suggest a cycle comprised of acquiring, applying, and acting upon knowledge in order to sustain (systemize) a culture of professional learning. Acquiring knowledge begins with developing an understanding of what cultures of learning that result in mature PLCs look and feel like. Application of understanding links what is being learned by professionals with the district's and the school's current status (vision, values, and goals). This phase includes administrators and teachers generating actionable plans comprised of visions, measurable goals, acting upon commitments, and collecting data and evidence. Analyzing application includes determining emergent themes, what has been learned through application, identifying strengths and challenges, and establishing what must be done to move forward.

The phases do not necessarily indicate a linear process in practice, most particularly because new teachers and administrators come and go. Significant efforts are in place for mentoring and coaching and bringing new colleagues up to speed. Deepening knowledge, understanding, application, and analysis are ongoing processes that ultimately lead to a culture of learning that is aligned to the vision, values, and goals and keeps student achievement always at the forefront.

Phase I: Acquisition of knowledge, deepening understanding, and leadership transfer from district to site administrators

The Whitnall School District spent three years in a pre-change stage where the district established a preliminary need for change, identified the nature of the change, developed the appropriate conditions for change, and then committed to the change before moving into the initiation stage of the change process. Principals and teachers attended a training session with Richard DuFour, engaged in book studies, and discussed possible actions, but follow-through was limited and no systemic action resulted at either the school or district levels. According to one elementary principal, "It was great stuff. It made sense. We knew we had to work together and get out of our silos, but we just didn't really know where to go next." In order to begin the district's efforts toward initiation, however, administrators needed to bring in an outside expert, a consultant on PLCs and professional learning, to guide and support strategic efforts and ongoing practical applications of PLC theory beginning with the 2012–2013 academic year.

The expert consultant, in partnership with the EDAA, began by re-culturing and re-teaching all staff through a series of keynote addresses, workshops, and meetings. Having developed a clear understanding of the District's situation, the consultant built upon prior knowledge and then deepened both the individual and collective understandings of the staff. This was accomplished by focusing on a central framework intended to not only identify and explain the facets of a PLC, but also direct action toward the development of effective practices. The Six Dimensions Framework, as represented in the PLCO (see Figure 6.1), enabled teachers and administrators to refocus on the underlying cultural needs and nuances of the organization, rather than simply attempting to brainstorm the next steps of technical change (Hipp & Huffman, 2010).

The district learned more about its own functionality as a PLC through the district–wide 100 percent response rate to teachers completing the Professional Learning Community Assessment – Revised (PLCA-R) survey. The survey identified current teacher and administrator perceptions regarding the six dimensions of PLCs (Hipp & Huffman, 2010). The district's partnership with an external neutral expert provided unbiased, yet meaningful and relevant data and information regarding the district's capacity as a PLC. The results from the PLCA-R became the essential foundation upon which was built an effective professional learning culture and furthered the growth of leadership capacity throughout the organization.

To empower principals to lead PLC efforts, the consultant and EDAA met with each site principal to review the PLCA-R results. The interviews (see Table 6.1) afforded principals ample opportunity to deepen their own understandings of the Framework and, more importantly, to determine how the Framework related to their particular sites' levels of readiness. The interviews also established a professional learning relationship among the principals, the district administrator, and the consultant. This was a crucial first step toward the transfer of leadership from the district to site-level administrators.

The expert consultant then focused on deepening the understanding of teachers at individual sites by linking the PLCO Framework to the PLCA-R results through all-staff, on-site workshops. At each site, the teachers gathered in small groups by the six dimensions and were tasked with making meaning of the quantitative results from the survey. Teacher teams studied dimension scores, discussed the indicators affiliated with those scores, and then articulated actions to "stop" and "start" doing to positively affect scores in the future.

The results of each team were reported to the entire group, and then synthesized to focus on only three "key take-aways" for each dimension. Establishing priorities was important for later discussion and action planning among principals and the district. Each team's work was transcribed by the district and shared with principals and staff. Similar to the principal interviews, teachers began to understand the connection between PLC theory and the necessary components of building a culture of learning that could affect PLC development. One teacher approached a principal after a workshop and said, "This is the first time in my 15 plus years in this district that we actually followed up on a survey. I hope something gets done with it now." The teacher, unbeknownst to her, identified a central indicator of the transfer of leadership from the consultant and district to the principals.

Once the site information was compiled, the consultant and EDAA interviewed the principals. This time, however, principals were asked to synthesize and share their own "key take-aways." Principals contextualized their interpretations within those articulated by their staff to compare, contrast, and draw conclusions. These sessions deepened understanding and produced actionable results through which principals assumed primary leadership responsibilities. Principals committed to short-term technical and structural changes to support PLCs at their sites and generated awareness among staff reinforcing that their voices, through this Framework and these efforts, were being heard. A culture of teacher empowerment and professional learning was born, and principals were encouraged by the positive responses of their staff.

Toward the end of the first year of initiation and Phase I, the consultant and the EDAA observed teacher team meetings in order to establish baseline qualitative data for future comparative analyses. The consultant also met with the Superintendent to provide an update and summary of PLC and leadership efforts throughout the year. Most importantly, she facilitated a meeting among all district and site administrators around the "key take-aways," thereby eliciting common and contrasting issues, needs, and efforts across the district. Resulting from this work, the district reconfigured the district-wide professional development calendar, and the specific structures of professional development days. As one principal suggested,

> We [principals] couldn't believe that we had so many of the same simple issues. One meeting, where we were allowed to be honest and trust that what we needed to get done would get done, was all it took. It worked out for all of us at our buildings and the district. Even the teachers saw that things were changing in a good way.

After the final professional development day, a self-identified "district office skeptic" and 22-year teaching veteran stopped the consultant on her way out the back door. The teacher leaned in for a hug and said, "Thank you for all that you've done for us." This statement validates prior feedback that positive momentum was emerging as teachers became empowered and leadership transferred from administrators to their PLC teams.

Phase II: Application of and deepened understanding and leadership transfer from site administrators to teacher leaders

Year 2 focused on building teacher leadership around PLC practices. Site-level PLC Teams, comprised of teachers and principals, were formed and tasked with: deepening their knowledge of the PLC dimensions; collecting and reporting evidence of teacher application; analyzing practices; and developing plans to assure meaningful professional practices aligned to visions, values, and goals. Each PLC Team met onsite for a full day with the consultant and EDAA to develop: a) a purpose; b) Team norms; c) perceptions of the current reality, preferred future, and pathway from the current reality to a preferred future; and d) Team roles and responsibilities.

In November of 2013, teachers completed the PLCA-R a second time and met with the consultant to review the analyzed data and discuss comparisons of mean scores across the first two years. Teachers expressed appreciations to not only have access to these results, but also to voice what was promoting and hindering progress toward a culture of learning. The consultant then interviewed principals with the EDAA. The interviews focused on themes from the PLCA-R data comparing the two years, how leadership was exercised and by whom, the PLC Team's impact, significant strengths and challenges, and what the Team could do to address the challenges. In turn, the consultant facilitated half-day PLC Team workshops to clarify, validate, negate, or add to the principal's perceptions to create action plans. The Teams' commitments were encouraging as some suggested actions took place immediately in the schools. With efforts being realized at the site level, the next steps of Phase II focused on meaningful systemic change.

A District PLC Team, including a principal and teacher representative from each site team and the EDAA, formed to co-ordinate actions, ideas, and insights. Specifically, teams used the PLCA-R results to share areas of focus, progress and successes, challenges, and resources and activities focused on PLC efforts. Feedback across site teams generated further understanding and insight, resulting in a "key take-away document" that was shared district-wide.

Moreover, the District PLC Team realized that it needed to augment the results with qualitative data from their colleagues to gain more clarity. Each site PLC Team developed questions that were brought to faculty meetings and facilitated small group discussions to enhance the clarity of the quantitative data. Feedback from teachers provided rich data, and the process generated more clarity, voice, and direction for future planning. Action plans at both the site and district levels became "living documents," promoting sustainability through ownership and commitment among teachers and administrators across the district. An intentional shift was occurring in shared decision-making, responsibility, and accountability. Teachers were recognizing the necessity of a PLC Framework to develop a culture of professional learning.

Phase III: Analysis of application, strategic action, and equalization of leadership among site administrators and teacher leaders

The purpose of Phase III was twofold: 1) to develop in-district expertise that nurtures a culture of professional learning that reflects a mature, district-wide PLC; and 2) to further develop leadership capacity that positions site administrators and teacher leaders equally to advance student learning through adult learning. Both the site and District PLC Teams effectively engaged in PLCA-R data-based action planning, goal-setting, and progress monitoring. During these processses, the Teams discovered a need to deepen their understandings of the underlying components of the PLC Framework in order to continue to effectively focus efforts on improving the culture of professional learning.

Additionally, Teams required training in the analysis of the PLCA-R data itself. The consultant expressed that, in order for the District to continue its growth, she needed to "work [herself] right out of a job." Phase III transitioned the consultant from facilitator to mentor, where she empowered teacher leaders by guiding them through processes to be replicated at their sites. Also, she coached a new principal and continues to provide workshops, guidance, and support services related to site and district needs. Although the district's direct involvement lessened, strong support *from*, advocacy *by*, and presence *of* district-level administrators remained necessary to support and advance efforts toward sustainability.

Phase III began by circling back to Phase I to deepen knowledge among PLC Teams through application of the critical attributes of the Dimensions of the Framework. These attributes reflect the finest threads woven into the fabric of an effective professional learning culture, underpinning the consultant's analyses and conclusions drawn from three years of PLCA-R quantitative data. The consultant empowered PLC Teams by teaching the intricacies of the Framework to enable future analyses and systematic efforts to be led, facilitated, and studied in-house *by* teachers and *for* teachers. In turn, PLC Teams planned and conducted professional development workshops prior to the fourth dissemination of the PLCA-R in January 2016. One teacher leader commented, "I feel more like a professional as a member of this [PLC] team. We've made changes and seen results, and that's contagious. Now we know how to keep this going." Such sentiment is supported by comprehensive results across the District and at each site.

Outcomes and impact

The following comprehensive and systematic (across the District) outcomes are presented in reference to the PLC Framework and its six dimensions.

Shared and supportive leadership

- Each site is led by teacher leader teams (PLC Teams) in partnership with principals where shared decisions are made and based upon meaningful data.
- Systematically, the vision, professional development activities, and efforts of the school district are developed and led by the Academic Achievement Team. Decision-making is shared equally among all members. The team's composition reflects shared leadership where 75 percent (18) are teacher leaders and 25 percent (6) are administrators.

Shared vision and values

- Comprehensively, every PLC Team established site culture norms, assessed its school's current reality, imagined a preferred future, and developed action plans to address the gaps. The preferred future served as the vision by which PLC Teams measured and monitored progress.

- Systematic reform was evident as the School Board collaboratively engaged in a strategic planning process with administrators resulting in support for PLCs. The Board publicly committed to support a culture of professional learning: "The district is committed to a culture of continuous growth, student achievement, and celebration of success." Further, the Board articulated a specific strategy aimed at "District Culture and Climate: Enhance a sense of ownership, belonging, and respect among all members of the Whitnall community" (Whitnall Public School District, 2015).
- The Academic Achievement Team established a systemic model and vision for continual professional growth, leadership development, and developing into a culture of professional learning. Professional development was designed and conducted *for* teachers, *by* teachers.

Collective learning and application

- PLC Teams collaborated with staff around PLCA-R results, which required strategic actions of instructional staff input and efforts to satisfy goals and intended outcomes. All schools identified underlying issues of trust, concertedly approached them directly and collectively, and monitored progress through quantitative survey results and anecdotal evidence to determine next steps.
- Comprehensive efforts were quantifiably reflected, over time, by the positive effect on the specific PLCA-R categories targeted by the PLC Team and school staff.
- The most significant comprehensive evidence was drawn from a kindergarten teacher team. The team fully engaged as a PLC and targeted emergent reading scores throughout the school year. The end-of-year student achievement results indicated that 100 percent of the students were proficient or advanced emergent readers.
- The District systematically engaged all teachers in a State initiative to incorporate new English Language Arts (ELA) and mathematics standards. Guided by a long-range plan and short-term goals, teachers collaboratively deconstructed the standards, articulated specific learning targets, and developed assessments to determine student performance.

Shared personal practice

- Site PLC Teams developed activities and tools to support teachers in sharing classroom experiences and ideas. High school teachers engaged in a "speed dating" ice-breaker activity during a staff meeting, which encouraged teachers to follow up with their "dates" via classroom observations during the school day. This form of teacher observation removed any perceived threat of evaluation as the visiting teacher selected an area of interest or need to observe a colleague with notable expertise. Elementary and middle school teachers collaborated with instructional coaches to observe their grade-level colleagues, interventionists, and specialists. Following visits, the teachers met to discuss the lessons.

- Systematically, instructional coaches, K-12 coordinators, and instructional technology leaders were hired to support ongoing dialogue and collaboration among staff around curriculum, instruction, and learning.

Supportive conditions – structures

- Comprehensively, site schedules were retooled to allow for collaboration time within the regular school day. High school teams were assigned common planning by department and/or course. Daily common middle school planning time was reallocated by grade level, as well as by subject level, about once per week. Elementary grade-level team planning time was scheduled to occur about three times per week.
- In order to systematically support a culture of professional learning and in collaboration with teachers, the District designed and the Board approved school calendars to include vertically and horizontally aligned collaboration time, teacher induction and support, and end-of-year transition activities. Time was allocated for district-wide, site-level, and teacher team activities and continues to be reallocated and reconfigured to meet the needs of staff.

Supportive conditions – relationships

- By simply walking the halls of schools, evidence of comprehensive reform was apparent. Not only was structured common planning time regularly used by teachers, but collaboration had become the norm, replacing previously common daily work done in isolation.
- Both systematically and comprehensively, staff expressed increased satisfaction with professional relationships across the district and schools through the PLCA-R and qualitative feedback data. Staff participated in collaborative planning sessions addressing the school calendar, health and wellness, climate, and a modified compensation structure. The resulting policies, practices, and structures reflected the effective problem-solving and critical thinking of the teams.
- Resulting from the establishment of the Academic Achievement Team, staff expressed increased feelings of support from and connection to the school district as a system. Evidence was most prominent as staff approached their colleagues more willing to problem-solve than simply problem-identify. They viewed themselves as having an active role and impact on situations or issues.
- Finally, teachers across the District expressed that their voices, collectively and individually, were being heard. Not only did they feel as though someone was listening, but teachers were also seeing action resulting from

their ideas. This led to richer dialogue with a more laser-like focus on issues directly impacting student achievement.

Having measurable and celebrated results, the District's momentum continues as PLC Teams forge ahead.

Next steps

With a greater understanding of the PLC Framework among teacher leaders and principals, the District is shifting focus to strengthen the tie between teacher leaders and what was being learned and practiced. To promote sustainability, the consultant will conduct a rigorous workshop with the District PLC Team using the fourth administration of the PLCA-R results. The goal of the workshop is to teach participants how to analyze the raw results of the PLCA-R. PLC Teams will be informed and highly trained, enabling the school organization, at teacher-leader, principal, and district levels, to take control of the professional learning culture analyses. This crucial step will promote the District's movement toward sustainability. As one high school principal suggested,

> We know good PLCs … and can keep it going ourselves. We all own it. My PLC Team tells ME what to pay attention to and should be done. It's not me telling them what they have to do anymore.

The PLC Teams will engage their sites in qualitative data sessions similar to the Phase I workshops. Site PLC Teams will then convene to strategically plan and determine continued actions needed to improve and support the district's professional learning culture. These plans, goals, and actions will be shared with building staff for feedback and modifications. While teacher leaders and principals share equal leadership responsibilities regarding site cultures, the district is focusing on systems to support continued efforts. Knowing that the most significant risk to sustainability is the loss of key leadership and knowledge, the district initiated plans for mentoring new administrators and teachers. The former middle school principal left the district at the end of Year 3, so the new leader engaged both a district mentor and the expert consultant. Further adjustments were made in the school year calendar to accommodate district-wide issues impacting the professional learning culture. Although the work and direction of professional learning efforts continue to shift in focus and scope, the shared leadership structure and professional learning culture of the Whitnall School District enables continued positive growth of staff and students alike.

Conclusion

The leadership practices and processes of the Whitnall School District reflect Hipp and Huffman's (2010) definition of a functioning PLC: "Professional educators working collectively and purposefully to create and sustain a culture of learning for all students and adults" (p. 12). Sustainability of a PLC depends upon commitment to vision, shared responsibility, and an undeviating focus on learning results. Through the incremental empowerment of District to principals and then, ultimately, to teacher leaders, this organization is shifting toward sustainability. "Energetic-enthusiastic-hopeful leaders 'cause' greater moral purpose in themselves, bury themselves in change, naturally build relationships and knowledge, and seek coherence" (Fullan, 2001, p. 7).

PLC Team leadership at district and site levels enabled continuous goal-setting, action planning, and progress monitoring, resulting in measurable gains among staff learning as well as early indications of effects on student learning. Evidence suggests that teacher attitudes and beliefs have changed as a result of meaningful staff development, but more importantly resulting from changed classroom practices. "A key factor in the endurance of any change in instructional practices is demonstrable results of the learning success of a teacher's students" (Guskey, 1986, p. 7). Comprehensive and systematic reform, therefore, is reflected in the resulting behaviours of stakeholders within the organization and permeates the district-wide culture, values, efforts, and vision.

The purpose of this chapter was to share how one mid-size district utilized a PLC Framework to develop a comprehensive, systematic process for creating and sustaining a district-wide culture of learning. Comprehensive reform meaningfully affects every member of the district. It extends through principals into classrooms, thereby permeating every level of the organization. This type of reform involves individual actions in accordance with the accepted norms. Systematic reform is evident on a larger scale and entails standardized district-wide efforts, processes, and public commitments. Systematic components are the norms by which our culture operates. As Heifetz and Linsky (2002) assert, "The *sustainability* of change depends on having the people internalize the change" (p. 13). Such reform manifests in changed daily instructional practices across the District.

Leadership is pervasive, and deeply evident within the teacher ranks in the site and District PLC Teams, the Academic Achievement Team, council chairs, and grade level and subject area leaders. Teachers' voices are heard and acted upon accordingly. Although the District guides actions through common processes, structures, parameters, and expectations, each teacher exercises flexibility and freedom to engage in building an organic, meaningful culture of professional learning affecting student outcomes.

In addition, the School Board's public support solidifies the message to educators and the greater school community that creating and sustaining a culture of learning requires support and resources toward sustaining a mature PLC. As efforts continue, teacher leadership will surely deepen within the organization. Norms of collaboration and commitment, rather than isolation, now exist voluntarily and permeate the District. Above all else, the transfer of leadership from District administrators to principals to teachers is powerful.

The unwavering comprehensive commitment *to* and support *of* PLCs over extended time has resulted in an emergent sense of ownership. There is a culture of professional learning across all stakeholders within the District and collaboration and professional growth is sustained *by* teachers *for* teachers.

References

Brazouski, A. E. (2015). *A Phenomenological case study of leadership impacting the implementation of standards-based grading in a public high school.* Milwaukee, WI: Cardinal Stritch University.

Denzin, N. K., & Lincoln, Y. S. (2011). *The Sage handbook of qualitative research* (4th ed.). Thousand Oak, CA: Sage.

Fullan, M. (1985). Change processes and strategies at the local level. *The Elementary School Journal, 85*(3), *Special Issue: Policy Implications of Effective Schools Research*, 390–421.

Fullan, M. (1995). *Change forces.* London: Falmer Press.

Fullan, M. (2001). *Leading in a culture of change.* San Francisco, CA: Jossey-Bass.

Fullan, M. (2007). *Leading in a culture of change: Personal action guide and workbook.* San Francisco, CA: Jossey-Bass.

Guskey, T. R. (1986). Staff development and the process of teacher change. *Educational Researcher, 15*(5), 5–12.

Heifetz, R. A., & Linsky, M. (2002). *Leadership on the line: Staying alive through the dangers of leading.* Boston, MA: Harvard Business School Press.

Hipp, K. K., & Huffman, J. B. (2010). *Demystifying professional learning communities: School leadership at its best.* Lanham, MD: Rowman & Littlefield Publishers, Inc.

Hord, S. M. (1997). *Professional learning communities: Communities of continuous inquiry and improvement.* Austin, TX: Southwest Educational Development Laboratory.

Huffman, J. B., & Hipp, K. K. (2003). *Reculturing schools as professional learning communities.* Lanham, MD: The Scarecrow Press.

Katzenmeyer, M. H., & Moller, G. V. (2001). *Awakening the sleeping giant: Helping teachers develop as leaders* (1st ed.). Thousand Oaks, CA: Corwin, a Sage Company.

Miles, M., Huberman, A. M., & Saldana, J. (2014). *Qualitative data analysis: A Methods sourcebook* (3rd ed.). Thousand Oaks, CA: Sage Publications, Inc.

Olivier, D. F., & Hipp, K. K. (2006). Leadership capacity and collective efficacy: Interacting to sustain student learning in a professional learning community. *Journal of School Leadership, 16*(5), 505–519. *Special Edition: Leadership and Student Learning in Professional Learning Communities.*

Olivier, D. F., Hipp, K. K., & Huffman, J. B. (2010). Professional learning community assessment – revised. In K. K. Hipp & J. B. Huffman (Eds.), *Demystifying professional learning communities: School leadership at its best.* Lanham, MD: Rowman & Littlefield Publishers, Inc.

Seidman, I. (2006). *Interviewing as qualitative research: A Guide for researchers in education and the social sciences* (2nd ed.). New York: Teachers College Press.

Whitnall Public School District. (2015). *WSD School District Mission, Vision, and Strategies.* Retrieved from: www.whitnall.com/ourpages/auto/2012/1/11/52402481/WSD%20Mission_%20Vision_%20Strategies.pdf.

7 From PLC implementation to PLC sustainability
The pivotal role of district support

Dianne F. Olivier, Patrice B. Pujol, Steve V. Westbrook and Jennifer G. Tuttleton

Introduction

Collaborative district and principal leadership, focused on teacher empowerment, is at the heart of any professional learning community and is integral to scalable, sustainable school improvement efforts. The purpose of this chapter is to share findings from a qualitative research study designed to explore district-level support of the professional learning community process within and across all district schools by supporting teacher collaborative practices. This study sought to investigate the intentions, actions, and practices occurring in initiating, implementing, and sustaining teacher and student improvement through the PLC process.

The study focuses on the Ascension Parish School System (APSS) and its attempts to embed the PLC process into the district-wide culture. This chapter also examines a focus on PLC implementation and how this work impacted upon policies, accountability and autonomy, transparency and trust, capacity building, modeling collaborative learning, proactive district involvement, and sustainability of progress. Additionally, this case study illustrates the re-culturing of a district as a professional learning community and the overall district transformation to a culture of learning. This transformational process highlights district and school level administrators' collaborative work with teachers to sustain a strong professional culture fostering ongoing learning for all.

Research design

This case study describes a district transformational process based on data gathered through qualitative methodology including observations, document analyses, and individual and focus group interviews. The interviews were conducted using an interview protocol designed to address the identified professional learning community dimensions. Individuals were selected through purposeful samplings and included district and school administrators and teacher leaders. The district leaders included superintendent, assistant superintendent, and curriculum and school improvement directors. School and teacher leaders interviewed were principals along with teachers representing primary/elementary, middle, and high school levels. The teacher leader group incorporated both formal and informal teacher leaders, including department-, grade-, and content-level chairs, as well as teachers who stepped forward to actively assume responsibility for improvement of overall school performance. Documents analysis incorporated reviews of district vision and mission statements, policies procedures, and professional development and collaborative session files.

Data analysis involved a constant comparative analysis whereby themes were identified and coded as they surfaced across all interview questions. Major findings were identified in relation to themes and indicators within each specific dimension, as well as across all dimensions, all grade levels, and all personnel levels. Study findings presented are based on summative analyses and assertions through analyses of observations, document review, and interview summaries resulting in recognition of common language, vision, strategic planning, and major findings.

Initiation to implementation to sustainability

This case study illustrates the re-culturing of a district as a professional learning community and the overall district transformation to a culture of learning centered on district and school level administrators' collaborative work with teachers to sustain a strong professional culture fostering ongoing learning for all.

Ascension Parish School System is located in the petro-chemical corridor of southwest Louisiana along the Mississippi River and represents one of the fastest-growing parishes in Louisiana. Serving 27 schools accounting for over 21,000 students, APSS is recognized by the State Department of Education as an *"A"* level district and ranks as the 4th highest performing public school district in Louisiana (Louisiana State Department of Education, 2015). The mission of APSS is "to provide each student the high quality education necessary to succeed in an ever changing world" (Ascension Public School, 2015).

Leadership development, collaboration, and school improvement processes have been part of Ascension Parish's strategic instructional goals for a number of years. During that time, a common language and vision have gained traction through building capacity among instructional leaders at the district and school level through collaborative practices with teachers. The targeted system approach adopted by the district resulted in a shared understanding within and across all schools in relation to district support through specified protocols, practices, actions, and resources. This strategic systems approach offering support in developing shared and supportive leadership, shared values and vision, collective learning and application, shared personal practice, and providing supportive conditions (i.e. relationships and structures) (Hipp & Huffman, 2010) began around 2010. As part of this system's approach, professional learning communities (PLCs) were declared a non-negotiable for all schools in the district.

All district- and school-level personnel clearly understood the PLC concept as *"professional educators working collectively and purposefully to create and sustain a culture of learning for all students and adults"* (Hipp & Huffman, 2010, p. 12). This non-negotiable status resulted in a mandate for all schools to adopt the PLC process while allowing each school to determine the most appropriate transition to embed the process within their individual school. Thus, while the district leaders identified policy, procedures, and practices, such as guidelines for required professional learning within each school and collaboration between school and district leaders, each school was able to address the parameters within their own context and schedule. As part of this PLC transition, district- and school-level leaders, as well as teacher leaders, engaged in professional learning focused on implementing PLCs in schools and at the district level, such that a culture of job-embedded professional development resulting in high-quality teacher and student performance would be sustained.

Creating a culture of collaboration

The district's first attempts at school improvement efforts were to engage teacher leaders at the district level, knowing the importance of a high-quality classroom teacher. The district leadership team members who directed the PLC process through collaboration with teacher leaders coordinated these initial efforts. Figure 7.1 illustrates the district framework designed to generate a culture of collaboration. As the district provided opportunities for teachers to assume leadership roles, such as curriculum writing, benchmark writing, and instructional coaching, teacher leaders became the conduit for all the district's improvement efforts. The most traction for those efforts came where principals provided those teacher leaders a forum to replicate best practices through coaching and mentoring other teachers, collaborating around assessments and curriculum, and doing peer observations. These schools had the structures and supportive conditions which the district has since come to recognize as the dimensions of professional learning communities: Shared and Supportive Leadership, Shared Values and Vision, Collective Learning and Application, Shared Personal Practice, and Supportive Conditions (Hipp & Huffman, 2010).

One key responsibility of the principal is to reduce the disparity of instructional quality from classroom to classroom within the school (Aseltine, Faryniarz & Rigazio-DiGilio, 2006; Haycock, 2011). Similarly, it is the responsibility of the district to reduce disparity among schools. Consequently, district leaders made the conscious decision to actively engage principals in the same work in which teacher leaders were involved through professional learning, thus developing principals' capacity to re-create this work on their campuses. District leaders understood they could not charge principals with this responsibility without helping them develop the skills they needed for success, operating under the principle of reciprocal accountability; that is, "for every increment of performance I demand from you, I have an equal responsibility to provide you with the capacity to meet that expectation" (Elmore, 2006, p. 93).

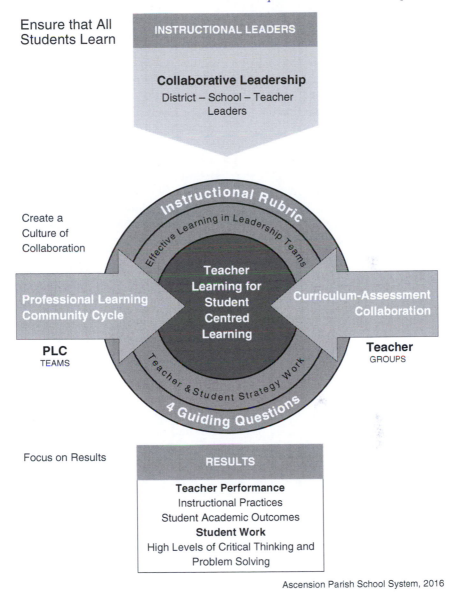

Ensure that All
Students Learn

Create a
Culture of
Collaboration

Focus on Results

Ascension Parish School System, 2016

Figure 7.1 Culture of collaboration framework

In order for sustainable school and district improvement to occur, a priority focus was placed on scaling up those school-based practices that were rendering the highest academic outcomes for all students. This focus resulted in teacher leaders sharing best teaching and new learning practices across all schools. These highly successful practices were supported by research and included professional development that was: job-embedded; involved the analysis of student performance data; provided follow-up and coaching to help teachers implement new learning; and included a form of accountability for implementation (Aseltine et al., 2006; Hipp & Huffman, 2010; Jerald, 2009; Waters, 2011).

An example of a successful practice shared by teacher leaders was the analysis of student data performance based on standardized tests. While collaboration among teachers within schools was a routine practice for the purpose of reviewing and discussing student performance and planning for student improvement, collaboration across the district was not a normal practice. The district leadership team worked in partnership with school and teacher leaders during the transition to the PLC process to support teachers reaching out across the district to those teachers who were achieving high levels of student success. Rather than keeping strategies deemed successful for improving student performance within their own schools, content teacher leaders began to connect with teachers from other schools to share effective strategies for student improvement. Thus, teachers in schools throughout the district were able to incorporate those most effective practices resulting in improved student performance across the district.

District leaders sought to establish a community of professionals who embraced a growth mindset in and among all schools through the implementation of professional learning communities. The leadership capacity among teachers was critical to sustaining this collaborative, problem solving approach to school and district improvement (Guskey, 2009). Equally as important, district leaders understood the importance of a principal's ability to focus on instruction and ability to foster strong collegial communities utilizing teacher leaders within the school (Reeves, 2009; Supovitz, Sirinides, & May, 2010). This required the principal to have a strong instructional leadership capacity and a unique understanding of followership. District leaders accepted this notion and recognized that strengthening their own leadership capacity, and the leadership capacity in schools, held promise for cultivating rapid and long-term school and district improvement.

Thus, the process of district-wide implementation of PLCs began during the summer of 2011 when district leaders educated themselves about what characterized the PLC process. They also read and discussed articles about the subject as they decided how to successfully implement the PLC process district-wide. District leaders then communicated the vision for PLCs to school-level leaders including principals, assistant principals, and teacher leaders from each school. These personnel were also introduced to the literature on the concept of PLCs.

During the first year of this process, the district leadership team focused on developing leadership capacity among school-level leaders so they could create on every school campus the vision and supportive conditions for the type of professional learning/teacher collaboration associated with highly productive PLCs. During the second year of district-wide implementation, the focus was on producing results. As the district deepened its understanding and refined its practices during the 3rd and 4th focus years, the implementation of PLCs has rendered impressive results. Focal points during this transition of embedding the PLC process within the school culture are highlighted in Figure 7.2.

The principals' survey results from a research-based leadership instrument designed to assess leaders' perceptions of these school improvement efforts indicated continued and dramatic improvement in principals' actions. Students continued to produce higher results on statewide assessments with more students scoring in the advanced and mastery categories, and fewer students scoring in the unsatisfactory and approaching basic categories. In the Louisiana accountability system, over the course of four years, the district grew from having six A-labeled schools (high-performing) to having sixteen A-labeled schools, and from having seven D- or F-labeled schools (low-performing) to today having no failing schools (Louisiana Department of Education, 2015). These results show the impact resulting from this district's transformation into a culture of learning centered on the creation and implementation of PLCs.

The following sections highlight the qualitative findings that surfaced across all data analyzed including: thematic coding of individual interviews of district, school, and teacher leaders; focus group interviews of teacher leaders; district and school document analyses; and observations of leaders in action during professional learning and collaborative session.

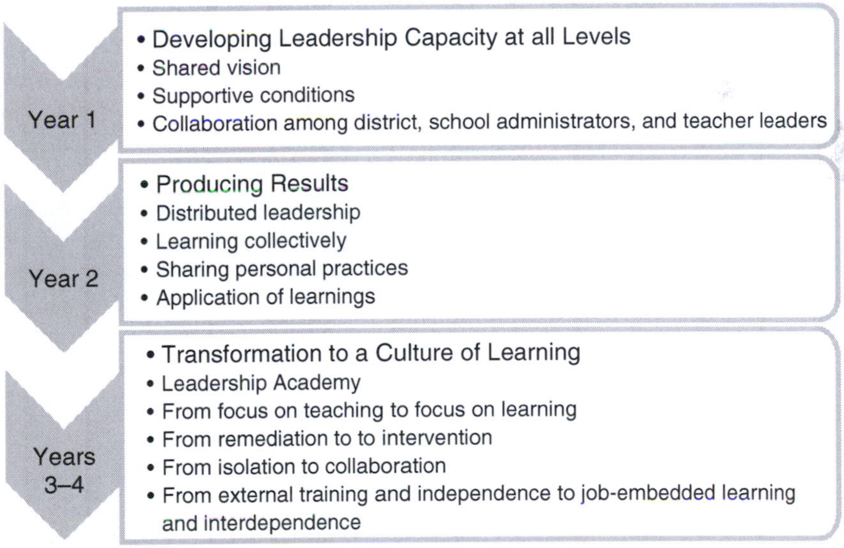

Year 1
- Developing Leadership Capacity at all Levels
- Shared vision
- Supportive conditions
- Collaboration among district, school administrators, and teacher leaders

Year 2
- Producing Results
- Distributed leadership
- Learning collectively
- Sharing personal practices
- Application of learnings

Years 3–4
- Transformation to a Culture of Learning
- Leadership Academy
- From focus on teaching to focus on learning
- From remediation to to intervention
- From isolation to collaboration
- From external training and independence to job-embedded learning and interdependence

Figure 7.2 Focus during the PLC transition process

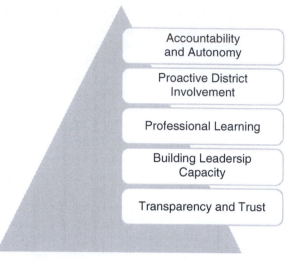

Figure 7.3 Major findings contributing to a culture of learning

Accountability and autonomy

Throughout this process, district leaders fully subscribed to the philosophy of *defined autonomy* (Marzano & Waters, 2009). The district gave school leaders the autonomy to lead their schools and implement PLC initiatives within the district's vision and instructional cohesiveness and held them highly accountable for producing results. Marzano and Waters (2009) described the construct of *defined autonomy* as giving principals complete autonomy to lead as long as they lead within the parameters set by the district goals. For example, when Ascension first initiated the professional learning community philosophy, district leaders gave principals the broad non-negotiable that every school would have teachers collaborate around the Three Big Ideas and the Four Questions (DuFour, DuFour, Eaker & Karhanek, 2009). The district based its cultural transformation on the belief that all children will learn to high levels, that collaboration would be at the heart of all professional work, and there would be a strong focus on results. Thus, teachers began their collaboration centered on four questions posed by DuFour et al. (2009):

- What do we want each student to learn?
- How will we know when each student has learned?
- How will we respond when a student experiences initial difficulty in learning?
- How will we enrich and extend the learning of a student who is already proficient?

The organization of teacher collaboration, the utilization of specific structures, and the interaction between principals and teacher leaders to support teachers, were all at the total discretion of the principals and their leadership teams. The district provided resources and models for how this collaboration could be structured and implemented, but school personnel had the autonomy to make decisions as to what would work on their campus. While the school's staff retained autonomy, district leaders held school leaders (administrators and teachers) highly accountable for results through tracking quarterly district benchmark assessment data and monitoring the quality of student work.

As the implementation of PLCs progressed in the district, other non-negotiables were established. For example, each principal and teacher collaborative PLC team was asked to develop quarterly short-term wins so progress toward yearly goals could be tracked and efficacy could be built through success. The principals and PLC teams could set these short-term wins; however, they were determined by focusing on the needs of each school and each set of teachers. The first year almost everyone set short-term wins around processes and structures for implementing PLCs. The following year, the non-negotiable became that the short-term win had to be measurable in terms of student academic outcomes.

Again, which academic outcomes were measured was entirely determined by school-level personnel based on their data. As it became clear school staff were struggling with shared decision making and the effective use of leadership teams, district staff set the non-negotiable that each school would have a leadership team with teacher leaders who met frequently to guide the school improvement processes and PLC implementation. School personnel were given training and support on how leadership teams should function and the roles teachers should play in decision making, but all determinations around who served on the team, what decisions they made, and how they functioned were made at the school level. The latest non-negotiable given to the school staff was that each teacher and PLC team would have individual student growth plans (IGPs) through which individual student progress would be tracked. The principals and teacher leaders were tasked with making decisions around what standards would be tracked, which students would be tracked, what tracking form or mechanism would be used, and how teachers would be supported and monitored in the implementation.

This approach of maintaining accountability while offering autonomy is not without challenges. There is a delicate balance between too much autonomy and too many district expectations. Eck and Goodwin (2010) suggested that the appropriate amount of autonomy districts should give to schools should be differentiated. The key to success is in balancing the amount of autonomy given with strong accountability for improved student outcomes and then providing the appropriate amount of support to each school to assure success with some schools requiring more support than others.

Early in the PLC process implementation, district leaders found that school principals and teacher leaders' readiness varied widely. Some principals wanted to be left alone to run their schools. Conversely, others wanted to be told step-by-step exactly what to do. The same was true of teachers. Some wanted to shut the doors of the classroom and do their own thing. Others wanted someone to provide the magic formula for success. Other teachers wanted to hide behind a cloak of "*the district said we had to do it this way.*" This range of attitudes was indicative of the difficulty of moving organizational structures and leadership from a hierarchal model to a collaborative one. In a study on district organizational restructuring to empower leaders and teachers throughout the system to make decisions, researchers found that some leaders both at the district and school level did not embrace the change in that they saw it as a threat to their power and position (Bjork & Blasé, 2009).

To that end, the district provided appropriate training and support regardless of the spectrum of readiness of the principal or teacher leader. District leaders worked with principals to empower teachers to make curriculum decisions collaboratively in their PLCs and tried to remove barriers and clarify misconceptions along the way. For example, the primary school culture was very much about "rule following," and among teachers there was often a sense of "*the district says we have to.*" District leaders continued to work in schools with principals and teacher leaders to dispel the misconceptions and provided permission for teachers to make professional decisions based on the needs of students. All of these integral, moving parts required continuous monitoring and support by district leaders such that a culture of success and collective efficacy was built among all principals and teachers and across the entire district.

A highly effective strategy utilized by district leaders in supporting schools is the assignment of an Instructional Leadership Partner (ILP) from the district office to each school. The role of the ILP was to coach the principal and leadership teams, consisting of other administrators and teacher leaders in the school, on their leadership behaviours so that school improvement processes and PLC processes continued to be the focus of everyone on the campus. Additionally, other district leaders performed classroom walk-throughs and provided feedback on such things as curriculum implementation, rigor of the curriculum, and the quality of student thinking seen in classrooms.

Proactive district involvement

The culture necessary to foster a high level of shared leadership and collaboration across the entire district could only be accomplished through very strategic, deliberate actions on the part of district leaders. Fullan (2005b) suggests "Leadership at the school level must be framed in terms of the district's role" (p. 176). He concluded that a *compelling conceptualization* by all district leaders that included both a deep understanding of the content of the reform, as well as a strong commitment to building the leadership capacity of school teams, was necessary to implement any sustainable improvement efforts. Thus, when central office administrators, school administrators, and teacher leaders collaborated around improvement efforts, capacity was built at every level and district collective efficacy increased. This type of collaboration among all leaders assured common understanding and built on the collective wisdom of leaders at all levels. When the expertise of all leaders was tapped through collaborative processes, the shared vision of the district and the exact means of achieving the vision were understood equally by all.

One of the first actions undertaken by district leaders to begin this cultural evolution was to change the format and focus of principal and staff meetings. Historically in the district, these monthly meetings had revolved around procedures and information delivered from the superintendent and directors to the principals. Principals dutifully took notes and tried not to ask too many questions. The district leadership strongly believed that this time set aside monthly was an opportunity for collaboration and new learning around improving student academic outcomes. Informational topics were handled in emails and newsletters, and principal and staff meetings became strategically-planned learning opportunities where district leaders and principals and teacher leaders engaged in collaborative dialogue around best practices and next steps in their learning around PLCs and their implementation across the district.

Principals and teacher leaders had an active voice in shaping the implementation and the district as a whole profited from the collective wisdom of the entire team. The interview and document analyses, as well as observations of district, school, and teacher leaders' actions, provided clear evidence of the role of leaders throughout the district and at all levels of leadership. While the district leadership team introduced the initial steps to transition schools and the district to higher performance levels, the district leadership teams' proactive involvement generated high levels of participation by school administrators and teacher leaders.

The district leadership was uniquely positioned to create shared leadership for teachers, school level leaders, and central office personnel to engage collaboratively in practices such as principal professional learning communities, curriculum writing, district-wide benchmark creation, analysis of data, determining common proficiency standards for student work, and doing peer observations across schools. This focus on sustainable district-school reform was framed by a strong relationship between the district as a whole and the individual schools in the district.

Professional learning

A community of professional learning developed in this district from a commitment to continuous learning on the part of all professional staff. PLCs were the infrastructure enabling high quality and focused learning through collaboration. Additionally, leaders from across the district attended professional conferences with PLCs as the focus, always with the intention of promoting shared and supportive leadership that would engage teacher leaders in activities designed to sustain a culture of learning in the district (Hipp & Huffman, 2010).

District leaders, including Instructional Leadership Partners, formed into PLCs, meeting regularly, as mentioned previously, to focus on their leadership development and to understand how principals can use their influence in the school building to develop teacher leaders. Principals were then asked to create their own Principal Professional Learning Communities (PPLCs) in order to truly focus on increasing the academic achievement of students. This served to create networks of PLCs, as described by Fullan (2005a), at the administrative level, and these networks ultimately brought together teacher leaders and PLCs from the various schools to focus on their professional learning, all centered on student work. This focus on student performance was now being shared not only beyond individual classroom walls but beyond the confines of any individual school campus. District leaders modeled behaviours that cultivated and transformed cultures into strong learning communities by working directly with skilled PPLC facilitators chosen by the members of each PPLC. PPLC facilitators were provided with formal learning opportunities based on the district's identified needs.

Today in this district, hundreds of teacher leaders have engaged in the professional learning required to become certified evaluators. This phenomenon arose as a result of district and school leaders, including teachers, recognizing the importance of the district vision becoming part of the culture of the schools. Part of that vision included having teacher leaders deeply understand the teacher observation rubric since these teacher leaders would lead the way in providing feedback about professional practice in the classroom. This is another example of how professional learning has become the culture of this district.

Thus, PLCs have become the process within which the content of all new learning is embedded in this district (Olivier & Huffman, 2014). Whether that was ensuring that teachers understood and could use effectively the Seven Strategies of Assessment for Learning, focusing on students improving their ability to respond to higher order thinking prompts in association with nonfiction texts, the Five Steps for Effective Learning in Leadership Teams, or a school improvement strategy by any other name, professional learning occurs and the work gets accomplished through the PLC process and professional learning teams.

Leadership development/capacity building

Leadership is absolutely critical to the success of this type of collaborative culture. To that end, a Leadership Academy was created in Year 3 of the culture transformation to assure a pipeline of leaders at all levels. The development of the Ascension Leadership Academy was the district staff's commitment to, and investment in, developing leaders with high potential to positively impact the educational experiences of all students. The academy serves to develop a talent pool of internal candidates who are actively interested in growing the organization, promoting its success, and are engaged over time to fill formal and informal leadership positions at the school and district-level.

Participants, teacher leaders and named administrators, are engaged in developing their own competencies associated with transformational leadership and aligned to leadership behaviours that show a statistically significant correlation to student academic success (Goldring, Porter, Murphy, Elliot & Cravens, 2009).

During the first year of the academy's existence, 20 of the district's 28 schools and programs directly benefited from the academy work. However, all schools were indirectly impacted by the energy created from the professional learning of the academy facilitators and participants. Teacher leaders were demonstrating a stronger ability to lead outside of their classroom on campus and at the district level. School and district leaders were more capable of demonstrating the ability to drive results, build relationships, and manage people. The academy work provided robust insight into the district's improvement efforts while posing thought-provoking questions about the importance of building teacher and instructional leadership capacity through job-embedded professional development with a focus on instructional strategies to meet student needs. This work helped teachers and school leaders meet student learning needs by connecting research-based, data-driven best practices to daily classroom instruction. Hipp and Huffman (2010) defined this type of professional learning as neither a program nor a prescription, but rather an infrastructure that fosters school improvement and change through professional development.

Transparency and trust

While leadership capacity is important, the effectiveness will be limited unless trust and transparency serve as the foundation to continued progress. Based on the research, district leaders were aware of the necessity of creating the supportive conditions critical for transparency and trust to exist among district- and school-level professional staff (Cranston, 2009; Hipp & Huffman, 2010; Hord & Sommers, 2008; Louis, 2008; Printy, 2008; Rasberry & Mahajan, 2008; Tschannen-Moran, 2009). In order for this to occur, schools' professional staff needed to be united around how they would attain future goals (Hipp & Huffman, 2010). They would need to collaboratively develop and share agreed-upon values and vision for school improvement (Doolittle, Sudeck, & Rattigan, 2008; Giles & Hargreaves, 2006; Hipp & Huffman, 2010; Pascal & Blankstein, 2008; Vescio, Ross, & Adams, 2008). With that end in mind, district leaders created opportunities for teachers to share personal practice and make high-quality decisions based on data as noted by researchers as effective characteristics of PLCs (Hord & Sommers, 2008; Leithwood, Patten, & Jantzi, 2010; Louis, 2006).

The Instructional Leadership Partners (ILPs) served a vital role in ensuring transparency and trust between district- and school-level leaders. This movement toward PLCs becoming the process for this district's culture of learning began with ensuring that school improvement priorities were consistently communicated to the Instructional Leadership Partners. This also required a high level of trust since specific needs of leaders, teachers, and students would be openly discussed resulting in the group working to collectively problem solve around the identified needs (Tschannen-Moran, 2009). In order to extend that transparency and trust while communicating the district vision of high expectations and data-driven decision making to all professional staff, district leaders established quarterly *Principal Data Sharing Sessions* (PDSS).

Principals shared with district leaders personal thoughts about organizing their data presentations, delivering the information to colleagues and district leaders, and their feeling and perceptions upon completion of the data-sharing process. Even though they experienced nervousness during the data-sharing process, due to trust established through integral work with ILP, principals overwhelmingly expressed how this analysis and sharing process assisted them individually in identifying behaviours that moved results in a positive direction. These positive behaviours included things like communicating the vision for examining student work in PLCs and monitoring to ensure that teachers understood how to accomplish this goal. When principals did not specifically plan for this kind of teacher support, they reported poor results. As a result of this examination of their practice, they specifically planned for opportunities to interact with PLC groups and provide the kind of follow-up support needed to sustain best practices in the classroom.

They reflected on this process in the context of necessary actions for creating the same supportive conditions for transparency and trust on their campuses. While principals reported being in different places in regard to teacher *readiness* for such data sharing practices, they worked with their ILPs and collaborated with their leadership teams to move forward. These leadership teams included assistant principals and teacher leaders (such as PLC facilitators). Leadership team members would initiate steps to re-create the same sharing of personal practice at the teacher PLC level. The leadership teams understood that this type of collective learning and application of best practices served as a vital part of school improvement efforts designed to support leadership development among teachers (Hipp & Huffman, 2010).

Continued steps toward sustainability

In order to ensure sustainability of the transformation to a culture of learning through the PLC process, next steps are continually reviewed for effectiveness. Teacher Data Sharing Sessions have become the norm in this district, to the point where teacher leaders describe how the process has become self-sustaining because of the results they observe. Their practice in PLCs has expanded to analysis of common formative assessments, a practice engaged in not just quarterly but as a matter of course when teachers gather in their PLCs. Gathering in PLCs has become not just an event scheduled for a particular day of the week, but a process – a vision – that unites them to attain future goals. Teacher leaders have described how their collaboration in PLCs has been elevated beyond mere sharing of lesson plans, beyond sharing of tests and quizzes to serious, focused analysis of individual student achievement and working collectively to ensure that students master essential learning, as described by DuFour et al. (2009).

Summary

The initial intentional focus by Ascension district staff and the subsequent actions by district, school, and teacher leaders resulted in a reculturing of the district as a professional learning community. In adhering to the PLC concept and a high level of commitment to student achievement and continuous learning by all, the district truly transformed into a *culture of learning*. Thus, the PLC process has become embedded throughout the district with a culture focusing on a learning process that is utilized to address any and all issues at the school level and system-wide.

It is important to note, Ascension district leaders established non-negotiables throughout this process. They offered *autonomy* to school leaders for implementation of the PLC process while still promoting *accountability*. District and school leaders promoted a sense of shared responsibility for all staff and student learning. District and school leaders consistently monitored progress to maintain focus on alignment of district and school vision, goals, and objectives.

Ascension district leaders were *proactive* in their involvement as active participants in the learning process. Through efforts by district staff, such as consistently modeling shared leadership and vision, district and school leaders became partners in the learning process. In working hand-in-hand, district personnel were directly involved in school-level collaborative groups and reinforced the necessary collective learning and application of learning. District personnel provided support and resources to schools based on identified individual needs.

Ascension School System used the PLC process as an infrastructure for continuous *professional learning*. District leaders modeled and clarified expectations of collaboration as an essential component of professional learning, thus transitioning to continuous learning as the norm and an integral part of the culture. Relevant job-embedded professional learning and the provision of time and resources to enable high-quality and focused collaboration were supported and reinforced.

Ascension utilized multiple layers of leadership to accomplish district and school goals. Various opportunities and resources for *leadership development and capacity building* were provided to strengthen current leadership and to create an avenue for teachers to transition from informal to formal leadership positions. District leaders fostered leadership succession in order to sustain a culture of learning by targeting personnel at multiple levels and providing smooth transitions and thus continuity in moving forward. District leaders modeled highly effective leadership practices through interactions among all professional staff.

Ascension's vision was clearly articulated and regularly reviewed. In an effort to be *transparent* from the district level and to maintain high levels of *trust*, a focus remained on being clear and consistent through communication, thus ensuring everyone was on the same page. District leaders clearly delineated high levels of expectations, decision making by all through quality data-driven decisions, and use of common and consistent language to communicate and maintain district priorities.

District leaders credit their investment in professional learning communities for the continuous improvement that has occurred over the past several years. Teachers and leaders, actively engaged in collaborative teams, are holding one another mutually accountable for making significant student achievement gains while growing professionally. This emphasis by district leaders has transformed the professional culture by placing teachers at the helm of school improvement. District leaders acknowledge that the cultural transformation has created a strong alignment between student goals, teacher goals, school goals, and district goals. This tight alignment, coupled with the balance between professional autonomy and accountability, has provided conditions that are fostering teacher collaboration.

The level of transparency and trust that exists in this district today has heightened collaboration and placed a higher value on teachers' professional knowledge and instructional practices. Professional learning communities have been the driver for cultural transformation with district leaders directly and explicitly building capacity for sustained school improvement through teacher leadership. "In recent years, districts have become increasingly accountable for the learning outcomes of students in the schools within the districts" (Cowan, Joyner, & Beckwith, 2012, p. 9). Researchers note that sustainability of school reform is dependent on district support (Appelbaum, 2002) and "districts matter fundamentally to what goes on in schools and classrooms" (McLaughlin & Talbert, 2003, p. 5). Our research supports this clear involvement by districts to positively influence school improvement and specifically the success of students.

The intense focus by district, school, and teacher leaders within Ascension School System has resulted in sustainability of effort as evident by the district's continual growth, increasing levels of student performance, and recognition as one of the state's highest performing districts. Ascension School System serves as an excellent model of the pivotal role of district support and the ability and feasibility to transition from PLC implementation to PLC sustainability and to promote a culture of learning among all leaders throughout the system.

References

Appelbaum, D. (2002). *The need for district support for school reform: What the researchers say. Research Brief.* Washington, D.C.: National Clearinghouse for Comprehensive School Reform.

Ascension Public School. (2015). *Welcome to Ascension Public Schools*. Retrieved from www.apsb.org/page/superintendent-pujol/

Aseltine, J., Faryniarz, J., & Rigazio-DiGilio, A. (2006). *Supervision for learning – a performance-based approach to teacher development and school improvement*. Alexandria, VA: Association for Supervision and Curriculum Development.

Bjork, L. G., & Blasé, J. (2009). The micropolitics of school district decentralization. *Educational Assessment, Evaluation, and Accountability, 21*(3), 195–208.

Cowan, D., Joyner, S., & Beckwith, S. (2012). *Getting serious about the system: A fieldbook for district and school leaders*. Thousand Oaks, CA: Corwin Press.

Cranston, J. (2009). Holding the reins of the professional learning community: Eight themes from research on principals' perceptions of professional learning communities. *Canadian Journal of Educational Administration and Policy, 90,* 1–22. Retrieved from www.umanitoba.ca/publications/cjeap/pdf_files/cranston.pdf \

Doolittle, G., Sudeck, M., & Rattigan, P. (2008). Creating professional learning communities: The work of professional development schools. *Theory Into Practice, 47,* 303–310. doi: 10.1080/004058402329276

DuFour, R., DuFour, R., Eaker, R., & Karhanek, G. (2009). *Raising the bar and closing the gap: Whatever it takes*. Bloomington, IN: Solution Tree Press.

Eck, J., & Goodwin, B. (2010). Autonomy for school leaders. *The School Administrator, 67*(1), 24–27.

Elmore, R. (2006). *Bridging the gap between standards and achievement: The imperative for professional development in education*. Washington, D.C.: The Albert Shanker Institute.

Fullan, M. (2005a). *Leadership and sustainability: System thinkers in action*. Thousand Oaks, CA: Corwin Press.

Fullan, M. (2005b). Turnaround leadership. *Educational Forum, 69*(2), 174–181.

Giles, C., & Hargreaves, A. (2006). The sustainability of innovative schools as learning organizations and professional learning communities during standardized reform. *Educational Administration Quarterly, 42*(1), 124–156.

Goldring, E., Porter, A., Murphy, J., Elliott, S., & Cravens, X. (2009). Assessing learning-centered leadership: Connections to research, professional standards, and current practices. *Leadership and Policy in Schools, 8*(1), 1–36.

Guskey, T. R. (2009). Closing the knowledge gap on effective professional development. *Educational Horizons, 87*(4), 224–233.

Haycock, K. (2011). *Raising achievement and closing gaps between groups: Lessons from schools and districts*. Jacksonville, FL: Duval County Public Schools.

Hipp, K. K., & Huffman, J. B. (2010). *Demystifying professional learning communities*. New York: Rowman & Littlefield Education.

Hord, S. M., & Sommers, W. A. (2008). *Leading professional learning communities*. Thousand Oaks, CA: Corwin Press.

Jerald, C. (2009). *Aligned by design: How teacher compensation reform can support and reinforce other educational reforms*. Washington, D.C.: Center for American Progress.

Leithwood, K., Patten, S., & Jantzi, D. (2010). Testing a conception of how school leadership influences student learning. *Educational Administration Quarterly, 46*(5), 671–706.

Louis, K. S. (2006). Changing the culture of schools: Professional community, organizational learning, and trust. *Journal of School Leadership 16*(5), 1–20. Retrieved from http://pdfs.scarecroweducation.com/SC/TJS/SCTJSLSep2006.pdf\

Louis, K. S. (2008). Creating and sustaining professional communities. In A. Blankstein, P. Houston, & R. Cole (Eds.), *Sustaining professional learning communities* (pp. 41–57). Thousand Oaks, CA: Corwin Press.

Louisiana State Department of Education. (2015). *Student information system report.* Retrieved from www.louisianabelieves.com

Marzano, R., & Waters, J. T. (2009). *District leadership that works: Striking the right balance.* Bloomington, IN: Solution Tree Press.

McLaughlin, M., & Talbert, J. (2003). *Reforming districts: How districts support school reform.* Center for the Study of Teaching and Policy, University of Washington.

Olivier, D. F., & Huffman, J. B. (2014). *Professional learning community process in the United States: Conceptualization and role of district in supporting schools.* Paper presented at the International Congress for School Effectiveness and Improvement, Cincinnati, Ohio.

Pascal, N. S., & Blankstein, A. M. (2008). Communities committed to learning. In A. Blankstein, P. Houston, & R. Cole (Eds.), *Sustaining professional learning communities* (pp. 5–21). Thousand Oaks, CA: Corwin Press.

Printy, S. (2008). Leadership for teacher learning: A community of practice perspective. *Educational Administration Quarterly, 44*(2), 187–226.

Rasberry, M. A., & Mahajan, G. (2008). *From isolation to collaboration: Promoting teacher leadership through PLCs.* Hillsboro, NC: Center for Teaching Quality.

Reeves, D. (2009). *Leading change in your school: How to conquer myths, build commitment, and get results.* Alexandria, VA: Association for Supervision and Curriculum Development.

Supovitz, J., Sirinides, P., & May, H. (2010). How principals and peers influence teaching and learning. *Educational Administration Quarterly, 46*(1), 31–56.

Tschannen-Moran, M. (2009). Fostering teacher professionalism in schools: The role of leadership orientation and trust. *Educational Administration Quarterly, 45*(2), 217–247.

Vescio, V., Ross, D., & Adams, A. (2008). A review of research on the impact of professional learning communities on teaching practice and student learning. *Teaching and Teacher Education: An International Journal of Research, 24*(1), 80–91.

Waters, T. (2011). *Accountability for what works, what matters, and what's next: Accountability for high reliability education.* Paper presented at the AASA National Education Conference, Denver, CO. Retrieved from www.mcrel.org/PDF/LeadershipOrganization Development/S102WM_AASA_Accountability.pdf

8 District efforts to support the professional learning community framework in schools

Transformation of learning

Jane B. Huffman, James K. Wilson and Mike Mattingly

Introduction and context

The professional learning community (PLC) term is used in a variety of ways throughout the world. In the United States, it is defined by Hipp and Huffman (2010) as "Professional educators working collectively and purposefully to create and sustain a culture of learning for all students and adults" (p. 12). The development of a successful PLC culture involves intentional and ongoing work in five dimensions: Shared and Supportive Leadership, Shared Values and Vision, Collective Learning, Shared Personal Practice, and Supportive Conditions – Relational and Structural (Hord, 1997). Thus, the PLC is used to refer to a school-based framework centered on adult learning and collaboration for the purpose of student learning. The focus of this chapter is to report findings about how this framework was implemented in one Texas district. Evidence will be presented related to how the PLC culture developed and how it continued to be sustained *over time*. By working together, yet focusing on the essential work of the teacher teams, districts and leaders collaboratively aligned and focused support strategies for student achievement.

The district

Denton Independent School District (DISD) has a history of strong student achievement and innovative research-based practices. Their interest in the PLC framework over many years provided the context for this research. DISD is a fast growth district just north of the Dallas/Ft. Worth metro area serving 38,000 students, and situated within 180 square miles. The student population has steadily increased over the past seven years at an average growth rate of 4.7 percent annually. Approximately one-third of the student population qualify for free or reduced lunch classifying these students as economically disadvantaged. The ethnic distribution of students attending DISD schools is 11.7 percent African American, 31.3 percent Hispanic, 51.9 percent White, 1.0 percent Native American, 2.7 percent Asian, and 1.45 percent reported 2 or more races. As the district continues to grow, so does student achievement. Every DISD campus met all requirements in all areas in the most recent state accountability system.

In the beginning – initial efforts

The PLC framework began to emerge in the mid-2000s with initial interest of principals and central office staff. In early years, the school district depended on principals to ensure teaching was effective. Most principals visited classrooms, reviewed teaching practices, and looked for evidence of student learning, but rarely intervened in the work of the teacher. The principal knew if student performance was acceptable then teaching was acceptable. If student performance was poor, then the teaching must be below par. Only in rare instances were principals prepared to assist the teaching-learning process. Often, teachers did not have a mechanism for receiving effective feedback about good teaching, and found themselves tied to their classrooms with little time to meet.

In the absence of collaboration, isolated teachers were dependent on their own knowledge of teaching practice and student performance. Further, drawing conclusions about teaching practices and resulting student outcomes proved difficult. School district professional development was in place; however, large-scale impact was absent. Clearly, the school district needed a process to transition a culture of isolation and independent teaching practice to a culture focusing on learning and collaboration. The transition needed to include the expertise already existing in the district's teaching force, yet was not pervasive across all schools. The district leadership realized a monumental change would be necessary to adjust the way teaching and learning would be addressed.

After a number of district, school, and teacher leaders attended introductory PLC professional development opportunities, it was resolved that district-wide reform could be achieved with a strong commitment to utilizing a PLC framework. This initiative serves to reculture school learning based on effective teacher leadership. Hord (1997) notes school reform can be enacted when organizations practice effective collaboration centered on common goals for student learning.

The success of any school system is dependent on the work of its teachers, and as teachers experience the successes of mutual discovery and collective action, changes begin to occur inside classrooms and eventually across the school. Teachers lead the way as they influence school reform through collaborative study of teaching and learning practices. The following sections of the chapter report evidence related to how teachers impacted upon reform. When teachers engage in a successful PLC culture, the evidence shows that powerful educational reform takes place (Katzenmeyer & Moller, 2001; Olivier & Hipp, 2006).

The research: methodology, data collection and analysis

The overarching research question for this qualitative study is: *How do school district personnel (central office staff) support schools in the professional learning community framework?* The participants of this study included principals, teacher leaders, and central office staff from a district in Texas. The researchers developed the interview protocol based on the five PLC dimensions and descriptors for each dimension. The support for data use to enhance teaching and learning and challenges related to support of the PLC process were investigated.

Data were collected through both individual interviews, focus groups, observations, and document analysis. Individuals were selected through purposeful samplings and interviews were conducted with principals, teacher leaders, and central office staff. In selecting the teacher leader representatives it was determined that, due to their leadership responsibilities (grade level, content, and department chairs), they would be aware of actions and support by district-level personnel for the professional learning community process. Interviews and focus group responses were captured through audio taping, recording of notes, and transcriptions. Each interview was read by two of the three researchers to individually analyze responses and margin notes. Observations and document analysis also assisted in providing relevant information. Data analysis utilized a constant comparative analysis whereby themes were identified and coded as they surfaced across all interview questions and other documentation.

Findings related to teachers

The findings are represented under three headings: the emergence of the professional learning team, how the teachers' practice was changed, and the development of teacher and school collective capacity.

a) Reforming the teaching community: the professional learning team

As teachers began engaging and participating in professional learning communities in schools, they soon reported an unexpected outcome. It was the community that formed. Teachers began meeting, sharing, collaborating, discussing, reflecting, contributing, listening. Coming together to plan and share ideas was not, in itself, uncommon, but this interaction was different. The meetings were not the lesson-planning meetings they had grown accustomed to through the years, where ideas were shared and batted around to either include or not, depending on whether it seemed to fit the objective, theme, or time-frame of the lesson. Now there are expectations, and these expectations are tied to a bigger purpose. The work from these collaborative meetings is expected to provide support and direction for the mission and vision of the school. Also, the work of this new community, the PLC, aligns the vision, the teaching, and the assessments to student learning outcomes.

In many cases, the professional learning team (PLT) forms based on the course or grade level taught, as principals organize schools into a number of professional learning teams. This brings people together who may not have collaborated in the past. Formerly, teachers just found a colleague they felt comfortable with and they would plan together. Now, working in a PLT, comfort zones are challenged. Each member of the PLT contributes his or her own personalities and views about collaboration.

Now teachers report they contribute and add value to discussions, and they expect to do this in a team environment with unfamiliar members. A certain amount of natural risk is present in every meeting as members learn how to add to a discussion with the knowledge that others in the group may have opposing viewpoints. The risk level for someone to speak out in the beginning is high, but as time passes and meetings are held, the comfort increases and the risks decrease. Teachers are able to maneuver through discussions with ease. Team members accept the roles that each play, yet they welcome any contribution as an attempt to add value to work of the PLT. As the risk level dissipates over time, freedom to share opinions and viewpoints are honored by individuals and the group. Eventually, the team realizes not everything reviewed or analyzed in a PLT is received with a positive reaction. Being able to consider alternative viewpoints, however, makes the team stronger, is a positive part of the collaborative process, and is an important step in building a community in a culture of learning.

The community functions well because relationships form over time. Team members participate without fear of judgment or negative backlash, and trust is built over time among the team members. The outcomes from the PLT are more important than the process and it is understood that PLT members will feel uneasy in the beginning. However, with a commitment to PLC framework, schools that keep pushing through the early stages emerge with teachers working toward a common goal in a community of respect with their peers.

b) Reforming the work of teachers: the practice

Schmoker (2006) explains that isolation is the enemy of improvement. In a PLC culture, teachers are no longer isolated. They are part of a team that creates, responds, and reflects upon their work. Veteran teachers report that the PLC culture now gives them a support system that did not exist in the past. They have found comfort in knowing that there are others facing the same challenges in the classroom and that they can safely communicate about these challenges.

There are many ways teachers believe they have changed as a result of shifting to a PLC culture. A veteran high school science teacher comments:

> It is a unique opportunity to bond with others who share their daily experiences in the same context as mine, and have similar objectives and visions. Over the years, PLCs have made me a better teacher because they have allowed me to open my eyes to the understanding of what it truly means to be a real and committed educator.

An essential way the PLC framework has changed teachers is how they view their work. There is a shift in the emphasis; the focus is *learning* rather than teaching. Document review revealed that when teachers began assessing the results of their teaching, it altered their approach to problem solving. All actions considered as possible solutions were viewed through the lens of learning rather than teaching. Teachers report this shift is the primary change once a successful school-wide PLC is operational.

A teacher of only two years shared that PLTs became the built-in safety net for her. She reports that she "remains more focused on learning strategies rather than teaching activities." It has made her more aware of student outcomes and being able to recognize student success and failure. During professional learning team time she is able to bounce ideas off of her peers in a way that would not have existed before. The experienced teachers give practical advice and help their younger peers to avoid pitfalls in the teaching process. Working through the deep conversations in a PLT meeting gives younger or less experienced teachers the confidence they need when they return to the classroom and implement a new instructional strategy.

Another change involved teachers reviewing practices and determining what did or did not work based on results. Focus group interviews substantiate that, unless the collaborative team is focused on the work that makes a difference with learning, they risk not delivering coherent and collective results (Fullan & Quinn, 2015). Thus most often the PLTs examine student performance data by reviewing data and considering what is most important. The process is not sidelined by egos or personal agendas as teachers focus on teaching and learning practices with student learning outcomes in mind. Thus, teachers emphasize worthwhile learning activities and eliminate extraneous actions. One social studies teacher remarks:

> PLCs have shifted my thinking process from a teaching focus to a learning focus. I have learned how to collaborate with my colleagues, and use data in a meaningful way, to assess the effectiveness of what I'm doing in my classroom based on results rather than intentions.

Without the PLC framework, a teacher working in isolation could easily lose focus on effective practices.

An additional change that was observed is in the way teachers work and how teachers collaborate. Teachers share ideas, and now they understand the importance of studying their work and giving honest and complete feedback with every conversation. A positive interdependency is created as some teachers fill in the gaps where other teachers do not possess certain skill sets. The trust factor reinforces a professional confidence that all members contribute different qualities and can learn from each other without hesitation.

The teachers learn they are more willing to open the door to their colleagues. For instance, the practice observed in one middle school revealed a team of special education teachers struggling with math co-teaching. Special education teachers were invited to observe the teachers within the math department. They visited each classroom and made observational notes, reflecting first individually, and then together. Further, they shared with the special education

PLT the new understanding of their role in a co-teaching model. Through the action and study of both groups, the math and special education teachers became owners of a solution that could have easily lingered in the school without any helpful change.

A significant way PLTs have changed teachers is in their work with students. Teachers report they are better equipped to know what students have learned. PLTs allow teachers to become expert assessment developers. By frequently monitoring student progress, teachers stay on top of identifying students making adequate progress or merely coasting. Teachers plan for assessment, and through ongoing PLC work they help each other create formative assessments that reveal what students know or are able to do. Planning has changed from what will I teach, to *what do I expect my students to learn?* Moreover, the question becomes *how do I know they know it?*

Engaging in the work of PLCs, a middle school science teacher suggests, "I have the opportunity to study the curriculum and analyze the success or weakness of my instruction." PLC work provides the chance to strengthen her areas of weakness with instructional success of other teachers. She shares, "PLCs enhance my teaching skills because it is no longer just about me. All of the lessons, instructions, and ideas come from collaboration among colleagues." Kouzes and Posner (2003) note that, without collaboration, people can't get extraordinary things done.

c) Building individual and school collective capacity

The thought, effort, and time teachers put into school improvement can be directly tied to their work with professional learning communities. When teachers focus and use the PLC framework with fidelity, the results can transform the work of the teachers, and reform the teaching and learning process within a school. Collective capacity in schools is defined by Fullan (2007) as "actions that lead to an increase in the collective power of a group to improve student achievement" (p. 97).

For lasting changes to occur, however, the change must come not only from outside the school but also from within (Barth, 2001). Through careful examination of both longitudinal and real-time data, teacher teams are able to identify strengths and weaknesses in student performance, appropriate instructional strategies, curriculum units, teaching resources, and teacher content expertise. Teachers are then equipped to understand and comprehend the needs of the students and school community. Consequently, by engaging in effective school-wide professional learning communities, teachers build collective capacity when the work is focused on the core work of teaching and learning (Darling-Hammond & McLaughlin, 1995).

Teachers also report one of the primary ways they impact change on the campus is through the rich discussion that ensues as student data are examined. In a small group team, teachers spend time together reviewing student performance data and comparing expectations with outcomes. In the process of the review, the discussion considers three areas: instructional practices, organization of the curriculum, and assessments used along the way. Alignment among the three areas becomes the foundation for comprehensive analysis of data. Teachers question each aspect of the teaching and learning cycle, and through collaborative dialogue begin to unravel strengths and weaknesses of current practices. This conversation and resulting shared decision-making contribute to the capacity-building efforts of teachers in the school.

Impact on student learning: the use of data, formative assessments, and vertical alignment

One of the strongest arguments that can be made for implementing school-wide professional learning communities is teachers' impact on student learning (Huffman & Hipp, 2003). Teachers report that working together in PLTs gives them the time and tools to address instructional needs based on student performance data. Initially teachers spent time studying learning objectives and unpacking learning standards. Then, teachers determined which strategies to use with each data set and continued the process of analyzing which strategies produce positive results. Further, the teachers, working together, begin to develop formative assessments that when administered will accurately capture student progress during the teaching unit. As assessments occur throughout the learning process, teachers know they will receive immediate and accurate feedback throughout the teaching unit. With this feedback, teachers then consider three areas: past student performance data, teaching strategies, and instructional resources, to better understand the alignment or misalignment of teaching and student learning (see Figure 8.1).

Teacher conversations in PLTs, around these areas, helped them to design future lesson strategies by focusing on the alignment to standards and what works for students.

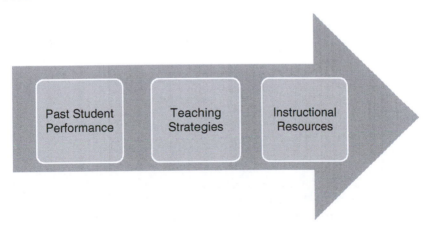

Figure 8.1 PLT review process for alignment

English teachers reported that the manner in which they teach thesis and position statements was changed based on common formative assessments. The teachers spent time together studying various approaches to teaching thesis statements and determining an approach that aligns to the students' needs based on the common assessments. Teachers' work to simplify the language of the standardized tests and to ensure common vocabulary is emphasized across learning tasks. Additionally, key academic vocabulary is identified and background knowledge established for students with gaps in learning. Further analysis includes summative results. Teachers shared that student performance increased by 5 percent in one year, and the economically disadvantaged students' passing rate increased by 9 percent.

A middle school science department had similar experiences by using professional learning community teams as the basis for school improvement. By participating in PLTs, the science department uses time together to study student science assessment data to guide future learning goals and lesson plans. When teachers create lesson plans with precise objectives that align with standards, the goals are more likely to be met across classrooms. Through a number of years of this practice in the middle school, significant student performance improvements occurred. In four years, the middle school percentage of students meeting satisfactory performance on the state assessment improved 24 percent and the commended performance improved 14 percent in the same four years (see Figure 8.2).

The science teachers collaborated over time with a specific goal in mind – to create scientifically literate critical thinkers. To accomplish this, they know the teaching strategies must focus on raising the level of thinking in their students. Again, the responsibilities of the science teachers include analysis of the outcomes of common assessments and adjusting rigor through teaching and questioning strategies. PLTs empower the teachers to set goals, develop common assessments based on careful study of the standards, use student performance data to adjust teaching, and create differentiated teaching approaches. They reach their instructional goals because they use time together to identify goals and explore options relevant to the goals. Professional

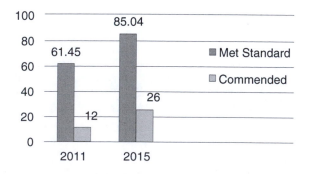

Figure 8.2 STAAR science assessment gains

development is considered only if it meets the needs of the team as it relates to their instructional goal – developing scientifically literate critical thinkers.

Campus PLTs allow the science teachers across grade levels to examine the components of state-mandated tests together. Many standards continue into the next year and teachers are able to implement spiraling standards and teaching strategies from year to year to help ensure successful science instruction. Thus the science PLTs enable vertical curriculum alignment and oversight of fundamental objectives that span multiple grade levels.

Another example of collaboration is how teachers layered questions. When teachers question why students are not grasping key concepts, the team works to investigate explanations. In this case, the teachers discover layered questions help students. Instead of low-level concept questions that lead to low-level thinking, teachers layer content questions with higher-level questions including reasoning and investigation process skills. Using this layering questioning as a key instructional approach, the students' thinking process improves. Also, by using the formative assessments, the learning is confirmed throughout the unit.

Observations support the idea that teachers agree the knowledge they now have of standards and formative and summative assessments has given them the opportunity to advance a student's understanding of science. After the rigorous analysis of the common assessments, unit summative assessments, and state-mandated standardized assessments, the teachers are better equipped to develop differentiated instruction that meets the needs of all students regardless of their learning challenges. Combined with a comprehensive approach to assessment and instruction using vertical alignment, the opportunities for student success at all levels increase.

Transformation of learning: the bigger picture

As a result of the accountability era in American education, principals and teachers now assume more responsibility for continuous school improvement and student achievement. Professional development of teachers, oriented towards the improvement of instruction and student learning, has become the expectation in American education. Thus, over the last decade, several critical outcomes have emerged to support these expectations. One outcome is that an operational structure within schools and districts for the delivery of professional development has become more defined.

Another outcome relates to the development of a culture of learning to provide a safe and trusting atmosphere so meaningful interaction and conversation occurs for both students and teachers. Such work provides a process for teacher collaboration and reflection. As a result, researchers document that professional learning community schools have positive impacts on student learning and teacher efficacy (Burdett, 2009; DuFour & Eaker, 1998; Hord, 1997).

Teachers in this study indicated that through the professional learning community framework they are better able to impact upon their own learning.

Unlike traditional professional development whereby teachers attend sessions after school or during the summer, teachers have found the power of learning at their own school and *with their colleagues*. Professional collaboration creates a support system among teachers. The reliance on school administrators for guidance and decision-making has decreased because teachers have learned to find solutions to their work among themselves. Team members are willing to help others in whatever ways possible, and assistance ranges from understanding the curriculum standards to using the newest technology. Interview and observation data confirm new learning comes from teacher professionalism situated within a PLC culture of learning.

For example, in the Denton schools, when teachers realized that scoring student writing is inconsistent from teacher to teacher, the PLT initiated a learning practice that brought teachers together to score and rate student writing samples jointly. The teachers created universal rubrics to use across content areas and grade levels. The reliability of scoring increased as they discussed the elements of each paper in the scoring process. Not only is inter-rater reliability created across classrooms, but teachers also develop ownership of their own learning. They share their work and they include everyone's contributions. Thus the learning practice is initiated by teachers and conducted voluntarily as they learn together for the benefit of students.

A Denton elementary teacher reports she desires to learn more about the writer's workshop based on what she observes happening in another teacher's classroom. She observes that her colleague brings writing samples from her classroom to a PLT collaboration meeting that are impressive and evidence of effective teaching practices. This sparks a need in the teacher to pursue additional professional learning in writing and she visits her colleague's classroom to watch demonstration lessons in writing instruction. The learning process is personalized, based on the teacher's needs, and as she develops confidence she too shares her new skills with other teachers in the district. She credits the PLT time as an opportunity to learn from each other and take advantage of the expertise of other teachers.

Professional development no longer requires a district mandate, attendance at a meeting, or even a book study for a teacher's learning to transpire. Now, teachers can impact their own learning by taking advantage of opportunities that emerge through the professional learning community culture. Darling-Hammond and McLaughlin (1995) suggest one of the most effective professional development models is when teachers are collaborating and sharing with other teachers. Teachers are empowered to make changes in teaching based on new learning related to personal and professional needs. The professional learning transcends the classroom walls through a collaborative system involving committed educators working toward common goals and supporting each other.

How did this happen?

Governance: School Board, District Office, and principals

The changes described in this chapter developed both from the bottom–up and the top-down, and over many years. The district context merges not only with state accountability expectations, but also federal regulations. In the United States, historically, federally mandated decision-making has often directed school reform efforts. The No Child Left Behind (NCLB) Act (2001) was one such example. NCLB required schools to examine the performance of students representing all groups and demographics. Undoubtedly, teachers have monitored individual student progress over time by differentiating instruction, forming literacy groups, and designing lessons to meet individual needs. However, now, as a result, schools and classrooms are held accountable and measured on the performance of these student groups.

Role of school board

To achieve federal and state mandates, campus leaders acknowledge the need for district awareness and system support. Communicating this need to the governing body is an essential step for the learning organization. The school board, the governing body of Denton ISD, has oversight of board, district, campus, and classroom goals. For teachers to make changes necessary to meet student needs, it is important for the district's board members to understand how the decisions for modifications are made. Such an understanding of how teachers do their work in the district provides the board members insight into the learning process and helps to monitor goal setting.

While many districts set aside time for teachers, campus leaders, and district staff to learn and work collaboratively in professional learning teams, such learning has not traditionally been extended to the school board. Though the majority of state and local taxes are spent on schools, most Americans do not understand the roles and responsibilities of the school board or their governance functions (Maeroff, 2010). If our schools are to embrace the potential of highly functioning PLCs, local governing bodies must have an understanding of the framework, the time commitment, and the resource needs of teachers and campus leaders.

In Texas, school boards are required to complete a session of team building on an annual basis. In an effort to provide a clear understanding of the PLC framework to the local school board, the Denton ISD school superintendent and the senior leadership team conducted board member training in 2009 on the role, function, and expected outcomes of the PLC framework. In this training, board members participated in a review of the PLC model and how it is implemented in schools. Building on this introductory learning, the district leaders began organizing the annual campus improvement planning workshop using a PLC presentation structure.

During this yearly workshop, the board room is transformed into a quasi-conference room designed to facilitate dialogue and conversation. About forty campus leaders representing all schools, all board members, and the superintendent, participate in the workshop with campus support personnel, community members, parents, the local media, and students sitting in the audience. Although not at the table, audience members are often called upon for information and/or participation depending on the topic. The purpose of the workshop is to review campus needs assessment, set performance indicators, and develop a plan of action for the coming year.

These plans have been developed at the campus level with input from all campus stakeholders. In addition to the academic goals outlined, the plans also meet all of the federal, state and local requirements of campus goal setting. This inclusive workshop is one way this district has shifted from the traditional roles of campus improvement with a primary focus on regulatory and business functions to a focus of supporting teaching and district-wide learning. As a result of this work, in 2011, the governing body established the following goal: "In pursuit of excellence, the district will establish quality staff development programs that promote professional learning communities."

Role of Central Office

Each year, in preparation for PLC work, the district's assistant superintendent for curriculum and instruction, curriculum coordinators, and the assistant superintendent for academic programs work with campus leaders to ensure each campus leader's voice is included. As conversations continue, it is clear the system of support for the schools is the responsibility of the district personnel. This assistance and support can be in the form of resource allocation, scheduling, framework for discussion, monitoring, or direct assistance. Often one will hear, "when implementing PLCs system wide," however PLCs are not really implemented. The PLC is a framework, not a program, or something you do at a certain time; it is more of a set of values and behaviors, which results in a dynamic culture of learning embedded throughout the school.

For this culture to be established, district leaders involve teachers and campus leaders in developing and leading the PLC efforts. This includes teaching both groups how to work together effectively so the PLC culture can be developed and refined. In addition, leaders show how PLCs fit into the overall district improvement process. The district incorporates a comprehensive leadership development process that includes PLC as the central component of the framework (see Figure 8.3). However, not all schools are in the same place at the same time, and support from the district recognizes such differentiation needs.

One significant area of negotiation is the value of time allocation. As each school begins initial steps, common time is identified in the schedule for such work to take place, and for professional learning teams and grade level teams to work together. The conversation in these meetings shifts from administrative

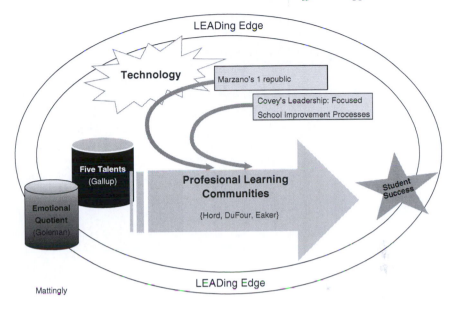

Figure 8.3 Denton ISD plan for leadership development

topics, such as tardiness, attendance, or lunch counts, to student assessments, teaching strategies, and differentiation of learning outcomes.

Once the PLC framework is established, the focus of district support continues, but it also shifts. In order for the conversations to be even more successful, both teachers and campus leaders need access to high-quality data. Initially, data sets are summative in nature, including standardized test scores, locally developed benchmark exams, and other testing. However, once teachers and campus leaders began to see the value in using data during collaborative dialogue, formative assessments, and sharing of practice, PLC conversations related to student learning and teaching strategies became much more robust and meaningful. The conversations change from what we teach to how are the students learning, and how can we ensure they are learning what we want them to learn. Hord (2009) indicates learning "is a habitual activity where the group learns how to learn together continuously" (p. 40). As each PLT grows and develops, the level of learning and understanding grows with it. Such growth requires continuous learning, not only on the part of the teacher but also on the part of campus administrators and district instructional personnel.

Another shift relates to grade reporting in the schools. Instead of the traditional letter grade reporting, the district modifies reporting to parents to include more formative assessment, standards–based grading, and a general understanding that student learning is not negotiable (Blankstein, 2004). All students will learn; however, some students will learn at a different pace. Currently, each K-12 student receives a report card communicating exactly what the student knows and understands *as it relates to the learning standard.*

Reporting would not be possible without a thorough understanding of *what do we want our students to learn?* and *how will we know when they have learned it?* (DuFour & Eaker, 1998).

These two questions seem to be the simplest to answer; however, determining high priority learning standards and developing reliable formative assessments are very difficult, yet are the backbone of effective PLC conversations. As teachers discuss student learning, district personnel should assist in developing the learning standards and meaningful assessments. Reporting to parents about their student's progress is an integral step into the robust learning experiences we desire for all children. Once developed, implemented, and refined, students begin to own their learning by participating in goal setting, achieving their personalized learning outcomes, and seeing the connections between their learning and the world in which they live.

Role of principals

Principals are the gatekeepers for reform in schools, and they play one of the most important roles in a highly functioning learning community. Traditionally, principals focused mostly on teacher performance when evaluating the effectiveness of a classroom teacher. Working in a PLC school shifts the focus from teaching to learning. Such a shift requires a change in mindset for the building principal. In a PLC school, principals learn that the focus is not on what one intends to do, but rather the results of collective actions related to student learning.

Principals are also involved in another major shift that relates to how data are incorporated in decisions about teaching. During PLT meetings, the focus is not necessarily on the teacher whose performance indicators are low, but the focus is on creating an atmosphere where the success of others can be shared and replicated. Principals in PLC schools must have the courage to deal with facing the reality of the data, and have the skills to lead conversations about the data – even if it is not favorable. Everything in a PLC school is about continuous improvement, and when principals and teachers work collaboratively they maximize efforts targeted for student achievement.

Another task of the principal is building capacity in teacher leaders. The principal often serves as a strong advocate and supporter for the teacher to develop leadership and facilitative skills. The principal's role in a PLC is to find people's talents, aspirations, and skills, and showcase them. The goal is to *leave a legacy of leaders*, not to create a legacy for one's self.

Final thoughts

The impact teachers have on school reform can be closely related to effective school-wide professional learning communities. As active members in a PLC culture, teachers and administrators of a school share the same mission, vision, and goals. Schools embrace student learning as a key element of their mission;

however, when PLC schools are effective, the impact on student learning is found to be the essential outcome.

Reformed practices occur as teachers collaborate, supported by the district, about student data, student work, and teaching practices. Teachers report that PLC work has been the most appropriate vehicle for teachers to identify and refine best practices as they reculture their school. Further, teachers know that personal learning must come first so they can improve their instructional practices as they engage in professional development.

Observations confirm that teachers who engage in PLC collaboration and also take charge of professional development decisions have a strong and active voice in school improvement (Harris & Jones, 2010). This is reinforced by Calvert (2016), as she describes teacher agency as "the capacity of teachers to act purposefully and constructively to direct their professional growth and contribute to the growth of their colleagues" (p. 4). Teachers consistently report more satisfaction, and thus have higher retention rates, when they interact professionally with colleagues as they work together for student learning. Teachers credit the intentional actions of district leaders and instructional staff, as well as the reinforcement provided throughout the PLC culture, for these learning opportunities. This engagement, support, and learning, in turn, contributes directly to improved classroom practices and student success.

References

Barth, R. (2001). *Improving schools from within: Teachers, parents, and principals can make the difference.* San Francisco, CA: Jossey-Bass.

Blankstein, A. M. (2004). *Failure is not an option: Six principles that guide student achievement in high performing schools.* Thousand Oaks, CA: Corwin Press, Inc.

Burdett, J. (2009). *The effects of professional learning communities on student achievement* (Unpublished Doctoral Dissertation). Denton, TX: University of North Texas.

Calvert, L. (2016). *Moving from compliance to agency: What teachers need to make professional learning work.* Oxford, OH: Learning Forward and NCTAF.

Darling-Hammond, L., & McLaughlin, M. (1995). Policies that support professional development in an era of reform. *Phi Delta Kappan, 76*(8), 597–604.

DuFour, R., & Eaker, R. (1998). *Professional learning communities at work: Best practices for enhancing student achievement.* Bloomington, IN: Solution Tree.

Fullan, M. (2007). *The new meaning of educational change.* Thousand Oaks, CA: Corwin Press, Inc.

Fullan, M., & Quinn, J. (2015). *Coherence: The right drivers in action for schools, districts, and systems.* Thousand Oaks, CA: Corwin Press, Inc.

Harris, A., & Jones, M. (2010). Professional learning communities and system improvement. *Improving Schools, 13*(2), 172–181.

Hipp, K. K., & Huffman, J. B. (2010). *Demystifying professional learning communities: School leadership at its best.* Lanham, MD: Rowman & Littlefield Publishers, Inc.

Hord, S. (1997). *Professional learning communities: Communities of continuous inquiry and improvement.* Austin, TX: Southwest Educational Development Laboratory.

Hord, S. M. (2009). Professional learning communities. *Journal of Staff Development,* 30(1), 40–43.

Huffman, J. B., & Hipp, K. K. (2003). *Reculturing schools as professional learning communities.* Lanham, MD: The Scarecrow Press.

Katzenmeyer, M. H., & Moller, G. V. (2001). *Awakening the sleeping giant: Helping teachers develop as leaders* (1st ed.). Thousand Oaks, CA: Corwin, a Sage Company.

Kouzes, J., & Posner, B. (2003). *The leadership challenge: How to make extraordinary things happen in organizations.* San Francisco, CA: Jossey-Bass.

Maeroff, G. I. (2010). *School boards in America: A flawed exercise in democracy.* New York: Palgrave Macmillan.

Olivier, D. F., & Hipp, K. K. (2006). Leadership capacity and collective efficacy: Interacting to sustain student learning in a professional learning community. *Journal of School Leadership, 16*(5), 505–519. *Special Edition: Leadership and Student Learning in Professional Learning Communities.*

Schmoker, M. (2006). *Results now: How we can achieve unprecedented improvements in teaching and learning.* Boston, MA: Houghton Mifflin Harcourt.

9 Creating a network for teacher-led reform and pedagogical innovation in Taiwan

Peiying Chen

Introduction

Global demand for workers who possess flexible competencies and can adapt to a changing social and economic environment has forced schools to redefine themselves as engines for creativity and agents of change (Cheng, 2011; Fullan, 2007; Ng, 2012). Schools and educators are required to transform themselves into organizations with cultures of collaborative learning and reflective practice to improve educational quality (Bryk & Schneider, 1996; Muijs & Harris, 2007; Opfer, Pedder, & Lavicza, 2011).

In 2014, Taiwan's government launched a systemic and comprehensive reform of 12-year Basic Education to prepare all students for the challenges of work and life, in the 21st century and beyond. The empowerment of teaching professionals became the core agenda in response to the new challenges (Chen, 2012). Since 2006, top-down professional training programs and workshops have been provided to support teachers' development. Nevertheless, few changes have occurred. It was not until 2013, when teacher-led reform through professional learning communities (PLCs) began to develop, that changes in teacher practice became more widespread. These self-motivated teachers took collective responsibility to experiment with learner-centred pedagogy and disseminated new practices through PLCs within and across schools. The reasons why this teacher-led reform emerged and evolved and the actions that were taken to influence instructional practices deserve exploration.

This chapter outlines the formation of and the meaning behind teacher-led initiatives in the context of Taiwan's education reform. It first discusses the development of PLCs in Taiwan and depicts how networked learning communities (NLCs) of teachers generated expansive learning spaces in which teachers created and experimented with learner-centred pedagogy. This chapter then examines why such border-crossing collaboration of teachers from different schools happened and how the collaboration has evolved over time. Last, the study reveals why these teachers were willing to take a bottom–up approach for change, and what impact such collective efforts have brought about on the system as a whole.

The research was mainly conducted in Taiwan's capital city, Taipei. The researcher observed the primary activities of the NLCs, and interviewed the Taipei educational commissioner and two curriculum supervisors at the Taipei Ministry of Education. Facebook messages and relevant documents were also collected with the permission of NLC participants. One case study, the Navigators, was chosen for an in-depth exploration into school-crossing formation and the practices of NLCs. The case study spanned from 2013 to 2015, and data collection consisted of field observation, an NLC survey, interviews with seven participants and one Taipei government officer, Facebook messages, video and audio records, reflective notes, and documents (government documents, meeting notes, and teacher reflection notes).

Educational reform in Taiwan and the rise of PLCs

Taiwan's educational reforms have moved along two trajectories since the 1990s: first, the deregulation of the educational system; and second, a focus on innovation to meet the demands of the 21st century global economy (Pan & Chen, 2011). Although the cultivation of Taiwan's human resources and international competitiveness have been at the top of the agenda since 2000, a prevailing practice that persists is test-oriented teaching. Core competencies of students, such as problem-solving, critical thinking, creativity, and collaboration, have not been genuinely integrated into curricular reform in the past decade (Huang, 2012).

Reform cannot be achieved without changing the culture of schools. The school culture in Taiwan is characterized by isolation, which often discourages collaboration or support among teachers. Hargreaves and Fullan (2012) identified six kinds of professional culture in schools: individualism; balkanization; contrived collegiality; collaborative culture; PLCs; and clusters, networks, and federations. Only collaborative culture, PLCs, and clusters and networks might generate fertile soil for positive change. In particular, 'developing professional learning communities appears to hold a considerable promise for capacity building and sustainable improvement' (Stoll, Bolam, McMahon, Wallace, & Thomas, 2006). PLCs have thus become a hot topic for education reform in Taiwan, as well as in other countries.

The concept of PLCs gained the attention of Taiwan's academic and government circles in the early 2000s. Because of government policies such as 'Teacher Professional Development Evaluation' and the 'School Actualization Program', formation of PLCs has been one method for curricular and pedagogical innovation and teacher development in Taiwanese basic schools (Chen, 2012). Nevertheless, the practice of 'collaboration' in general has not yet found its way into the conventional teacher culture. Every school is like a beehive with each worker in his or her own cell rarely interacting with neighbours (Hord & Sommers, 2008, p. 21). Therefore, instead of collaborative engagement, Taiwanese teachers usually work and teach independently.

Teachers even sometimes compete against each other due to class rankings being based on student test performance (Chen & Wang, 2015).

In addition, as Hargreaves and Shirley (2009) indicated, the failure of large-scale education reform is often associated with the reckless speed of change and the high expectations of scaling up reform far too quickly. Taiwan's teachers sometimes feel disoriented when faced with endless waves of reform. Enhancing teaching quality and renewing professionalism were intensified through a series of policies, including teacher education, teacher training, teacher evaluation for professional development, and school-based PLC programs (Pan & Chen, 2011). However, of the myriad of programs, the push for school-based PLC programs seemed to have an effect. In 2010, the Ministry of Education (MOE) published a handbook of PLC models adopted from the United States, and provided PLC funding for teachers to collaborate and innovate instruction (Chang, 2011). As a result, the program enabled an increase in the number of PLC teams in schools, from only a few PLCs in schools before 2010 to a total of 828 PLCs in 311 elementary schools by 2011. Additionally, 85 junior high schools had a total of 227 PLCs, and 66 high schools had obtained PLC funding from the MOE (2011). However, the influence and impact of such teacher-led reform have not been fully explored.

Currently, PLC practices in Taiwan have spurred other kinds of teacher-led initiatives, such as specialized curriculum development, action learning, and flipped classrooms. Teachers have also joined in teams crossing subject or school boundaries to form interdisciplinary PLCs or cross-school NLCs. Since 2012, networks of cross-school PLCs have emerged and have gradually gained momentum, playing a critical role as boundary spanners that connect teachers across the entire country (Chen, Zheng, Huang, Zheng & Lin, 2016b). Whether the new path of teacher networked learning could bring about the desired reform outcomes is still unknown in Taiwan's context; and the reasons for the development of collaborative endeavours of shared practices among teachers deserves to be explored.

Teacher-led action: from PLCs to NLCs

Teacher professional development as a form of joint agency emerged in the 1990s. The evolvement of PLC structure and processes to a certain extent reflects the ever-changing roles and functions of school leaders and teaching professionals to meet the higher expectations of the new education environment. Most researchers define PLCs according to a number of dimensions, which often include shared and supportive leadership, shared values and vision, a commitment to continuous improvement, collective responsibility for pupils' learning, reflective professional inquiry, results orientation, supportive conditions, and shared personal practices (Department for Education and Skills [DfES], 2005; DuFour, DuFour & Eaker, 2008; Hord, 1997). Huffman and Hipp (2003) examined these dimensions and added the need for interaction with external support systems such as a central office, parents, and the extended community. Huffman et al. (2015) further proposed overarching ideas that arose from common elements of global PLCs across the United States, China, Taiwan, Hong Kong, and Singapore. Essentially, studies of PLCs depict educators in a community collaboratively engaging to foster a culture that enhances teaching and learning for all.

Based on literature review, this study characterizes PLCs as members of a school community sharing common vision and values, building collegial trust, constantly discussing, collaborating, and reflecting on their shared practices, and aiming to improve instruction and student learning. These PLC features were used to develop a measure of PLCs and conduct an investigation of PLC practices in Taiwan. The results showed that a shared vision along with supportive and shared leadership, through collegiality and trust relationships, to a certain extent enabled school members to collectively learn, collaborate, innovate, inquire, reflect, and give feedback to one another in the form of shared PLC practices. Nevertheless, few schools developed the conditions necessary for effective PLC implementation (Chen, Lee, Lin & Zhang, 2016a).

Effective implementation of PLCs can be hampered by an over-emphasis on teacher performance through student assessments (Hairon & Dimmock, 2012) or the contrived collegiality oftentimes resulting from enforcement by state-granted programs (Fullan, 2007). Such enforced collaboration has little chance to sustain school improvement efforts or build lateral capacity and connection between schools. Because school-based PLCs produced little systemic change, some teachers in Taiwan sought opportunities to develop cross-school networks, or NLCs. The emergent NLCs in Taiwan indicated that an alternative path of teacher professional learning might be more welcome among teachers.

The rise of NLCs

Since the turn of the 21st century, networking has been adopted as a policy instrument for educational reform. The OECD proposed NLCs with the purpose of scaling up school improvement efforts and sustaining lateral capacity building. The organization promoted NLCs as 'an instrument to disseminate good practice, enhance the professional development of teachers, support capacity building in schools, mediate between centralized and decentralized structures, and assist in the process of restructuring and reculturing educational organizational systems' (OECD, 2003, p. 154).

The strength of NLCs to build lateral capacity for educational systemic changes was also recognized by the United Kingdom government. The National College of School Leadership in England established the Network Learning Group in 2002 and launched a funding program for NLCs in the following year to enhance the quality of professional learning and sustain school improvement capacity. Between 2002 and 2006, 137 NLCs were set up in England with more than 1500 school participants (Jackson & Temperley, 2006). Similar employment of NLCs to change classroom practice can also be found in the Netherlands, Singapore, and the United States (McCormick, Fox, Carmichael, & Procter, 2011).

The meaning and practices of NLCs

The volunteerism and pro-action of NLCs render networking as a less controlling mechanism to enhance lateral capacity building and school improvement, and at the same time reduce management cost or conflict between governments and schools. In studying networked collaboration, Jackson and Temperley (2006) found that networking was associated with school cultures. Schools with strong organizational cultures could share their improvement strategies through networking between schools, which in turn could enhance collaboration of teachers at their own home schools. Hadfield and Chapman (2009) posited that networking also facilitated professional learning, knowledge creation, and transfer, which travelled not only between individuals and groups, but also between schools.

At the system level, NLCs may play a bridging role between schools and government to translate and implement policies and thus help schools make a meaningful link between local action and central government policies. Liberman and Wood (2004) agreed that networking was more likely to support professional development of staff, ease the inertia of bureaucracy, and bring new technology into practice. The flexible, borderless, and innovative features of networks could help to change organizational culture from static to dynamic, from passive to active, and from isolated to collaborative. Networks also helped local government and schools work together to develop issues with a common focus and build a peer support culture for learning and changes.

While comparing NLCs with PLCs, Stoll (2004) posited that emergent NLC practices were an extension and enlargement of the PLC function. Both PLCs and NLCs are groups belonging to members and represent a collective effort by teachers to collaborate. Both promote shared vision and collegiality to enact teacher-led reform through individual and organizational learning. Learning communities within and across schools also help to create a platform where educators could experiment with new practices and allow pedagogical innovation to emerge by exchange of ideas. That is, the common threads between PLCs and NLCs are shared vision or values, team collaboration and capacity building, collective inquiry and reflection on core practices, collegiality or trust relation, and shared leadership for initiatives (Harris, 2008; Spillane, Halverson, & Diamond, 2004).

What makes the practices of NLCs different from those of PLCs is the scale and density of interconnections. Networking promotes system-wide horizontal connection across school boundaries (National College for School Leadership [NCSL], 2002). It also plays a role as a boundary spanner mediating between individuals and organizations (Earl & Katz, 2005). The professional links and collaboration within and between schools may help to break down the inertial culture embedded in school contexts. The NLC platform provides a learning environment for frequent exchanges of ideas and practices, which probably support and sustain border-crossing efforts. It therefore encourages bottom–up production and transfer of knowledge creation across school boundaries. This study therefore describes NLCs as a networked community with educators who share common vision and values and build lateral capacity to generate collective efforts that enhance teaching and learning for all.

Emergent NLCs in Taipei

The new path for professional development

Educational reform turned a new page beginning in 2012 with a series of events and activities. Parenting Magazine in Taiwan published a book, 'Learning Revolution', in April 2012 and then held three conferences with about 3000 participants in September. Within a year, the publisher drew thousands of book readers and audience members to engage in discussion forums on student learning issues and teachers' professional learning. In 2013, a high school Chinese Language teacher advocated his own innovative instruction called 'learning–thinking–expressing', with the purpose of cultivating students' self-regulated learning, thinking, and expression competencies. He soon attracted a great number of followers. In the same year, the non-government organization Junyi Academy advocated a flipped classroom mode of learning, and established a virtual learning platform to provide teachers and students with online learning materials.

Taipei, the capital city of Taiwan, has 280 schools ranging from primary to senior high schools. There are about 3000 teachers, 1000 in each level of schooling. In the face of the 12-year Basic Education reform policy and the implementation of the new 2018 curriculum guidelines, Taipei city government accelerated the continuing professional development of teachers. The government sent about 300 educators overseas for a week of professional learning between 2011 and 2013. Among them, 75 high school teachers went to Japan and Korea for study tours in 2012 and 2013. The commissioner of the Taipei City Government Education Department explained this policy in her interview in 2013:

> We need to empower teachers to make changes in classroom practice … The teachers not only require professional development, … but also are willing to set up PLCs for achieving consensus about how to develop curriculum and innovate instruction. I also hope these joint efforts could gradually build a city-wide consensus on pedagogical innovation.

The city government then launched the Learning Community Program to encourage teachers to develop school-based learning communities with a shared focus on lesson study. Some participants of the study tour groups then voluntarily set up a Facebook learning community in 2012. The members built a network to exchange information and engage teachers across school districts to disseminate new ideas and innovative practices. The number of teachers involved in open classrooms and instructional experiments increased rapidly within a year. Two teachers shared their thoughts on social media after a study tour trip. The Chinese teacher said:

> After the trip to Korea … we realized that learning in a community is not a kind of technique but a journey of learning through long-term practice. The teacher must return the right to learn to students, and students also have to accept that they are responsible for their own learning … then the reciprocal relation of teaching and learning will gradually appear.
>
> (Facebook message by MJ (female teacher), 23 October 2012)

After attending a class observation, a physics teacher reported:

> As I stepped into class 107, I saw students divided into several groups. They held learning sheets in hand and listened to one student answering questions in front. Some of them jotted down some notes while listening … Most of the students had already written down the answers by themselves … Some of them turned to their peers and spoke in a low voice.
>
> (Facebook message by YD (male teacher), 25 October 2012)

Social networking helped to 'keep warm' the teacher-led initiatives. The flow of online conversation increasingly encouraged more teachers to engage in instructional experiments and stimulated them to step outside their comfort zones. Between 2012 and 2014 five face-to face discussion forums were organized by teachers for exchanging ideas, sharing stories, and demonstrating innovative practices. Teacher-led professional learning snowballed soon after, with over 600 participants gathering in these Facebook conventions.

In 2012, 62 teachers opened up their classrooms for observation and held post-teaching reviews, which further inspired hundreds of teachers to engage in learning networks. The extension of city-wide teacher-led actions, including the study tour, social media networking, and open classroom observation, was fuelled by contagious imaginaries that shaped the path of individual changes from outside to inside. This transformation journey evolved from visible changes of teacher behaviours to shifts in invisible attitudes and pedagogical beliefs. Capacity building of professionals can only be sustained if teachers changed their mindset.

The increase of NLC members engaging in pedagogical imaginary practices shows the ripple effects of teacher-led reform. Currently in 2016, the Facebook Learning Community has about 1000 members. Almost every subject matter has established its own Facebook community for information exchange and contact. The smallest one is the English Facebook community with 25 members, while the largest one is the Social Studies Facebook group with 526 members.

In the summer of 2013 and spring of 2014, the Taipei City Government sponsored three rounds of Leadership for the Future workshops in Taipei. Ninety head teachers and middle-level teacher leaders voluntarily participated in leadership training. Most of these head teachers and teacher leaders had also joined study tours to Japan and Korea, and were involved in the Learning Communities Program. Compared with the 'keep warm' function of social media networking, the Leadership for the Future workshops were expected to tie passion with the action of practitioners. The workshops functioned as a driver to 'heat up' participants in the larger network. These activities provided opportunities for participants to meet and connect with practitioners from other schools that might foster willingness and capacity for borderless collaboration.

Networking of the Navigators NLC

The case of the Navigators represents a prototype of teacher-led reform through NLC practices and impact on home school PLC practices. Two Chinese Language teachers decided to set up an NLC in May 2013. They then invited another seven teachers from five schools to join. Two of them were male teachers who also held administrative positions during 2014 and 2015. They called themselves the 'Navigators' and publicly endorsed learner-centred pedagogy. They met at least twice a month in a coffee shop to plan lessons together. They took turns to develop a lesson, demonstrate their teaching, and review student learning right after observation.

The Navigators used Google, Facebook, and Messenger constantly to manage their instructional materials and documents, and ubiquitously exchange ideas. Between 2013 and 2014, this NLC held 29 lesson study seminars to experiment with a variety of instructional methods and co-designed collaborative learning activities for students. They also brought new ideas and practices they learned from NLC peers back to their home schools and set up PLCs for disseminating learner-centred pedagogy. They generously shared their learning experiences with other NLCs and schools to influence the larger community of teachers. In 2015, the Navigators invited five new members to join, thus expanding their networking impact.

When reflecting on the process, all of the members positively recognized the usefulness of mutual support and collaborative inquiry. They particularly appreciated the power of interconnectedness and interdependence. The youngest member, YL, who had seven years of teaching experience, was sceptical of joining the Navigators in the beginning. After one year, however, she was engaged deeply in the community. She recalled:

> I had enjoyed very much the comfort zone of doing my own teaching duty as long as I did not fail my job. That was quite enough for me. However, after practising lesson study in the Navigators' experiment, I witnessed how this group created a very inspiring scene of collaborative

learning among students, which quickly transformed the classroom landscape. This really struck me and I knew in my heart I wanted to make changes as well. I was so sure that it was the right path to travel even though daunting challenges were waiting ahead.

The last person to join the Navigators in 2013 was a male teacher who strongly felt isolated and lonely at his home school. He appreciated the collaborative learning opportunities offered by the Navigators. He commented at the end of the first year:

> The Navigators group is an independent and warm network where subtle feeling and interconnected affection could be solidified. Oftentimes, after I absorbed new ideas from the Navigators, I was eager to make a trial run in my school. I am quite sure that collegiality, reciprocity, and mutual trust were the critical factors that successfully hold us together.

The seven members of the Navigators either set up PLCs or scaled up the PLC practice in their home schools in the second year (2015). One of the Navigators' founders, PS, engaged in multiple NLCs and did her best to establish an interdisciplinary PLC in her school. At the end of the second year, she reflected:

> As we so choose, nothing can't be changed … We do want to share responsibilities in response to collective needs … For me, no matter which group I join, be it the Navigators, book study clubs, or my school PLC, these communities create a space like a revolving door for teacher learning. Many ideas, beliefs, professional knowledge, practice, and affective connection could be revolved round and round, connected and converged together. In such a space, through continuing dialogues and brainstorming our experiences, we upgrade our knowledge, 'constantly + 1'. We boost up our energy and turn it into a bright light that shines on many people and places … and by means of incessant connection and extension, we create an invisible but naturally growing eco-network.

Expansion of NLCs in Taipei

In January, 2014, Taipei City Government set up the High School Taskforce (HST) to sponsor school-crossing NLCs, which was inspired by the practice of the Navigators. The HST encouraged teachers to form their own networked teacher communities, set up their own schedules, and build a common focus on learner-centred instruction.

The curriculum supervisor of Taipei City Government posted her observation on Facebook in February 2014:

National Science teachers from all over the country voluntarily set up a lesson-planning NLC last year, and experimented with various ways of teaching. We then formally established our group this year. We invited new members. Although we come from different schools and are not acquainted with one another yet, the purpose is surely shared. It is to improve our students' learning ... The wave of passionate emotion triggered by sharing touching stories has gradually cooled down. That passion has currently turned into the calm stream of deep learning action and rooted these new practices in our soil (context), which makes these collective endeavours more meaningful and probably more sustainable.

At the time, there were 17 NLCs, with the smallest having six members and the largest with 16 members. Among these NLCs, five of them regularly met once a month, while the rest met at least once a month. About 150 teachers, representing 23 percent of the total, engaged in NLC activities. Between January 2014 and August 2015, the HST called 12 meetings to coordinate NLC activities. It held 17 workshops with over 1000 participants to 'upgrade' professional knowledge and leadership skills. The themes and content of the workshops included curriculum mapping and development, learning-by-doing pedagogy, digital learning material design, assessment for learning, and middle-level leadership empowerment for NLCs.

By 2015, the number of Taipei NLCs increased to 28. NLC practices then galvanized more energy, enabling teachers to build social capital across schools. The right climate in favour of change gradually emerged. The successful stories travelled across schools and inspired more teachers to join. The scale of change was magnified by the extension and intensity of teacher-led initiatives through NLC activities of lesson planning, class observation, and post-teaching review.

In April of 2016, over 400 teachers from the entire country gathered at the Stadium of National Nei-Li High School to participate in a curriculum-mapping workshop that prepared them for implementing the 2018 Curriculum Guidelines. The facilitation team consisted of eight teachers who were engaged with multiple NLC groups. This team had contributed to many nationwide teacher training workshops and were instrumental in promoting learner-centred pedagogy. This bottom-up teacher action for curriculum reform and development brought about significant change in the culture of teacher learning and collaboration.

Discussion

The formation of an epistemic community

The emergence of school-crossing NLCs in Taipei was, on the one hand, supported by the City Government and, on the other hand, initiated by teachers experimenting with learner-centred pedagogy. The original 17 NLCs formed the city-wide network, and then the lesson study activities within each NLC and the empowerment workshops held by the HST created networking that turned into larger epistemic communities. Teacher-led reform through NLCs opens up an alternative space for practitioners to meet, share, and collaborate, which enlarged their instructional resources and deepened their professional learning to facilitate changes in classroom practices.

Taking the Navigators as an example, the successive cycles of lesson study accumulated into a reservoir of learner-centred instructional resources. Through the process of collaborative enquiry, the Navigators concretized the ideal pedagogy into classroom practices. Each micro cycle of collaborative inquiry and reflective review slowly changed the members' habitual behaviours, thinking, attitudes, assumptions, and beliefs such that they became aligned with learner-centred pedagogy and 21st century educational goals. The collaborative inquiry cycle expanded common understanding and collective learning capacity on learner-centred instruction, by which the members could unlearn conventional teaching and, at the same time, adopt differential and multiple ways of stimulating students to learn. This was also a process of co-constructing pedagogical imaginaries and epistemic communities. It could be said that the relation embedded in collective inquiry activities wove the bonds between members of the Navigators. The expansive learning of the Navigators not only empowered each member through networked activities but also built social capital through reciprocity of the members.

The experiences of the Navigators were echoed by the findings of Hadfield and Jopling (2007) on effective school networks. They concluded that the initial stages of creating a shared focus were important for the positive effects of networking. The processes concerned 'articulating shared values and a common focus, building trust and mutual knowledge, and developing a strategic approach to continuing professional knowledge' (cited by Hadfield & Chapman, 2009, p. 29).

As a result of the affinity between NLCs and PLCs, it was not difficult for four Navigators to successfully build PLCs at their home schools and extend the impact of NLC practices. In the years 2014 and 2015, Navigators delivered 35 public speeches to schools, seminars, and conferences. Through sharing professional practices, they disseminated inquiry-based learning and encouraged school-based PLCs to experiment with learner-centred pedagogy. Four of them also joined other networks of teachers to serve schools in remote areas or to conduct workshops for professional training. Five of them participated in the Curriculum Development team, which was organized by NLC teachers across schools to help numerous teachers and schools implement the 2018 Curriculum Guidelines. The horizontal connection across NLCs and PLCs intensified meaning making and action taking of teacher-led reform and thus generated capacity building and knowledge transfer throughout the circle of teachers.

Expanding epistemological spaces for pedagogical innovation

Figure 9.1 shows the loose coordination of NLCs in Taipei. Each NLC was formed for the purpose of pedagogical innovation. These NLCs were on the whole voluntarily organized and 'magnetically' attracted by learner-centred pedagogy (the shared vision). Pedagogical imaginaries played a role in gaining public attention, which brought all kinds of innovative practice into a discourse of the learner-centred paradigm. As Wenger posited,

> Educational imagination is ... about not accepting things the way they are, about experimenting and exploring possibilities, reinventing the self, and in the process reinventing the world. It is daring to try on something really different, to open new trajectories, to seek different experiences, and to conceive of different futures.
>
> (Wenger, 1998, p. 273)

With the support of the city government, additional resources and an ad-hoc HST came into existence and created a policy space for innovation. The policy space also legitimized NLC and PLC members in their effort to make meaningful links with teachers across subject matter and schools. The expansion of NLCs then helped to generate the right climate for instructional experiments. The co-ordination of the HST allowed teacher-led initiatives to become boundary spanners in response to the needs of each NLC and the PLCs in local schools.

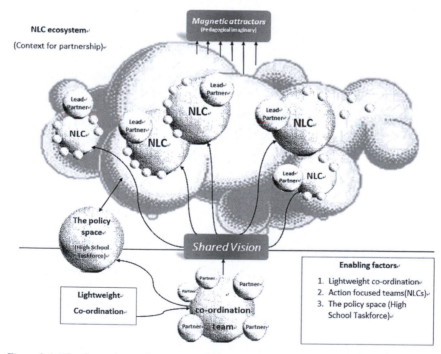

Figure 9.1 The formation and practices of Taipei NLCs, adapted and revised from Surman & Surman, 2008

The connection within and among NLCs germinated pedagogical imaginaries through teacher-led sharing, convening, presenting, and publishing. As Taylor (2002) interpreted, social imaginaries incorporate 'a sense of the normal expectations that we have of each other; the kind of common understanding which enables us to carry out the collective practices which make up our social life' (p. 106). The common understanding of learner-centred pedagogy enabled NLC participants to engage in collective activities that made the paradigm shift possible.

The pedagogical imaginaries are enacted within policy space and substantialized in NLC epistemological spaces. It can be said that the 17 NLCs in Taipei evolved themselves into a larger epistemic community. It was therefore able to engender multiple epistemological spaces or 'third spaces' where alternative or hybrid ideas or practices were allowed to develop (Gutiérrez, Baquedano-López & Tejeda, 1999). The possibility of making change was situated in the third space, where change agents intentionally search for alternatives by means of effectively connecting actors with resources to legitimize their new initiatives. Through working on differences, problems, and conflicts, transformation of classroom practices can be expected to happen, and alternative ideas, values, and paradigms could be repositioned or created (pp. 286–287). The third spaces provide room for creativity while epistemological spaces generate ideas for pedagogical experiments and innovation.

The formation of NLCs as an ecosystem of epistemological spaces co-evolved by unplanned extension, like a rhizome. The empowerment of teacher-led action was derived from a bottom–up connection of scattered activities, in essence a rhizomatic approach to networking (Deleuze & Guattari, 1987, p. 46). This rhizomatic phenomenon of NLC expansion and its ripple effects further enabled teacher-led reform action. The emergent epistemological spaces in Taipei showed that the interconnection of teachers by means of NLCs not only enhanced inquiry-based teacher learning, but also nurtured a culture of professional collaboration. The connection, interdependence, and collaboration of professional learning may raise the social capital of teachers and empower them to become agents for systemic capacity building and change in education. The pedagogical shift from teacher-centred to learner-centred has been made and continues to engage teachers in collective inquiry. As Church et al. (2002) stated,

> It is the activity (beyond the communication, information-sharing, relationships) that gives the network its meaning. It also gives the network a living feel, one dependent on the commitment and input of its participants (p. 17).

The case of Taipei NLCs and Navigators has shown that shared practices and responsibilities of teachers provide the means for open communication, collegial trust and rapport, and continuous improvement of pedagogical work.

Such bottom-up initiatives were characterized as an evolving process of parallel, facilitative, or shared leadership using created artifacts to facilitate professional dialogue and solve instructional problems, which were both supported by previous PLC and NLC research outcomes (Chen & Wang, 2015; Hadfield & Chapman, 2009).

Conclusion

In conclusion, the results of this study revealed that a new form of networked learning could be used as a means to encourage teacher-led initiatives that nurtured a pro-change climate and strengthened a culture of professional collaboration. The activities of NLCs sowed the seeds for developing school-based PLCs and enlarged the impact of PLCs at the inter-organizational level through shared vision and values. A rhizomatic mode of interconnection characterized NLCs as a platform where epistemological spaces could be created and pedagogical imaginaries constructed by common understanding of how to realize learner-centred instruction. The positive effects imply that the new path of networked learning can be adopted elsewhere for enhancing lateral capacity building and systemic changes in education.

The case of Taipei NLCs, on the one hand, unleashed the energy of passion and enthusiasm of teacher-led initiatives that helped to spread new pedagogy via border-crossing collaboration. On the other hand, the collective efforts of NLCs may not be sustainable due to a lack of disciplined innovation or the stable support of government funding. The ad-hoc and loose coordination of NLCs simultaneously constructed interconnections between schools and possibly destabilized the relations of educators within schools. The latter may also become an obstacle to the healthy development of school-based PLCs. In addition, NLCs tend to be more value-oriented rather than outcome-based guiding. It is thus difficult to measure and evaluate the success of NLCs because of the distributed features of unbounded relations and expanded activities. Broad support of NLCs may decline after a period of time due to unclear validation of lateral capacity building.

Nevertheless, the important but loose impact of NLCs on school-based PLC practices and nationwide curriculum innovation may generate a public discourse to emphasize the need for substantial coordination at the centralized governmental level. Several national reform programs, such as the High School Improvement Program, could be redesigned as a stable catalyst to support and sustain teacher-led initiatives over an extended time. In addition, collaboration between school-based PLCs and school-crossing NLCs need to be developed to expand dynamic capacities of schools and to build mutual reciprocity for both teachers and administrators. These future endeavours are certainly critical for strengthening organizational innovation, which, in turn, may provide a stronger collaborative culture within schools for student learning and success. Follow-up research is needed to evaluate PLC and NLC impact and the durable effects on teacher-led action and student learning.

References

Bryk, A. S., & Schneider, B. (1996). *Social trust: A moral resource for school improvement.* Chicago, IL: The University of Chicago Consortium on Chicago School Research.

Chang, S. J. (2011). The evolution of teacher's professional development and evaluation in Taiwan in the past 100 years. In Y. C. Fang, & P. Chen (Eds.), *A century retrospect on education: Heritage and innovation* (pp. 201–256). Taipei, Taiwan: Pro-Edu.

Chen, P. (2012). Empowering identity reconstruction of indigenous college students through transformative learning. *Educational Review, 64*(2), 161–180.

Chen, P., Lee, C., Lin, H., & Zhang, C., (2016a). Factors that develop effective professional learning communities in Taiwan. *Asia Pacific Journal of Education, 36*(2), 248–265. doi:10 .1080/02188791.2016.1148853

Chen, P. & Wang, T. (2015). Exploring the evolution of a teacher professional learning community: a longitudinal case study at a Taiwanese high school. *Teacher Development, 19*(4), 427–444.

Chen, P., Zheng, M., Huang, C., Zheng, Y., & Lin, Y. (2016b). Enabling pedagogical imaginary: Networked learning communities and school-based learning communities realizing shared visions. *Journal of Education Research, 265,* 91–109. doi: 10.3966/168063602016050265007

Cheng, Y. C. (2011). Towards the 3rd wave school leadership. *Revista de Investigacion Educativa, 29*(2), 253–275.

Church, M., Bitel, M., Armstrong, K., Fernando, P., Gould, H., Joss, … Vouhe, C. (2002). *Participation, Relationships and Dynamic Change: New Thinking on Evaluating the Work of International Networks* (Working Paper No. 121). Development Planning Unit, University College London. Retrieved from www.bartlett.ucl.ac.uk/dpu/publications/latest/ publications/dpu-working-papers/WP_121.pdf

Deleuze, G., & Guattari, F. (1987). *A thousand plateaus: Capitalism and schizophrenia.* Translated by Massumi, B. Minneapolis: University of Minnesota.

Department for Education and Skills (DfES). (2005). *Creating and Sustaining Effective Professional Learning Communities, Research Report RR 637.* London: Bolam, R., McMahon, A., Stoll, L., Thomas, S., Wallace, M., Greenwood, A., … Smith, R.

DuFour, R., DuFour, R., & Eaker, R. (2008). *Revisiting professional learning communities at work: New insights for improving schools.* Bloomington, IN: Solution Tree.

Earl, L., & Katz, S. (2005). Painting a data-rich picture. *Principal Leadership, 5*(5), 16–20.

Fullan, M. (2007). *The new meaning of educational change* (4th ed.). New York: Teachers College.

Gutiérrez, K. D., Baquedano-López, P., & Tejeda, C. (1999). Rethinking diversity: Hybridity and hybrid language practices in the third space. *Mind, Culture, and Activity, 6*(4), 286–303.

Hadfield, M., & Chapman, C. (2009). *Leading school-based networks.* New York: Routledge.

Hadfield, M., & Jopling. M. (2007). *The potential of collaboratives to support schools in complex and challenging circumstances.* Nottingham, UK: NCSL.

Hairon, S., & Dimmock, C. (2012). Singapore schools and professional learning communities: Teacher professional development and school leadership in an Asian hierarchical system. *Educational Review, 64*(4), 405–424.

Hargreaves, A., & Fullan, M. (2012). *Professional capital: Transforming teaching in every school.* New York: Teachers College Press.

Hargreaves, A., & Shirley, D. (Eds.). (2009). *The fourth way: The inspiring future for educational change.* Thousand Oaks, CA: SAGE.

Harris, A. (2008). *Distributed school leadership: Developing tomorrow's leaders.* London/New York: Routledge.

Hord, S. M. (1997). *Professional learning communities: Communities of continuous inquiry and improvement.* Austin, Texas: Southwest Educational Development Laboratory.

Hord, S. M., & Sommers, W. A. (2008). *Leading professional learning communities: Voices from research and practice.* Thousand Oaks, CA: Corwin Press.

Huang, T. (2012). Agents' social imagination: The 'invisible' hand of neoliberalism in Taiwan's curriculum reform. *International Journal of Educational Development, 32*(1), 39–45.

Huffman, J. B., & Hipp, K. K. (2003). *Reculturing schools as professional learning communities.* Lanham, MD: R&L Education.

Huffman, J., Olivier, D., Wang, T., Chen, P., Hairon, S., & Pang, N. (2015). Global conceptualization of the professional learning community process: Transitioning from country perspectives to international commonalities. *International Journal of Leadership in Education, 36*(2), 248–265. doi=10.1080/13603124.2015.102034

Jackson, D. & Temperley, J. (2006). From professional learning community to network learning community. In L. Stoll & K. Seashore Louis (Eds.), *Professional learning communities: Divergence, depth and dilemmas.* (pp. 45–62). Berkshire, England: Open University Press.

Liberman, A., & Wood, D. (2004). Untangling the threads: Networks, community and teacher training in the national writing projects. In H. McCarthy, P. Miller, & P. Skidmore (Eds.), *Network logic: Who governs in an interconnected world?* (pp. 63–76). London: Demos.

McCormick, R., Fox, A., Carmichael, P., & Procter, R. (2011). *Researching and understanding educational networks.* London: Routledge.

Muijs, D., & Harris, A. (2007). Teacher leadership in action: Three case studies of contrasting schools. *Educational Management Administration & Leadership, 35*(1), 111–134.

National College for School Leadership (NCSL). (2002). *Networked learning communities: 'Like no other initiative'.* Cranfield, UK: NCSL.

Ng, P. T. (2012). An examination of school leadership in Singapore through the lens of the fourth way. *Educational Research for Policy and Practice, 11*(1), 27–34.

OECD. (2003). *Networks of innovation: Towards new models for managing schools and systems.* Paris: Organisation for Economic Co-operation and Development. Retrieved from www.oecd-ilibrary.org/content/book/9789264100350-en

Opfer, V. D., Pedder, D. J., & Lavicza, Z. (2011). The influence of school orientation to learning on teachers' professional learning change. *School Effectiveness and School Improvement, 22*(2), 193–214.

Pan, H-L. W., & Chen, P. (2011). Challenges and research agenda of school leadership in Taiwan. *School Leadership Management, 31*(4), 339–353. doi:10.1080/13632434.2011.606270

Spillane, J. P., Halverson, R., & Diamond, J. B. (2004). Towards a theory of leadership practice: A distributed perspective. *Journal of Curriculum Studies, 36*(1), 3–34.

Stoll, L. (2004). *Networked learning communities as professional learning communities.* Paper presented at Aporia Consulting Ltd for Phase 1 of Evaluation of Networked Learning Communities Program Network Learning Communities Seminar, San Diego.

Stoll, L., Bolam, R., McMahon, A., Wallace, M., & Thomas, S. (2006). Professional learning communities: A review of the literature. *Journal of Educational Change, 7*(4), 221–258.

Surman, M. & Surman, T. (2008). Listening to the stars: The constellation model of collaborative social change. *Social Models, Social Space*, (2008), 24–29. Retrieved from https://marksurman.commons.ca/publications/listening-to-the-stars-the-constellation-model-of-collaborative-social-change/

Taylor, C. (2002). Modern social imaginaries. *Public Culture, 14*(1), 91–124.

Wenger, E. (1998). *Communities of practice: Learning, meaning, and identity*. Cambridge, UK: Cambridge University Press.

Section 3

Teachers leading educational reform within and across schools

The third section of this book moves to the micro level to consider school-based professional learning communities. While previous chapters have looked at change at scale, at the national, provincial or district level, the chapters in this final section of this book look at the development of PLCs from a starting point *within or between* individual schools. Ultimately, any effective reform process will require change at all three levels (macro, meso and micro) but the chapters in this section focus particularly on the school as the main unit of change.

The initial chapter in this section by Timperley, Ell and Le Fevre explores the idea of developing adaptive expertise through the medium of professional learning communities. It considers five conditions for developing adaptive expertise and highlights the importance of having a clear model of engagement for successful professional learning communities, at the school level. The chapter reinforces that the development of adaptive expertise should not be left to chance but rather that it needs to be fostered and developed as part of the PLC process. The chapter argues that adaptive expertise can generate teacher agency that in turn can contribute to effective PLCs and professional collaboration with impact in schools.

The next chapter by Thomas, Peng and Triggs outlines evidence about the introduction and implementation of PLCs into schools in China. Drawing upon case-study evidence from four schools, as part of a larger longitudinal study, the chapter outlines evidence relating to the operation of whole-school PLCs. The issue of cultural differences is raised by the authors and they suggest that the PLC concept, largely derived from the West, may need adaption for the Chinese context. The chapter suggests that teacher-led reform could be enacted through PLC development in schools in China although this is unlikely, at scale, without support from policy makers and school leaders.

The last chapter in this section, by Hadfield, focuses on the role of PLCs in supporting school collaboration in Wales. It considers the history of PLCs in Wales and explores how a move from centralized control to greater decentralization has provided a consortium-based platform for collaboration within and between schools. The chapter explores how School Improvement Groups (SIGs) have supported teachers' collaborative work and how small groups of teachers are working within and between schools in inquiry-based

PLCs. Deep engagement and experience of collaborative professional learning is highlighted as one of the essential components of effective PLC work. The chapter proposes that where PLCs work well they can provide a space in which classroom practitioners can take on the role of teacher leaders.

Overall, the chapters in this section highlight that, for PLCs to work most effectively within and between schools, it is important to ensure that there is shared understanding of the PLC process as well as considerable investment in professional development and training that develops teachers' collaborative skills. The chapters also reinforce the importance of having sufficient time to implement PLCs so that teachers feel confident enough to lead improvement and change.

10 Developing adaptive expertise through professional learning communities

Helen Timperley, Fiona Ell and Deidre Le Fevre

The failure of many reform efforts in our schooling systems has led to the realization that these efforts need to be developed and promoted by those most affected by them if systemic and sustainable change is to be realized (e.g. Fullan, 2011; Hargreaves & Fullan, 2012; Harris & Jones, 2010; Stoll & Louis, 2007). Most often, others make the direction and decisions of professional learning. Those most affected, of course, are the teachers who are expected to transform practices in their teaching and learning environments because, if no impact is made on the instructional core, little will improve for learners (Elmore, 2004).

Professional learning communities (PLCs) have been promoted as a way to provide teachers with greater agency and efficacy in making improvements to their practice (e.g. Louis & Kruse, 1995; Hargreaves & Fullan, 2012), but these expectations often occur in organizational and policy environments that explicitly or implicitly promote expectations of compliance with reforms that others are leading and developing. The resulting function of PLCs tends to be on enacting what others have developed with a focus on correct implementation of the advocated teaching practices, which is contradictory to the reasons for the original promotion of PLCs.

In this chapter we argue that, if PLCs are to realize their potential in reform efforts, they need to be explicitly and deliberately constructed in ways that promote teacher agency in *leading* reform rather than being used as a vehicle to ensure teachers enact mandated or imposed policy or organizational directives. Teachers need to be seen as a resource with the capacity to develop innovative solutions to the challenging and complex problems required of authentic reform efforts. To do this, they are likely to need access to particular expertise, but the process must enhance their professional agency in leading reform rather than diminishing it.

There is an increasing international consensus that "the term 'professional learning community' refers to an inclusive and mutually supportive group of people with a collaborative, reflective and growth oriented approach towards investigating and learning more about their practice in order to improve pupils' learning" (Stoll, 2011, p. 104). Our research and development work over the last three years has involved studying and working with a wide range of PLCs in schools both in New Zealand and Australia (Le Fevre, Ell, Timperley,

Twyford & Mayo, 2015a; Si'ilata et al., 2015). In this work we have identified that the attributes of PLCs described by Stoll more often lead to innovative solutions to enduring problems when they are deliberately constructed to promote and sustain the development of adaptive expertise among the participating teachers.

By adaptive expertise we mean the development of a deep understanding of the complexity of the interactions between learners and their learning environments as well as the capability to draw on a rich and deep knowledge base to address specific challenges in that environment, rather than learning to enact a generic set of standards or teaching practices that apply across contexts. Those with adaptive expertise are also committed to using this knowledge to make a difference for every learner, particularly those at risk of failure and dropping out intellectually or physically from formal learning environments. Adaptive expertise goes beyond a mindset or a set of skills and comes to form the essence of teachers' professional identities.

In the remainder of this chapter we contrast routine and adaptive expertise and identify the conditions from our research and development work in PLCs that were associated with developing adaptive expertise. We then describe a structured inquiry approach used within PLCs that has assisted in the development of adaptive expertise and illustrate the process with examples from our ongoing work in this area. We conclude the chapter by examining implications for policy and practice.

Routine and adaptive expertise

Conceptualizations of teacher professionalism that focused on teachers mastering particular routines and getting practice "right" have a 40–50-year history. One of the most extreme examples was a teaching reform promoted in the 1970s that focused on simplifying the notion of teaching by creating a teacher-proof curriculum and pedagogy that provided clear guidelines and practices for teachers to employ. It was thought that teachers simply needed to learn specified scripts in a given situation to become more effective. Parallel to this view was one of teacher development in which novice teachers became expert through supported practice (Dall'Alba & Sandberg, 2006). In this view of professionalism, skill development takes place in a stepwise, cumulative manner. Becoming a skilled professional, therefore, involves progressively developing a set of knowledge and skills relevant to the profession. Most of the models based on this understanding of professionalism follow a general pattern of an initial phase of survival and rule-following, one or more intermediate stages showing greater flexibility, experimentation and consolidation, and a final phase of mastery and fluency (e.g. Dreyfus & Dreyfus, 1986). By this final stage, the novice's rule-following has been transformed into skilful know-how in which problems are identified intuitively and holistically with appropriate strategies enacted to solve them. Most supporters of these models acknowledge that fully-fledged mastery is not necessarily attained by everyone.

This early depiction of effective teaching as following scripts faithfully, and teacher development as generic stage-like progress, has been largely discredited. However, we have taken the space to describe them because similar ideas have lately been revived in other forms with recent efforts to codify a generic set of knowledge, dispositions, competencies and skills required for effective teaching (MET Project, 2013). Within this vision of teaching, the teacher's main challenge is to develop these competencies and to master the enactment of desirable practices through developing adaptive expertise.

We do not want to dismiss the importance of advancements in knowledge about the effectiveness of particular teaching practices, or the importance of the knowledge base for teaching (Cochran-Smith et al., 2016). We are concerned, however, that such work might be used in unintended ways to codify a set of practices that teachers should follow. What we are seeking to advance is the view that real reform and innovation that addresses the enduring problem, of providing each student with a high-quality education, requires a vision of professionalism that we have defined above as adaptive expertise (Hatano & Inagaki, 1986; Le Fevre, Timperley & Ell, 2015b). Hatano and Inagaki (1986) identify a qualitative difference between routine and adaptive expertise and the types of environments in which each is appropriate. Stable environments provide opportunities for routine expertise in which people can be highly efficient without needing deep conceptual understanding about what they are doing and constantly testing its effectiveness. Standard operating procedures work for the most part. The above view of teaching as mastery of generic codified practices is underpinned by this idea of routine expertise.

In contrast, Hatano and Inagaki (1986) identify that environments that experience constant change and complexity often demand adaptive expertise. Teachers face complexity every day. To be effective teachers need to be responsive to the needs of diverse students in uncertain contexts. Students, particularly those most vulnerable to failure, do not necessarily arrive ready to learn what a teacher has prepared or what a curriculum dictates. Teachers must constantly make on-the-spot decisions, solve problems as they arise, juggle priorities, and attend to simultaneous and sometimes incompatible needs (Lampert, 1985).

Routine and adaptive expertise should not be seen in terms of a dichotomy, because routine expertise usually involves adaptations in response to situational demands while adaptive expertise requires the mastery of particular routines. Without routines in complex environments, cognitive overload is inevitable. One essential difference, however, is that adaptive expertise demands constant evaluation of the appropriateness of particular practices and routines, and does not just assume them to be appropriate because they form part of one's repertoire of practice. Rather, practice is constantly monitored for its effectiveness, and ongoing decisions are made about whether to continue, adjust or discard a particular practice in a given situation. In teaching, this means constantly evaluating the impact of practice on the learning and well-being of students. The focus is on how well students are learning, not on how well a particular teaching activity is executed.

Both routine and adaptive expertise require knowledge and skills but the type of knowledge differs. Routine expertise requires deep knowledge of the "what" and "how" of practice. Adaptive expertise demands deep conceptual understanding of the "why" of practice in ways that enable the creation of new solutions to existing problems and innovative solutions to new ones (Hatano & Inagaki, 1986). To illustrate the differences, we draw on the evidence from a national evaluation of schooling improvement in New Zealand (Parr, 2010). In this evaluation, teachers were asked what changes they had made to their practice and why they believed the new practices were more effective than what they did before. All were able to describe the specifics of new practice in a targeted curriculum context, consistent with the notion of routine expertise. Far fewer, however, were able to say why their new practice was more effective than their previous practice – a level of understanding required for adaptive expertise. This deeper conceptual understanding allowed these teachers to articulate how they had applied the principles of the new practice in novel ways in a range of situations.

Solving the complex problems of teaching and learning requires more than doing something different. It often requires questioning and challenging one's personal beliefs. For example, a colleague of ours, Rae Si'ilata, was working in a research and development capacity with a PLC in a New Zealand primary school when a teacher talked about the inability of her Samoan students, for whom English was a second language, to make inferences from text (Si'ilata, 2014). Concerned about the possible inaccurate diagnosis, our colleague spoke to the students in Samoan to find they were well able to make inferences, and that they used forms of metaphorical language valued by their culture far more than their English first-language counterparts. An alternative, more productive diagnosis was a problem of expressive language, not of conceptual understandings. By considering the evidence, the teacher came to realize that she had not taught in ways that utilized these first-language understandings and skills when teaching the students in English. This challenge to her assumptions about her students and how to teach them effectively led her to acquire new practices in a range of situations, resulting in rapid gains in her students' achievement.

Both routine and adaptive expertise perspectives assume teachers will continue to develop their expertise throughout their careers. One difference, however, is the expectation that those with adaptive expertise have a strongly agentic mindset and take responsibility for their own learning. They seek opportunities to learn in a variety of ways, such as requesting feedback by colleagues in a PLC about their classroom practice. These processes become central to both their identity and their professional lives.

Conditions for developing adaptive expertise through professional learning communities

Our understanding of the following conditions essential to the development of adaptive expertise in PLCs was influenced by our own research (Le Fevre et al., 2015b; Si'ilata et al., 2015; Le Fevre et al., 2016) and evidence from others. The first condition is responsiveness to the needs of both students and the participating teachers. At a minimum, responsiveness to students means that their perspectives and their learning are represented in some way in the PLC (Schildkamp & Poortman, 2015; Harris & Jones, 2010; Timperley, 2011). This may take a range of forms, such as their physical presence, a survey of their attitudes about the focus of the PLC, or their academic results. Canvassing the views of parents and the community can also create the conditions for responsiveness to learners, while responsiveness to teachers means addressing the challenges teachers face in promoting the learning of their students in context.

The second condition is that PLCs are driven by curiosity and an inquiry mindset which poses questions and seeks to understand deeply the student and teacher learning-related challenges evident in the learning context (Coburn, 2006; Dweck, 2008; Horn & Little, 2010; Kaser & Halbert, 2009). This shift involves moving from exchanging helpful hints to deep inquiry as those involved find compelling reasons to change what they are doing and take joint responsibility for doing it. Learners' intellectual disengagement is becoming a major challenge in many of our education systems, but we cannot foster the intellectual engagement of learners without stimulating the intellectual curiosity of their teachers (Timperley, Kaser & Halbert, 2014). Such engagement is fostered by creating safe spaces for exploring and challenging assumptions about what is leading to what and how things might be improved. False assertions of certainty and simple answers act against such engagement.

The third condition is that the discussions and deliberations within the PLCs are based on evidence of student, teacher and leader learning and well-being (Coburn & Turner, 2011; Kazemi & Franke, 2004; Lai & McNaughton, 2013; Schildkamp & Poortman, 2015). Without a strong grounding in evidence, responsiveness (our first condition) becomes weakly theorized personal beliefs, and our second condition (curiosity and inquiry) becomes no more than expressions of individual opinion. Testing assumptions about causal possibilities develops through the collective interpretation of carefully selected evidence.

Another source of evidence forms the fourth condition. This time, it is evidence from research theory and empirical studies as a lens through which to diagnose challenges, identify possible causal pathways and develop the most productive solutions (Hill, Rowan & Ball, 2005; Ikemoto & Honig, 2010). As Timperley et al. (2014) have written, "ignoring the current research evidence on what makes a difference to learners and to learning is the educational equivalent of malpractice" (p. 15). The conceptual knowledge needed for adaptive expertise requires a deep understanding of relevant research literature related to students, how they learn, their conceptions and misconceptions, their emotions, and effective processes for addressing them. It may be that this kind of evidence is brought to the group in the form of specialist expertise because teachers rarely have the opportunity to read widely across all relevant domains.

Finally, seeking transformative and sustainable change in the pursuit of educational innovation and reform rather than "adding on" to practice or temporarily changing how things are done (Lai, McNaughton, Timperley, & Hsiao, 2009) is key. PLCs become *learning laboratories* for transformed practice. The aim is to make irreversible shifts in thinking that will change the participating teachers' and students' approaches to all future problems, not just the immediate problem confronting them at the particular time. To achieve this shift, those who are involved in analysing and solving one problem need to be explicit about how a given solution might apply to different problems, and encourage both new mindsets and new skill sets to approaching practice.

These five conditions are closely interrelated. All are necessary for developing adaptive expertise within the professional community and none of them is sufficient in isolation. These conditions also need to be supported outside of the PLC in all practice contexts: the PLC needs to be well led, but so does the organizational context in which teachers are supported to try out the ideas developed in the PLC, with risks encouraged and failures accepted (Le Fevre, 2014). Effective transformation and innovation do not happen in hierarchically-dominated organizations where getting teaching practice "right" and incremental changes in test results are the only things that count.

Structuring inquiry in PLCs

These conditions require leadership and planning. As well as an organizational culture that creates the conditions for risk taking and innovation, practical aspects such as the time to meet and the availability of relevant evidence and expertise, together with the reduction in other demands that allows the PLC to focus, are essential to success. The PLC processes need to be carefully structured around an inquiry framework that integrates the conditions. Timperley et al. (2014) provide a "spiral of inquiry, learning and action" as a framework for transforming learning for students, teachers and leaders in schools that we have used successfully to frame the work of PLCs. The spiral encapsulates the five characteristics of professional learning environments identified above.

The spiral of inquiry opens up a new space for professional learning by beginning with learning challenges that the students are experiencing. Adaptive expertise is developed in this space as challenges are jointly defined and solution paths proposed and tested. The process is practical and grounded in real challenges arising from the participants' own students. It is also intrinsically theoretical, as it requires the development of hypotheses, and the examination of assumptions and personal practical theories together with the application of theory and evidence from research.

Working through the inquiry spiral builds adaptive expertise because it is grounded in noticing what is going on, thinking creatively about what can be done, deliberately selecting actions to take and evaluating those actions in terms of learners' experiences. Figure 10.1 shows the spiral of inquiry diagrammatically. Although portrayed as a series of stages, in reality they are more iterative and often overlap. "What's going on for learners?" and "How do we know?" are the two key questions that underpin and drive all phases of the spiral. The first question ensures that the process is responsive to learners, while the second ensures it is based on evidence.

The process in the PLC begins with "scanning". Scanning is a broad look at what is happening for learners that includes both the academic curriculum and personal competencies. Scanning leads to focusing: choosing where to begin taking action. There may be many interesting possibilities but what is chosen will depend on a number of factors: what is manageable; what will leverage the most change for improvement; and what is most urgent.

The aim of focusing is to make the learning process manageable because, in the initial engagement with the spiral, those participating are learning about systematic inquiry and about pedagogical changes that will make a difference to learners. The deep nature of focusing will probably mean that more information needs to be gathered by the participants in the PLC to ensure the process is responsive to students' needs in relation to the selected focus area. It is driven by the two key questions: "What is going on for our learners?" and "How do we know?"

Once a clearer idea of the student learning challenge is established, those involved can start to develop hunches and to think about what they believe might be contributing to the situation: what are their hunches about why

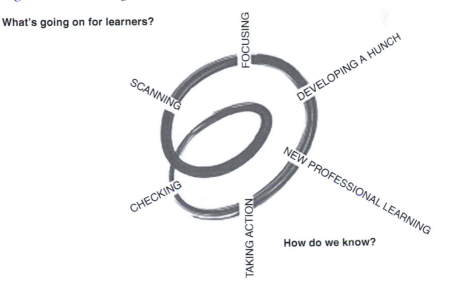

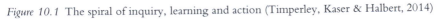

Figure 10.1 The spiral of inquiry, learning and action (Timperley, Kaser & Halbert, 2014)

things are as they are? Exploring hunches is a chance to surface underlying beliefs and ideas about how things work in relation to the learning challenge. These hunches are expressions of beliefs and theories about the situation. Practice is unlikely to change unless hunches are understood and addressed. Central to developing hunches is facing the question "How are we contributing to the situation?" Investigating this question is essential to developing adaptive expertise in that it requires agency – a sense that one can make a difference to the situation.

Learning is essential at this next point. Without new learning, teachers are unlikely to change and outcomes will remain the same. This is the space in which reference is made to relevant research and specialist expertise in the area of focus. Taking action is of critical importance here. Professional learning without action is pointless. Things must be done, and done differently from the past if changes in student experiences are to eventuate. The distinction between learning something new about a situation or problem and taking action to address it is slippery, because changing practice promotes deeper learning as ideas are revisited in context.

The checking phase is about evaluating progress. In reality, checking occurs throughout because this is what constitutes a curiosity mindset. The checking phase, however, is the time to take stock together. It involves looking broadly across students, school communities and teachers for evidence of impact, perhaps returning to some of the initial scanning and focusing activities. Checking does not signal the end of the process: the nature of the spiral is that new significant questions and insights will arise from checking and lead into further spirals of inquiry, becoming the basis of transformative and sustainable change.

Developing adaptive expertise in a PLC

Next we describe the development of adaptive expertise through an example of an Australian professional learning community context.

Teachers from a small semi-rural school in Australia, catering for students from Foundation to Year 7, began their PLC journey through the inquiry spiral under sufferance. They were working with a network of leaders and teachers from six other schools that were "invited" to work with the first two authors using the spiral of inquiry. It took this small school two years to achieve change – but when they did it was transformative, sustainable and professionally exciting. The difficulties they encountered highlight the necessity for the five conditions described above.

The size of the school meant that all teachers were included in the PLC. In the scanning phase of the inquiry spiral, they began with the formal assessment data they already had to hand. So many learning challenges arose from the assessment data that it was hard to know where to start. To resolve their confusion, they reverted to a familiar pattern of discussing what they had anecdotally noticed their students could not do. This led the teachers to focus on two different things in different parts of the school, guided not by evidence of student learning, but by the teachers' long-held concerns. The way the focus was selected served to reduce curiosity and commitment to change. Without further evidence from learners, their families or specialists, the teachers became stuck and ever more confused. When it came to examining their hunches, the team became trapped in a spiral of blaming the children's poor behaviour, disengagement, backgrounds and lack of parental support. They felt as though they were "going round and round in a fog".

At this point the teachers decided to "push the reset button" and try again. Some of the other schools in the network appeared to be energized and getting traction, so why weren't they? They took out their data and began again. This time they sought help from a facilitator who sat with the team, posed questions, made observations and clarified the messages from the data. When together they analysed the different curriculum data sets, it became apparent that mathematics required their attention. Through working with the facilitator a new focus emerged – place value in numeracy. This was not something they had considered before.

The teachers were intrigued by the new pattern that they saw in the data and decided to find out more from the learners about their place value understandings. They devised a simple common task that suited different ages at different levels of difficulty. Each child chose a number from a list and wrote all the ways they knew to represent that number. Each teacher used their laptop to video record some target learners talking about their response to the task. These one-on-one videoed interviews were shared with colleagues and prompted rich discussion about students' abilities, needs and attitudes. Features of the children's responses intrigued the teachers. Some common themes emerged across year levels: difficulties expressing place value concepts and problems with representing numbers in different ways.

From this point the PLC discussion was fuelled by enthusiasm and curiosity about a shared problem they now understood, in contrast with their first attempt which was confusing and frustrating. The teachers listed over 30 ideas about why the students might be struggling. Using the data and evidence from learners made the conversation more positive and productive. Two themes emerged in the teachers' hunches: concern about teacher knowledge of the curriculum for place value, and concern about knowledge of pedagogy for teaching place value. It was clear what new learning needed to take place.

Meeting weekly as a PLC, the staff began to tackle difficulties they were experiencing with their own knowledge of place value. As a team they unpacked the curriculum standards and worked out what each meant for place value. In this process some experts emerged from the PLC, people whose capacity had previously been untapped. They acted as guides and together the staff built a continuum of place value learning from the beginning of school (Foundation) to Year 7. The continuum described key concepts and skills in place value for each year level.

Their next step was to place every child in the school on the continuum. Rich discussion arose from this exercise – children who needed extension were made obvious, and clusters of children with similar knowledge and skills from different year levels emerged. The teachers talked about what could be done for children, shared resources and ideas for different concepts, reflected on what worked, focused on specific children and clearly identified needs. The continuum became a focal point of staff room discussion.

Collectively they used their new knowledge of place value and what children at each level needed to be able to do to plan and teach targeted lessons. There was a high level of purpose and excitement: teachers began to ask to watch each other trying new practices and to learn from one another. At the end of the three weeks' intensive work the teachers re-assessed the students and moved the students' names across the continuum to show their progress by marking where each learner started and drawing a line to their names on the sticky note showing their new level. They were rewarded with large amounts of progress. Figure 10.2 illustrates the concept of the place value continuum chart, though it only provides data for a few students for just three levels due to limitations of space.

The resulting graphic is a powerful illustration of how the teachers' curiosity, commitment, new learning and deliberate teaching affected student learning. The difference made for learners and the transformation of the staff in terms of their confidence and motivation was tangible.

In this example, teachers controlled their own learning. They developed adaptive expertise through their participation in their PLC by committing to deepening their knowledge base and professional practice to address specific challenges faced by their learners. They took the personal and professional risks around investigating the impact (or lack of it) of their own practice on student learning in ways that were confronting at times. They were motivated by the focused improvement in their students' learning over a short period of time to commit to an inquiry approach in their professional learning, both within and beyond the PLC, as the way they would collaboratively tackle their challenges in the future.

Conclusions

PLCs were originally designed to develop greater teacher agency and efficacy by promoting collegial learning through collaboration. This approach positions teachers as professionals, able to solve their problems of practice, rather than as dependent participants in external initiatives. Our argument here is that these aspirations for PLCs are consistent with the development of adaptive expertise, but unless this professional identity explicitly underpins their development, they may not realize their potential for teacher-led reform. They need to have a commitment to deepening their knowledge and working together to improve outcomes, and be prepared to constantly test if their efforts are making a difference.

If teachers and their leaders view their work as essentially requiring only routine expertise, then they will focus on the "what" and "how" of practice,

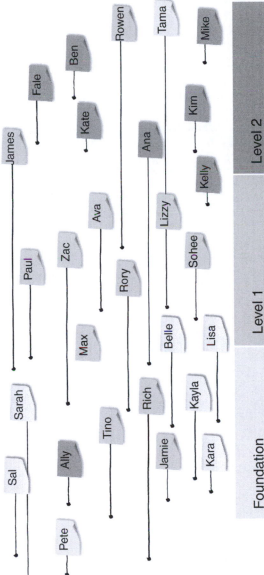

Figure 10.2 The place value continuum

rather than the deeper understanding of the "why" and the impact on learners. This is problematic because innovative and creative solutions that truly benefit learners are less likely to be developed within a routine expertise framing of professionalism. Teachers experience constant change and complexity in the contexts in which they work, and these complex environments demand adaptive expertise.

Adaptive expertise also demands the capability to use deep conceptual knowledge to work effectively and problem solve in novel, complex and uncertain situations (Hatano & Inagaki, 1986). We argue that PLCs that develop adaptive expertise need to be driven by curiosity and an inquiry mindset that poses the difficult questions. In particular, these questions are concerned with why some students are not successful in our education systems and how to tap into the perspectives of these learners. The process encourages those involved to seek creative answers that are, at the same time, grounded in what we know about learning and the curriculum.

Adaptive expertise develops deep conceptual and practical knowledge as teachers and leaders survey the research for likely solutions and apply them in a range of situations. Deep knowledge is transferrable knowledge (Pellegrino & Hilton, 2012). A PLC process that supports the development of adaptive expertise is highly metacognitive as professionals seek evidence about what is happening for student learners, how they, as professionals, might be contributing to a particular situation, and whether their efforts to change outcomes are any more effective than what they did before.

Fostering these kinds of attributes cannot be left to chance. Rather, they need systematic and focused processes within and outside of PLCs such as that promoted by the spiral of inquiry, and defined and illustrated through the analysis of the two examples in this chapter. Our vision of adaptive expertise promotes teacher agency and a responsibility for their own learning as critical properties of a PLC, but they do not exist independently of the organizational and policy environments in which teachers work. Environments that focus solely on the enactment of particular teaching practices, and on student attainment on basic skills test scores, are unlikely to foster the mindsets or the skill sets required for the development of adaptive expertise. It cannot be seen as an attribute of individuals alone, but must also permeate the norms of the PLCs and the wider environments in which teachers work.

Policy environments can be enabling or disrupt what happens in the everyday work of teachers and impact on their identity as professionals. Agencies within the New Zealand educational policy environment are increasingly articulating adaptive expertise as an underpinning conceptualization of professionalism in relevant documents (e.g. Education Review Office, 2015; Professional Development Advisory Group, 2014a; 2014b), in an effort to build consistency of a vision for the profession across the sector. Implementation strategies are being tested for their consistency with this vision. While these can be enabling conditions, translation into powerful teacher-led reforms requires that every PLC is underpinned by principles and practices consistent with adaptive expertise to build teacher agency and make a difference for every student learner.

Recently, the provision of nationally funded professional development across New Zealand has formally adopted the spiral of inquiry as its basis. Leaders and teachers will be expected to engage with an expert facilitator over a two-year time frame to investigate what is happening for learners, to focus in a specific area and to address hunches about what is contributing to the situation before engaging in knowledge and skill building designed to address identified problems. Similarly, a nationally contested teacher-led innovation fund has adopted the spiral of inquiry as the basis for teachers to investigate and research their practice. This fund specifically promotes the development of adaptive expertise as teachers work together in professional communities with researchers to figure out together how to make a difference to outcomes for learners.

In addition, schools across the country are being encouraged to join in cross-school professional collaborations called "Communities of Learners". Principals and teacher leaders are being appointed and recompensed for their efforts. Their role is to enhance professional expertise and collective responsibility through these professional collaborations to improve outcomes for the learners in their schools (New Zealand Ministry of Education, 2016). At this stage, it is too soon to assess the effectiveness of this changing educational landscape, but there is no doubt about the government's commitment to building collaborative expertise throughout the education system.

References

Coburn, C. E. (2006). Framing the problem of reading instruction: Using frame analysis to uncover the microprocesses of policy implementation. *American Educational Research Journal, 43*(3), 343–379.

Coburn, C. E. & Turner, E. O. (2011). Research on data use: A framework and analysis. *Measurement: Interdisciplinary Research and Perspectives, 9*(4), 173–206.

Cochran-Smith, M., Villegas, A. M., Abrams, L., Chavez-Moreno, L., Mills, T. & Stern, R. (2016). Research on teacher preparation: Charting the landscape of a sprawling field. In D. Gitomer & C. Bell (Eds.), *Handbook of research on teaching* (5th ed.). Washington, D.C.: AERA.

Dall'Alba, G. & Sandberg, J. (2006). Unveiling professional development: A critical review of stage models. *Review of Educational Research, 76*(3), 383–412.

Dreyfus, H. & Dreyfus, S. (1986). *Mind over machine: The power of human intuition and expertise in the era of the computer.* New York: Free Press.

Dweck, C. (2008). *Mindset: The new psychology of success.* New York: Ballantine Books.

Education Review Office (2015). *School evaluation indicators: Effective practice for improvement and learner success (Trial document).* Wellington, New Zealand: ERO.

Elmore, R. (2004). *School reform from the inside out: Policy, practice and performance.* Cambridge, MA: Harvard Education Press.

Fullan, M. (2011). *Choosing the wrong drivers for whole system reform. Seminar Series 204.* Melbourne, Australia: Centre for Strategic Education.

Hargreaves, A. & Fullan, M. (2012). *Professional capital: Transforming teaching in every school.* New York: Teachers College Press.

Harris, A. & Jones, M. (2010). Professional learning communities and system improvement. *Improving Schools, 13*(2), 172–181.

Hatano, G. & Inagaki, K. (1986). Two courses of expertise. In H. Stevenson, H. Azama & K. Hakuta (Eds.), *Child development and education in Japan* (pp. 262–272). New York: Freeman.

Hill, H. C., Rowan, B. & Ball, D. L. (2005). Effects of teachers' mathematical knowledge for teaching on student achievement. *American Educational Research Journal, 42*(2), 371–406.

Horn, I. S. & Little, J. W. (2010). Attending to problems of practice: Routines and resources for professional learning in teachers' workplace interactions. *American Educational Research Journal, 47*(1), 181–217.

Ikemoto, G. S. & Honig, M. I. (2010). Tools to deepen the practitioners' engagement with research: The case of the Institute for Learning. In C. E. Coburn & M. K. Stein (Eds.), *Research and practice in education: Building alliances, bridging the divide* (pp. 93–108). Lanham, MD: Rowman & Littlefield.

Kaser, L. & Halbert, J. (2009). *Leadership mindsets: Innovation and learning in the transformation of schools.* London and New York: Routledge.

Kazemi, E. & Franke, M. L. (2004). Teacher learning in mathematics: Using student work to promote collective inquiry. *Journal of Mathematics Teacher Education, 7*(3), 203–235.

Lai, M. K. & McNaughton, S. (2013). Analysis and discussion of classroom and achievement data to raise student achievement. In K. Schildkamp, M. K. Lai & L. Earl (Eds.), *Data-based decision making in education* (pp. 23–47). Dordrecht, The Netherlands: Springer.

Lai, M., McNaughton, S., Timperley, H. & Hsiao, S. (2009). Sustaining continued acceleration in reading comprehension achievement following an intervention. *Educational Assessment, Evaluation and Accountability, 21*(1), 81–100.

Lampert, M. (1985). How do teachers manage to teach? Perspectives on problems in practice. *Harvard Educational Review, 55*(2), 178–194.

Le Fevre, D. M. (2014). Barriers to implementing pedagogical change: The role of teachers' perceptions of risk. *Teaching and Teacher Education, 38*, 56–64.

Le Fevre, D. M., Ell, F., Timperley, H., Twyford, K. & Mayo, S. (2015a). *Developing adaptive expertise: The practice of effective facilitators.* Auckland, New Zealand: Consortium for Professional Development.

Le Fevre, D. M., Si'ilata, R., Timperley, H., Twyford, K., Mayo, S. & Ell, F. (2016). *Developing linguistically and culturally responsive practice.* Auckland, New Zealand: Consortium for Professional Development.

Le Fevre, D. M., Timperley, H. & Ell, F. (2015b). Curriculum and pedagogy: The future of teacher professional learning and the development of adaptive expertise. In D. Wyse, L. Hayward & J. Pandya (Eds.), *The SAGE handbook of curriculum, pedagogy and assessment* (pp. 309–324). London: Sage.

Louis, K. S. & Kruse, S. D. (1995). *Professionalism and community: Perspectives on reforming urban schools.* Thousand Oaks, CA: Corwin Press.

MET Project. (2013). *Ensuring fair and reliable measures of effective teaching: Culminating findings from the MET project's three-year study.* Bill and Melinda Gates Foundation. Retrieved from www.metproject.org/downloads/MET_Ensuring_Fair_and_Reliable_Measures_Practitioner_Brief.pdf

New Zealand Ministry of Education (2016). *Community of learners: Guide for schools and kura.* Wellington, New Zealand: Ministry of Education. Retrieved from www.education.govt.nz/assets/Documents/Ministry/Investing-in-Educational-Success/Communities-of-Schools/Communities-of-Learning-Guide-for-Schools-and-Kura-web-enabled.pdf

Parr, J. (2010). Inquiry into classroom practice for improvement. In H. Timperley & J. Parr (Eds.), *Weaving evidence, inquiry and standards to build better schools* (pp. 115–134). Wellington, New Zealand: NZCER Press.

Pellegrino, J. & Hilton, M. (2012). *Education for life and work: Developing transferable knowledge and skills in the 21st century*. Washington, D.C.: National Research Council.

Professional Development Advisory Group (2014a). *Professional learning and development across the compulsory school and kura sector: Report of the Professional Learning and Development Advisory Group*. Wellington, New Zealand: Ministry of Education.

Professional Development Advisory Group (2014b). *Professional learning and development across the compulsory school and kura sector: The future design of professional learning and development*. Wellington, New Zealand: Ministry of Education.

Schildkamp, K. & Poortman, C. (2015). Factors influencing the functioning of data teams. *Teachers College Record, 117*(4), 1–42.

Si'ilata, R. (2014). *Va'a Tele: Pasifika learners riding the success wave on linguistically and culturally responsive pedagogies* (Unpublished doctoral thesis). University of Auckland, New Zealand.

Si'ilata, R., Le Fevre, D. M., Ell, F., Timperley, H., Twyford, K. & Mayo, S. (2015). *Adaptive expertise in the facilitation of linguistic and cultural responsiveness*. Auckland, New Zealand: Consortium for Professional Development.

Stoll, L. (2011). Leading professional learning communities. In J. Robertson & H. Timperley (Eds.), *Leadership and learning* (pp. 103–117). Los Angeles, CA: Sage.

Stoll, L. & Louis, K. S. (Eds.). (2007). *Professional learning communities: Divergence, depth and dilemmas*. Maidenhead, UK: Open University Press.

Timperley, H. (2011). *Realizing the power of professional learning*. London: Open University Press.

Timperley, H., Kaser, L. & Halbert, J. (2014). *A framework for transforming learning in schools: Innovation and the spiral of inquiry. Seminar Series 234*. Melbourne, Australia: Centre for Strategic Education.

11 Professional learning communities in Chinese senior secondary schools

Sally M. Thomas, Wen-Jung Peng and Pat Triggs

Introduction

For more than three decades the idea of professional learning communities (PLCs) has been present within education. The concept has been variously defined and theorized but there is a broad consensus that it describes a group of people sharing and critically interrogating their practice to mutually enhance each other's and pupils' learning (Hord, 1997). Over time the notion of 'the reflective practitioner' (Schon, 1983) was linked with that of 'collegiality', 'community', 'collective learning' and 'shared vision' in a focus on school reform, school improvement and increasing teacher effectiveness through professional development.

More recently PLC definitions have been developed in different but overlapping ways, some emphasizing the role of within school PLCs (Harris & Jones, 2010) and others the involvement of all professional staff in both whole school and smaller PLCs (Department for Education and Skills [DfES], 2005). The purpose of this chapter is to examine the relevance and existence of the PLC concept in a context where relatively little research has been conducted on this topic – mainland China – by reporting new evidence from an ESRC DFID funded study, 'Improving Teacher Development and Educational Quality in China' (ITDEQC) (Thomas & Peng, 2014).

Importantly, the past 20 years has seen quantitative and qualitative research concerned to investigate not just the concept and function of PLCs but also the relationship between professional learning communities and student achievement (Akiba & Liang, 2016). However, the proposition that professional learning communities are a predictor of student success has seldom been tested directly, although some tentative positive associations have been found with students' academic performance in primary and secondary phases of education (Vescio, Ross & Adams, 2008; Thomas, 2010; Lomos, Hofman & Bosker, 2011). Furthermore, typically PLC studies have been conducted in the USA, the UK and the Netherlands and it is in 'the west' where the PLC concept has been most embedded. Therefore, given the evidence of the positive outcomes of schools operating as professional learning communities it is not surprising to find increasing interest in exploring the concept internationally, and specifically in China (Hannum, Park & Cheng, 2007; Sargent & Hannum, 2009; Wong 2010; Peng et al., 2013).

In 2010 a ten-year National Plan for Education Reform and Development in China (Chinese Ministry of Education [CMOE], 2010) included the requirement to 'renovate school operation and education administration, overhaul quality evaluation, [and] examinations … revamp teaching … methods and approaches, and put a modern school system in place'. Schools have been given greater autonomy and now have to design a school based curriculum to accompany the National Curriculum. In this context could the concept of PLCs contribute to achieving the desired reforms and change?

This chapter explores this issue by presenting findings from the ITDEQC project which investigates the existence and relevance of professional learning communities (PLCs) in China to promote student outcomes and teacher development (IEEQC/ITDEQC, 2016). However, before outlining the key ITDEQC findings and providing illustrations of the features of PLCs identified in the Chinese schools, we first provide a brief overview of Chinese literature on professional development and related policy and practice. The chapter concludes by discussing what we can learn from the Chinese experience generally about PLCs and how this relates to the potential for teacher-led reform and change in terms of impact, sustainability and support.

Professional development and PLCs in China

Regarding teacher development and the relevance of PLCs in the Chinese context a few studies have reported relevant findings, but there does not seem to be a consistent PLC definition or terminology used. Zhong (2005) indicates that a school learning community is constructed by four major elements: sense of belonging, sense of trust, sense of mutual benefit and sense of sharing. It can exist in an actual or virtual form but with two key features of distributed expertise and mutual appreciation. Chen (2005) also emphasizes that head teachers have to play a multiple role as a leading learner, a shared vision developer, innovative management designer as well as team relationship coordinator in the process of establishing a learning community. Walker (2016) and Wang (2015) have also emphasized the key role of educational leaders in promoting positive emotional relationships in schools and in binding together the key conditions of effective schooling.

As noted previously, the China mainland is carrying out a new basic education and development reform, which involves a new curriculum at national, local and school levels. As part of the new reforms schools are encouraged to create their own curriculum while also ensuring the implementation of national curriculum (The State Council of PRC, 2001). Li and Song (2006) consider that the process of a school developing their own curriculum ultimately leads to building the school as a professional learning community for it involves sharing leadership and practice, values and vision, group learning and application of learning. Wong (2010) has examined explicitly what makes a PLC in a Shanghai junior secondary school via interviews with mathematics and English teachers and pointed out that socio-cultural factors have played a role in promoting and shaping teaching research groups as PLCs in 'a different way from the Western practice'. The factors include examination-driven values and sense of collectivism, authoritarian-oriented practice and limited conflict, as well as interpersonal relationships being an important social capital of PLCs.

Wong (2010) suggests that more structural support is critical for constructing PLCs in Chinese schools, teacher learning has to go beyond schools and classrooms, and PLCs need to be contextualized for sustainability. Jiang and Liu (2009) also highlight that teaching research teams should play a more proactive role in promoting PLC development rather than just act administratively. Nevertheless, the existence of PLCs seems to be more evident in some Chinese regions than others. In highly affluent Shanghai, Sun (2010) reported that over 80 percent of 481 teachers who were surveyed indicated several features of effective PLCs and, specifically, they reported their learning is supported by external networks. Similarly, Thomas, Peng and Li (2015) reported high levels of recognition of the PLC concept amongst senior secondary school teachers, although this varied across Chinese regions, with less evidence apparent in the poorer west. Meanwhile, Li (2013) highlights some barriers to constructing Chinese schools as PLCs. He argues that head teachers may not provide an adequate role model of learning and typically teachers have fragile professional autonomy, lack teaching autonomy and have a weak awareness of collective learning, collaborative inquiry and self-reflection. This suggests that the nature of PLCs and opportunities for teacher led reform may be highly context specific in China and we seek to explore the issue further.

Overall, we aim to build on previous evidence and present a snapshot of the existence and relevance of professional learning communities (PLCs) in Chinese schools that are identified as either more or less effective in different contexts. If PLCs exist in Chinese schools a key issue is whether these are observed as more 'mature' PLCs in more effective schools, as suggested by previous research in UK (DfES, 2005). In the following sections we outline the ITDEQC study design, methods and key findings, followed by a discussion in relation to the literature and lessons learned.

ITDEQC research approach and methods

The purpose of the ITDEQC study was not to look for 'policy borrowing' (Phillips & Ochs, 2003) but rather to explore the views and experiences of Chinese stakeholders regarding the existence, relevance and utility of the concept of PLCs to improve teacher quality and student outcomes. The evidence reported comes from national and local policy makers as well as practitioners in four case study senior secondary schools (two more effective and two less effective) from two contrasting eastern and western provinces in mainland China.

One-to-one and focus group interviews were used as the main method of data collection, as well as follow up reports and telephone interviews conducted between October 2010 and March 2012. The range of participants was chosen to gain the perspectives of different groups in the school community, and all responded to an invitation to contribute. Interviews were conducted with senior leaders (Headteachers, Deputy Head Teachers, Heads of Subject or Year Groups), senior teachers with more than five years' teaching experience, junior teachers with five or fewer years' teaching experience, support staff not directly involved with teaching and students aged 18 or above.

In total there were 96 interviewees, including four national policy makers, four local policy makers and in each of four case study schools between 16–23 staff and between 2–5 students. Participants were specifically asked their views on the characteristic features and processes of professional learning communities in relation to the operation of their own school. Given the 'fuzzy' semantic history of the concept, it was necessary to agree a definition in order to discuss it with the participants:

> A professional learning community (PLC) is an inclusive group of people, motivated by a shared learning vision, who support and work with each other, finding ways, inside and outside their immediate community, to enquire on their practice and together learn new and better approaches that will enhance all students' learning.

This definition was created by UK government funded research into creating and sustaining effective professional learning communities (DfES, 2005; Stoll et al., 2006), which also identified eight characteristics of effective PLCs (Shared values and vision; Collective responsibility for students' learning; Collaboration focused on learning; Group as well as individual professional learning; Reflective professional enquiry; Openness, networks and partnerships; Inclusive membership; Mutual trust, respect and support). A key aim of the ITDEQC study was to explore and test out Chinese stakeholder perceptions of this formulation of PLC characteristics identified in the UK. The idea of stages of development in a PLC based on these characteristics was also used and participants were asked to consider whether their school as a PLC could be described as 'starting', 'developing' or 'mature'.

Overall the study was located within a large scale longitudinal quantitative research project (Thomas & Peng, 2014; Thomas, Peng & Li, 2015). Criteria for selection of the four case study schools were location, which broadly reflects higher or lower economic development (east/west region; urban or rural), and academic 'value added' performance. Schools A1 (urban; more/ average effective value added performance) and A2 (rural; less effective value added performance) are in a north-eastern city which covers a very large metropolitan area, comprising three municipal districts, four county level cities and 18 counties, and includes five universities and 12 colleges. The city has a population of over ten million people. In contrast, Schools B1 (rural;

more/average effective value added performance) and B2 (urban; less effective value added performance) are in a north-western city with nearly two million inhabitants. It comprises one central urban district, where half a million people live, and three counties. Much of the province is mountainous or plateaus, most at least 1,000m above sea level and agriculture is a major economic activity. With regard to the educational context, Chinese senior high schools provide three years of education beyond the nine years of compulsory education in China. Entry to an academic senior high school or a vocational high school at age 15–16 years is by a competitive entrance examination (zhongkao).

In the following sections we examine the ITDEQC evidence in relation to the existence and relevance of PLCs and specifically to various PLC characteristics. The views of policy makers are compared and contrasted to practitioners in the four case study schools, and where relevant any observed differences between the more and less effective schools are highlighted. However, overall, given the relative size of China, it is recognized that only a relatively small sample of schools and stakeholder interviewees were possible, and so the findings reported are intended to be exploratory and illustrative, rather than definitive.

Evidence of professional learning communities in more and less effective Chinese schools

All policy makers interviewed saw the relevance and existence of professional learning communities in relation to teachers' membership of teaching research groups (TRGs), as noted in previous research such as Wong (2010). A senior policy maker and academic in teacher education who had lived in the USA was very clear that these already constituted a form of within school sub-PLC:

> In my opinion the learning community of teachers, the professional community in China is relatively strong. I once managed five kinds of learning community – that is a lesson preparation group, a subject group, a year group, a teaching and research group and a research office; these were five professional learning communities. I don't think there is any such system abroad. I believe there are no learning communities abroad as sound as the ones we have in China.
>
> (NPM1).

However, an interviewee from the MoE was more guarded, arguing that there are huge disparities between areas in the effectiveness of TRGs. Nevertheless, he saw these groups as 'the major form' in relation to PLCs and went on to mention teachers taking an initiative and forming professional development communities based on a common interest which linked with their subject knowledge and teaching, pointing out that Chinese teachers naturally collaborate and more formally, at national level, schools are being required to work together.

With regard to the teachers in the four case study schools, the specific PLC concept was typically new to them but nevertheless they saw it as having relevance and value for their work. For example, a senior teacher in the most effective school (A1) also pointed to the tradition of TRGs as evidence of PLCs:

> In our school, teachers of the same subject belong to the same small group. These small groups form a big group, the school. Learning materials that we use in addition to exams and test papers are compiled and designed collectively by individual small groups.
>
> (Lea1Sch1ST2).

Another teacher in the same school also recognized the potential contribution of PLCs to whole school development and teachers' learning:

> It helps students' development, the development of school and society, improves teachers' professional development and life-long learning, improves the effectiveness of the work in the school, improves the co-ordination between various departments within school. For teachers this is an important route to their personal development.
>
> (Lea1Sch1Ex2).

Not surprisingly, all participants were in agreement that aspects of a PLC could be seen in their school, and in two schools (A2 and B1) staff depicted a common view of a developing PLC. However, interestingly, in the most and least effective schools (A1 and B2) there were differing views between staff, with some senior staff arguing the PLC was mature, while more junior teachers and support staff sensed the school was developing (A1) or just starting (B2).

For example, in the least effective school (B2) there was an almost unanimous consensus that for them the development of a formalized PLC was at the preliminary stage as indicated from these comments from the deputy head and English teacher:

> It's at an elementary stage … I think we have to learn more about this. [Teachers] have acted on their own to collaborate and exchange their experiences, but there was no sort of [PLC] climate. It's being formed now.
>
> (Lea2Sch2DH).

The one notable exception to this consensus was the Head of Teaching and Research who thought that from the perspective of regarding the PLC as a means of teacher development the school (B2) was a well-developed organization.

Meanwhile, some teachers were more likely to understand a PLC as a whole school undertaking. This was an aspiration for the head teacher of one school

(A2) but he noted so far '*we are actually in a process of exploration, and just got going*'. His understanding and that of other teachers was that a PLC was a continuously evolving process. An indication of a move to whole-school development activity is a weekly whole school staff meeting, seen as an opportunity for group professional learning. In the poorer western but more effective school (B1), the head teacher recognized the potential strengths of the whole school PLC and noted,

> all the staff, no matter whether they are admin staff, teaching staff, or support staff, should all be involved in [the community]. This point is very good.
>
> (Lea2Sch1HT).

But the Headteacher and Head of Research also thought that, although there were elements of the PLC in their established practice, aspects of a PLC defined as a whole school undertaking were missing:

> As for our school … I think there is such practice. But compared with your definition, there is a gap between our practice and what you mentioned. For example, support staff are not usually involved in teaching affairs.
>
> (Lea2Sch1HT).

Moreover, other interviewees agreed that various groups in the school (B1) could be regarded as sub-PLCs. However, some, including the deputy head, thought that in PLC terms the practice was weak in relation to the way the groups were formed and worked.

> If we take the teaching research group of our school as a PLC, it should be described as at the primary stage. Teachers are brought together and form the group just because of a requirement to achieve certain targets. To say it is matured, it is not even close to that yet. A matured group should be driven by [teachers'] own willingness. Teachers discuss and communicate with each other for the purpose of bettering students' scores, in order to improve overall results of a class. This kind of practice only qualifies as a primary stage.
>
> (Lea2Sch1DH).

> Teaching and research groups have existed in our school for a relatively long time. But in terms of the level of the form and content … the practice is still not good enough.
>
> (Lea2Sch1ET).

From the stakeholder perceptions outlined above it is clear that the overall concept and existence of PLCs in Chinese schools is familiar and relevant, although the terminology used may be different. Moreover, there are tentative indications that a school's own classification as a starting or mature PLC maps onto relative levels of value added effectiveness, thereby supporting similar conclusions in previous research in the UK (Thomas, 2010; Thomas et al., 2015; Lomos et al., 2011). Below we move on to examine in more detail the PLC characteristics identified from the DfES (2005) study to establish if the PLC features of English schools are also found to a greater or lesser extent in more and less effective Chinese schools.

Shared values, vision and collective responsibility for students' learning

The two PLC characteristics 'Shared values and vision' and 'Collective responsibility for students' learning' were typically seen as very closely aligned by Chinese stakeholders. However, policy makers on occasion differed in their perceptions of the 'shared values and vision' characteristic. One thought that teachers typically shared a common vision about their school and their students and this coincided with the nationally advocated view that school culture should reflect the values of the head and teachers, namely that everyone should work hard to teach students well and to run a school well. However, he saw this as a challenge that involved more than the display of 'empty slogans' around the school. In contrast was the view of another policy maker that, although in general terms SHS teachers might share values about the development of students, their individual priorities varied according to the year group they taught:

> For Year 3 teachers the value is all about improving students' scores in the entrance examination. This is a negative situation. By rights teachers' work should be about promoting the competence, thinking and ethics of the students, but in Year 3 all these are given up for the examination.
>
> (NPM1).

The tendency for SHS teachers to prioritize exam scores was also alluded to by a policy maker as a source of tension:

> A professional development community is easy to set up and can have impact where there is agreement between government requirements and teacher needs. It is not easy to establish a PLC when teacher's demands and expectations do not agree with what government advocates.
>
> (NPM4).

With regard to the four case study schools, shared values and a collective responsibility for students learning was typically evidenced by school staff via slogans and banners displayed on classroom walls, for example referring to 'helping each other', 'working hard' and 'effective performance is paramount'. The head teacher in the most effective school (A1) also referred to establishing a brand for the school as a means to reflect the shared values and vision and to prioritize excellent performance. However, like the policy makers, both senior and junior staff from the other three schools (A2, B1, B2) mentioned the challenge and tensions that arise from a performance based exam orientated system. Moreover, collective responsibility for student learning was noted in all four schools and is explicitly used as a mechanism to promote student performance. In the more effective western school (B1), the Head of Research and Teaching provided an example:

> If a senior third-year student performs well in math and Chinese … but not in English, this will affect the student's overall achievement in college entrance exam. Other teachers will ask the student's English teacher to give the student extra tutoring. The English teacher is very responsible and coaches the student alone. The student's English improves enough to pass the college entrance exam. This is common responsibility.
>
> (Lea2Sch1RH1).

A student in the most effective school (A1) also supported this and noted that all teachers are willing to help them.

> I think our teachers are all good. Sometimes when we have any queries and couldn't find our Physics or Chemistry teacher, we could seek other teachers' advice. They are very patient and kind in answering our queries. They won't reject us because we are not in the classes they teach.
>
> (Lea1Sch1ST3).

Nevertheless, both the schools in the poorer west also referred to the need for differentiation in teaching, learning and performance. A deputy head from the least effective school (B2) highlighted the need to recognize student progress not just raw outcomes and stated,

> Our student intake is pretty poor … It is unrealistic to hope all students will be able to get a place at Tsinghua, Peking, or other key universities. If a student can now get only a score of 100, and later on receive a score of 300 in the entrance examination, we regard this as an achievement too. Therefore, every teacher needs to implement the practice of teaching according to different levels of students in class so that students will be able to go to whatever university they can.
>
> (Lea2Sch2DH).

Thus, not surprisingly given cultural factors, the ITDEQC findings suggest that shared values and collective responsibility for students' learning are two PLC features that are typically strongly evidenced in the Chinese context.

Collaboration focused on learning and group as well as individual professional learning

The two PLC characteristics 'Collaboration focused on learning' and 'Group as well as individual professional learning' were also typically seen as very closely aligned by Chinese stakeholders. Policy makers and school staff generally agreed that group learning and collaborations focused on learning were evident in professional development of teachers in China, notably via TRGs and the well-established traditions of model demonstration lessons and mentoring. In the more effective western school (B1), two senior teachers gave examples:

> We require every teacher to sit in on other teachers' classes, and learn from them. Teachers you think have better teaching; you just bring a chair to their classes and sit down to listen to their teaching.
>
> (Lea2Sch1RH1).

> Another thing is to write a research proposal. Every year the teaching research groups have to identify research topics and to actively seek funds at district and/or provincial levels. Teachers then can conduct research collaboratively.
>
> (Lea2Sch1ET).

The less effective western school (A2) also followed the common practice of placing all teachers of the same subject in the same office to support collaboration, and the deputy head of the most effective school (A1) provided an illustration of how the national reforms in curriculum and assessment were having an impact on collaboration and group learning:

> In the curriculum reform and changes to college entrance exams, for example, the three different subjects, History, Politics and Geography, are blended into an interdisciplinary subject and tested in one exam paper … That means, teachers of the three subjects have to gather together to prepare lessons collectively.
>
> (Lea1Sch1DT).

Traditionally, mentoring in Chinese schools is seen as collaborative but hierarchical – a master and apprentice activity, although one policy maker had specific concerns about the mentoring system in Senior High Schools and argued good practice is declining. Indeed, in the least effective school (B2) it was clear that recent changes had been made to re-organize and to monitor much more closely the teaching group and mentoring activities in order to improve teacher collaboration, reflections and ultimately student outcomes. A senior teacher in the less effective eastern school (A2) also recognized the potential of mentoring to promote reciprocal learning and professional development for both participants:

I usually say, let's learn together. Sometimes … a paired senior teacher although more experienced has a lower educational qualification compared to the junior teacher. Therefore, mentoring is also a learning process for senior teachers. Sometimes we learn an advanced teaching idea from young teachers and we teach them the skill of effectively managing the classroom.

(Lea1Sch2Chinese).

Thus, overall and similar to the ITDEQC findings related to shared values and collective responsibility for students' learning, the two PLC features – collaboration focused on learning and Group as well as individual professional learning – are also typically strongly evidenced in the Chinese context. However, as we shall see below, this is not the case for the remaining four PLC factors.

Reflective professional enquiry

The process of reflective enquiry was perceived as important but stakeholder views suggested it was often confined to students' academic performance, mainly because this was a key indicator for evaluating teacher performance. In addition to the collaborative 'reflective activity' in the teaching and research groups, teachers also typically received regular feedback from students on their experiences of learning. For example, in the most effective school (A1), at the end of every semester students are required to complete a questionnaire which gives them opportunities to comment on, for example, which teachers they like most, whether they like the teaching approach and delivery, the amount of homework they receive, the learning environment, and their expectations of teachers. A student noted:

> Then teachers communicate and make adjustment according to our thoughts. This promotes better interaction between teachers and students as well as our learning.

(Lea1Sch1ST2).

Nevertheless teachers' reflection on their professional practice is typically formalized and monitored. In the more effective eastern school (B1), the Head of Research indicated that the depth of teacher reflection is monitored:

> Senior teachers are asked to give a model teaching class. All other teachers come to the class and learn from them. Then they gather to discuss the strengths and weaknesses of the class. After the discussion, each teacher writes down the reflection concerning what he/she has learned from the class and hands it in to the Office.

(Lea2Sch1RH1).

Moreover, in the less effective eastern school (A2) there was clearly a sustained focus on attainment outcomes which forces teachers to consider their practice with specific reference to the examination. As noted by an experienced teacher, this can be an uncomfortable process:

> Peer pressure is so huge. When the results of the monthly exam come out, the scores are there for you to compare. If your class did not achieve a good score, you feel pressure even though others do not judge you. In this case you would consider how to improve, how to communicate with your students and find out the problems. When thinking of all this, you feel so anxious.
>
> (Lea1Sch2ET1).

Similarly in the least effective school (B2), the stakes are high for teachers, given a teaching quality feedback assembly is regularly convened to provide information such as which class of which year grade did poorly in which subject. Teachers are expected to adjust their teaching based on the information received from the assembly and their students' marks. The Head of Research also said that the school was placing a particular emphasis on teachers' reflective inquiry:

> Teachers are required to write and attach their teaching reflections to the teaching plan after each class. Teachers must do reflection for each class in a serious manner to reflect their own teaching process and behaviour, and to find out what is and is not effective in order to promote their growth.
>
> (Lea2Sch2RH).

In spite of reference to numerous formal activities to promote teachers' reflective professional enquiry in all four schools, the head of research in the less effective eastern school (A2) admitted that this continued to be worked on to improve practice and has also become associated with teacher appraisal. This may be due to a point raised by another staff member in the same school arguing that reflection and discussion by teachers is mostly superficial:

> The teachers usually do the reflections only because it is required, and do not pay enough attention during the discussions of others' reflections about their practice.
>
> (LEA1Sch2RM).

Similarly, a policy maker interviewed was also not confident that teachers were equipped to reflect effectively on pedagogy:

> I think this aspect is weak ... Everyone in a lesson preparation group prepares lessons and analyses students collectively ... However, I do not think the approach to data collection and analysis is scientific. This is

probably to do with lack of equipping teachers with the ability to do research while we are training and nurturing them as a teacher.

(NPM1).

Thus, with regard to the PLC factor reflective professional inquiry, the ITDEQC findings suggest that often this activity is highly formalized and there may be a need to consider how to encourage teachers to take more individual responsibility for meaningful reflective practice.

Openness, networks and partnerships

In relation to openness, networks and partnerships, national policy makers noted some exchange and co-operation between schools in the same county or district, invariably initiated by LEAs in response to central requirements. However, they were most concerned about the lack of communication between schools and universities, especially in rural areas. This perception reflected the policy makers' view that the characteristics of a PLC were more frequently found in 'eastern areas, developed areas and cities'. The internet, it was felt, might be a factor in reducing the disadvantages interviewees felt were experienced by rural schools. It was emphasized that the government (MOE) intention was to use the potential of digital devices to support online communities and networks, for example those who were undertaking the National Training Programme.

With regard to the four case study schools only the less effective eastern school (A2) and more effective western school (B1) provided meaningful examples of external links, although both mentioned that developing networks and partnerships is limited by lack of funding. In the less effective eastern school (A2) a teacher argued,

> The school invests limited money in activities and it hopes to meet the requirements of development. It is really difficult to do it. We can't do as much as those schools with sufficient funds.
>
> (Lea1Sch2math).

This school provides some financial assistance to teachers who want to pursue higher degrees but some interviewees said that they were contributing to their own professional development through attending courses at the weekend and studying alone. However, similar to the view of policy makers, the head teacher saw the internet as the way to compensate for limited funding. In the more effective eastern school (B1), evidence of openness, networks and partnerships appeared in teachers' accounts of research projects in the district involving other schools. A junior teacher described visits to partner schools:

> Our teachers go to those schools to listen to their classes every year and discuss teaching.
>
> (Lea2Sch1JT1).

Yet, students in this school wanted more communication with city schools, which they described as '*more advanced*'. They thought that students of partnership schools should communicate more, specifically about the exam, and there should be comparison of exam results to compare schools.

Interestingly, neither the most nor the least effective schools (A1, B2) could provide much evidence of external networks or partnerships and reasons for this were unclear, even though the eastern school would have relatively easier access to universities. Teachers in the most effective school (A1) acknowledged that communication between schools and networking was something that should be promoted and saw their school as 'modernized' in terms of provision of ICT to support communication. Nevertheless, overall the ITDEQC findings related to the PLC factor openness, networks and partnerships were mixed across the four case study schools and also closely linked to funding opportunities, suggesting this feature is not necessarily very common practice in Chinese schools.

Inclusive membership

The concept of inclusiveness in relation to PLCs was somewhat unfamiliar for most stakeholders and otherwise was seen mostly as related to non-teaching staff. Support staff were seen by some as irrelevant to a PLC, as stated by a policy maker:

> They cannot join the teaching community; all they need to do is take care of their own job. Maybe librarians and clinic staff can be part of the community but they are marginalized and may feel like outsiders. This is related to our tradition. Clinical staff concern themselves about students' health. They seldom interfere in education.
>
> (NPM3).

However, evidence of varied practice in schools was provided from another policy maker:

> Some principals may regard non-teaching staff as part of the school and bring them in. Others may divide them from the teaching faculty. It all depends on the principal. In some schools I have been in every teacher has a project including the non-teaching staff.
>
> (NPM1).

Interestingly, participants in all of the case study schools mentioned that typically non-teaching staff shared a responsibility for students' learning which they discharged by doing the various jobs which contributed to creating a positive environment for learning. Support staff also felt empowered to contribute to students' moral education, especially in relation to discipline and behaviour. For example, in the more effective western school (B1) a non-teaching staff member who worked in the library and had no education beyond SHS described his relationship with the students:

> I get along well with our students ... I told them to call on me when they need me ... I say to them in a humorous way: like me, you are also from countryside. All the bread you've taken from home could pave the road from home to the school. If you were not studying hard, but playing around or doing irrelevant things in class, doesn't that let your parents down? Then they would say: Sorry sir. I was wrong. I now know what to do.
>
> (Lea2Sch1NTS).

In addition, staff in two case study schools (A1, B1) mentioned collaborations between ICT support staff and teachers as examples of including all school staff within the PLC, especially when a teacher's skills are not adequate for the demands to include the internet and computers in lessons. Moreover, a non-teaching member of staff in the most effective school (A1), from his administrative perspective, also saw inclusive aspects of a PLC developing within the school, as a result of national reforms:

> The teaching and educational reform has made the relationship between frontline and non-frontline staff, i.e. teaching and admin staff, closer.
>
> (Lea1Sch1NT).

In the less effective eastern school (A2), the Head of Maths also saw considerable potential for including support staff more closely in a learning community given they have a relatively wider view of the school. Nevertheless, although generally aspirations for a whole school PLC tended to be inclusive of all staff, in practical terms, many participants felt that collaborations focused on learning did not involve non-teaching staff. For example, the head teacher of the more effective western school (B1) observed:

> support staff are not usually involved in teaching affairs. They think their work is concerned with management, personnel, assisting teachers but not teaching.
>
> (Lea2Sch1HT).

Similarly, a non-teaching member of staff in the least effective school (B2), who was university educated and a first rank teacher who now worked in administration, thought that the PLC concept described very necessary practice to be more inclusive:

> I think it is essential, absolutely necessary ... but this kind of collaborative learning and collaborative exploration is not a habitual practice in our school. Teachers are still used to working separately.
>
> (Lea2Sch2NT).

Thus, similar to the PLC feature of reflective professional enquiry, the ITDEQC evidence of inclusive PLC membership was generally found to be somewhat weak in Chinese schools.

Mutual trust, respect and support

Policy makers' comments about the mutual trust, respect and support PLC characteristic included references to students and their families, although it was felt that relationships between students and teachers were better. A typical view was that '*Students respect teachers and teachers care for their students*'. However, the practice of teachers going to students' homes to talk with parents about a student's education was seen by some as problematic and less evident.

Interestingly, in all of the case study schools except the least effective (B2), teachers at all levels, non-teaching staff and students felt that there was mutual trust, respect and support in the school. For example, in the most effective school (A1), students felt encouraged and supported in how to improve their marks; teachers thought that students trusted teachers and teachers had a natural affection for students. A subject head thought that the school leaders were aware of teachers' concerns and had set up systems that showed regard for their well-being in and out of school. However, a teacher in the less effective eastern school (A2) highlighted there may be fear or caution amongst junior teachers in approaching senior staff, which may reflect the frequent monitoring of teachers' performance. Meanwhile, the Head of Teaching and Research in the more effective western school (B1) provided the bluntest view of relationships between teachers and students:

> There is basically no conflict among teachers themselves but there is positive competition, fair competition about results ... Do teachers treat students fairly? ... teachers usually show favouritism to good students. Basically, from the junior high school, teachers will show more concern for good students [than] slow ones.
>
> (Lea2Sch1RH1).

These comments and the lack of evidence from the least effective school (B2) suggest that the hierarchical nature of schools in China and the highly competitive exam oriented environment may limit in some cases the mutual trust, respect and support needed to support a well-functioning PLC.

What can be learned about PLCs in China and the potential for teacher-led reform?

In summary, the evidence from the ITDEQC study indicates that the concept of PLCs is relevant and useful in the Chinese context, both established sub-PLCs as well as whole school PLCs seem to exist, but participants' understanding of the concept varied, as did their view of how far features of a PLC were evident in their own schools or more generally in Chinese schools. Typically, and in line with previous research (Wong, 2010), stakeholders linked PLCs with their established practice of teachers working in teaching and research groups, and other existing professional development mechanisms such as strong support for mentoring, collaboration and model lessons. Although all the case study schools used teaching groups as an organizing mechanism for management, they differed in the ways these groups operated and in the ways participants described their involvement and purposes (e.g. more/less meaningful reflective enquiry). Nevertheless, students in all four schools said they felt supported by teachers – though these were all final year students and preparing for the college entrance exam. They all referred to giving regular formal feedback on teachers' practice. They expected, and saw, changes as a result of their feedback.

In terms of the particular PLC characteristics identified in English schools (DfES, 2005), there was generally strong consistent evidence from policy makers and across the four senior secondary schools on four out of eight characteristics. The most developed PLC features comprised: *shared value and visions, collective responsibility for student learning, collaboration focused on learning*, and *group as well as individual professional learning*. Meanwhile, the evidence was more mixed for two PLC features: *mutual trust, respect and support* and *openness, networks and partnerships*, with the latter feature clearly linked by school staff to the extent of funding opportunities. In contrast, the most challenging PLC features were found to be: *reflective professional enquiry* and *inclusive membership*. Inclusiveness was the least easily understood concept. The response of schools to this idea varied but typically was focused on the separate nature of support staff responsibilities. In terms of reflective professional enquiry, this appears to be highly formalized and monitored in Chinese schools and some stakeholders consequently considered teachers' reflections to be rather superficial or otherwise too focused on examination success. Teachers are regularly evaluated – analysis of test and exam results, scrutiny of reflections, student feedback, peer pressure, lesson observations and senior management appraisal. Some of this appears to be productive, some less so. The management of teachers is typically hierarchical and lacks opportunities for distributed leadership, which may result in teachers being motivated mainly by external incentives such as promotion criteria or fear of demotion. The impact of evaluation on career progression is huge which may encourage conformity rather than risk-taking. Interestingly, junior teachers and some non-teachers seemed to express the more progressive ideas but the social and organizational hierarchy may impede their contribution. Several stakeholders also alluded to the principle of damage limitation by constant monitoring and evaluation – avoiding teacher carelessness in not covering the knowledge required, or not doing things properly. The extent to which this is evident varies between schools and links to ideas of mutual trust, respect and support, a factor which also seemed to differ between the four Chinese schools but nevertheless is clearly evident in more mature PLCs. Similarly, Wang (2015) in her study of two northeastern high performing schools seems to describe those schools as mature PLCs given her observation that 'professional learning is ongoing, supported and fully integrated into the culture and operation of the school system. Emotional bonds, trust and an inclusive school culture contribute to genuine collegiality' (p. 908).

Overall, there are tentative indications that the categorizations of the four ITEDQC case study schools as more or less effective map onto the evidence reported by stakeholders of a stronger or less developed profile of the eight PLC characteristics, thereby supporting similar conclusions in previous western research (Thomas, 2010; Lomos et al., 2011). However, perceptions of the east/west or urban/rural divide are relevant here. Urban teachers often referred to any differences observed in terms of the characteristics of schools and teachers, usually to the detriment of rural teachers. Rural teachers refer more to lack of funding to support professional development and external networks. Nevertheless, the similar PLC features of the less effective (rural) eastern school (A2) and more effective (rural) western school (B1) were notable, suggesting that categorizations of effectiveness may be more complex in a country as diverse as China and may only be validly compared *within* a region or city (Thomas & Peng, 2014). This issue is underlined by University entrance examination scores, given it was apparent that the less effective school (A2) in the East actually obtained very similar results to the more effective school in the economically poorer West (B1).

In terms of how PLC development could be better supported in the Chinese context, policy makers indicated that the activity by leaders and educational administrative departments at all levels was key and closely involved with evaluation of teachers' professional development. This issue is important given Tan and Chua (2015) argue that 'there exist fundamental cultural differences between Western and Chinese perspectives on the nature and transmission of knowledge ... China borrow education policy judiciously by integrating foreign and indigenous sources of knowledge, teaching and learning' (p. 686). In other words, the PLC concept needs to be adapted to the Chinese context. Aspects that may need to be considered in refining the PLC concept in China include recognizing differences between east/west and rural/urban contexts, and the strength of existing pedagogies, hierarchies and competition, as well as reviewing the role of non-teaching support staff and parents. Moreover, in urban areas it seems that communications in the larger community are better, whereas in rural areas communication between individuals was a strength.

Finally, with regard to the potential for teacher led reform, the key focus of this book, it is clear from the ITDEQC findings that mature PLCs are likely to support this phenomenon, especially given the changes required by new curriculum reforms in China. Nevertheless, the leadership of the head and support from the whole district are key to empower teachers to take more responsibility themselves for their own learning and school improvement. Adequate time and training is also necessary for new habits to be cultivated, although it is likely that variations in funding across regions and schools are likely to constrain the opportunities for some teachers to be actively involved in reform efforts.

Overall it is apparent that impact, sustainability and support for teacher led reform could be enhanced through PLC development tailored for the Chinese context. Stakeholders clearly indicated that PLC evaluation tools and training could improve professional development practices and teacher agency given ITDEQC schools reported that staff who had received this have a better developed understanding of the features of more effective PLCs, such as reflective teaching practices and distributed leadership. In some cases, ITDEQC schools had also subsequently introduced more effective strategies to promote and sustain the school as a PLC, such as greater involvement of non-teaching support staff. Therefore, it seems from the ITDEQC and other research evidence that teacher led reform underpinned by contextualized PLC development has the potential to be very powerful in bringing about the changes needed to improve quality and equity in the Chinese education system. However, the bottom line is that this is unlikely to be achieved without explicit endorsement and support from policy makers and school leaders and impact may be patchy without a fairer distribution of resources across schools and regions.

References

Akiba, M. & Liang, G. (2016). Effects of teacher professional learning activities on student achievement growth. *The Journal of Educational Research, 109*(1), 99–110.

Chen (陈秋兰), Q-L. (2005). The role of principal in the learning-community school. 教育导刊 *Journal of Educational Development, 12*, 42–43.

Chinese Ministry of Education [CMOE]. (2010). The guidelines of the national plan for medium- and long-term educational reform and development (2010–2020). Retrieved on 30 July 2010 from www.moe.gov.cn/publicfiles/business/htmlfiles/moe/moe_838/201008/93704.html

Department for Education and Skills (DfES). (2005). *Creating and Sustaining Effective Professional Learning Communities, Research Report RR 637*. London: Bolam, R., McMahon, A., Stoll, L., Thomas, S., Wallace, M., Greenwood, A., … Smith, R.

Hannum, E., Park, A. & Cheng., K-M. (2007). Introduction: market reforms and educational opportunity in China. In E. Hannum & A. Park (Eds.), *Education and Reform in China*. Oxford, UK: Routledge.

Harris, A. & Jones, M. (2010). Professional learning communities and system improvement. *Improving Schools, 13*(2), 172–181.

Hord, S. M. (1997). *Professional Learning Communities: Communities of Continuous Inquiry and Improvement*. Austin, TX: Southwest Educational Development Laboratory.

IEEQC/ITDEQC. (2016). *Introduction and Related Materials of IEEQC and ITDEQC Projects*. Retrieved from www.bristol.ac.uk/education/research/sites/ieeqc/

Jiang (蒋福超), F. C. & Liu (刘正伟), Z. W. (2009). Innovation of teaching and researching group in the perspective professional learning community theory. 教育发展研究 *Exploring Education Development, 10*, 83–87.

Li Zijian (Lee, J.C.K.) (李子建) & Song, H. (宋萑). (2006). Professional learning community and curriculum development. 课程教材教法 *Curriculum, Teaching Material, and Method, 26*(12), 24–28.

Li (李清臣), Q-C. L. (2013). Construction of learning environment from the perspective of professional learning community. 河北师范大学学报(教育科学版) *Journal of Hebei Normal University (Educational Science Edition), 15*(2), 34–38.

Lomos, C., Hofman, R. H. & Bosker, R. J. (2011). Professional communities and student achievement – a meta-analysis. *School Effectiveness and School Improvement: An International Journal of Research, Policy and Practice, 22*(2), 121–148.

Peng, W-J., McNess, E., Thomas, S. M., Wu, X., Zhang, C., Li, J. & Tian, H. (2013). Emerging perceptions of teacher quality and teacher development in China. *International Journal of Educational Development, 34*, 77–89. http://dx.doi.org/10.1016/j.ijedudev.2013.04.005

Phillips, D. & Ochs, K. (2003). Processes of policy borrowing in education: some analytical and explanatory devices. *Comparative Education, 39*(4), 3.

Sargent, T. C. & Hannum, E. (2009). Doing more with less: teacher professional learning communities in resource-constrained primary schools in rural China. *Journal of Teacher Education, 60*(3), 258–276.

Schon, D. A. (1983). *The Reflective Practitioner: How Professionals Think in Action*. USA: Basic Books.

The State Council of PRC (中共中央国务院). (2001). *Decision of the State Council on Basic Education Reform and Development*. Retrieved on 15 March 2011 from www.edu.cn/20010907/3000665.shtml

Stoll, L., Bolam, R., McMahon, A., Thomas, S., Wallace, M., Greenwood, A. & Hawkey, K. (2006). *Professional Learning Communities: Source Materials for School Leaders and Other Leaders of Professional Learning*. London: Innovation Unit, DfES, NCSL and GTC.

Sun (孙传远), C-Y. (2010). A survey research into the status of teacher professional learning: Shanghai primary and middle school teachers as example. 基础教育 *Journal of Schooling Studies, 7*(12), 27–32.

Tan, C. & Chua, C. S. K. (2015). Education policy borrowing in China: has the West wind overpowered the East wind? *Compare: A Journal of Comparative and International Education, 45*(5), 686–704.

Thomas, S. M. (2010). Evaluating schools as learning communities. In P. Peterson, E. Baker & B. McGaw (Eds.), *International Encyclopaedia of Education* (3rd Edition). Oxford, UK: Elsevier.

Thomas, S. M. & Peng, W. J. (2014). *Final Report, ITDEQC project* (Final project report submitted to ESRC/DFID funding programme). University of Bristol. Retrieved from www.bristol.ac.uk/education/research/sites/ieeqc/

Thomas, S. M., Peng, W-J. & Li, J. (2015). Time trends in school value added performance and the relationship between value added and teachers professional development in China. *Educational Researcher, 35*(7), 64–72.

Vescio, V., Ross, D. & Adams, A. (2008). A review of research on the impact of professional learning communities on teaching practice and student learning. *Teaching and Teacher Education, 24*, 80–91.

Walker, A. (2016). *Keynote Address ICSEI*. Glasgow, January 2016.

Wang, T. (2015). Contrived collegiality versus genuine collegiality: demystifying professional learning communities in Chinese schools. *Compare: A Journal of Comparative and International Education, 45*(6), 908–930.

Wong, J. L. N. (2010). Searching for good practice in teaching: a comparison of two subject-based professional learning communities in a secondary school in Shanghai. *Compare: A Journal of Comparative and International Education, 40*(5), 623–639.

Zhong (钟志贤), Z. X. (2005). Understanding of the concept of knowledge construction, learning community and interaction. 电化教育研究 *E-Education Research, 11*, 20–24 & 29.

12 Decentralization, localism and the role of PLCs in supporting school collaborations in Wales

Mark Hadfield

Introduction

Policies promoting decentralization and a 'new localism' (Corry & Stoker, 2002) have had a significant impact on public services including education in the UK and internationally, giving rise to a pervasive but often under-defined commitment to partnership and collaboration (Glendinning, Powell & Rummery, 2002). This policy environment has resulted in increasingly divergent national and local education systems in the UK, with complex and fragmented educational landscapes particularly with regards to how they organize the support and development of schools and teachers (Simkins, Coldron, Crawford & Jones, 2015). Greater divergence between the UK education systems is the result of a number of policy changes, not least in Wales due to the devolution of powers to a National Assembly.

Decentralization and localism as drivers of policy reflect a growing belief in the efficacy of locally generated solutions to systemic issues, such as pupil under-achievement. The policy emphasis on locally 'bottom-up' solutions is part of a growing recognition of the limitations of centrally imposed change agendas with regards to their take up, ownership and sustainability (Fullan, 2009). Local solutions are often premised on increasing collaboration between aspects of the education system. Collaboration aims to cohere and align the existing capacity within a system and, if based around effective models of partnership working, to increase it over time.

The approaches to creating local conditions supportive of collaboration have varied depending on which aspects of a system are being brought together and the nature of their partnership working. In the UK, centrally and locally driven approaches have ranged from networks of schools being brought together around specific funded initiatives and shared approaches to school improvement (Hadfield & Chapman, 2009), 'chains' of academy schools with common governance arrangements that have tried to established shared education philosophies and common approaches to teaching and learning (Hill, Dunford, Parish, Rea & Sandals, 2012), to regional 'challenges' that have targeted systemic issues such as pupil under-achievement by drawing in partners from outside of the local education system (Claeys, Jempron & Paterson, 2014).

Collaborative reform efforts are an area of intense international interest and research (Rincon–Gallardo & Fullan, 2016) that has drawn heavily upon earlier work on the development of professional learning cultures and structures within schools (Jäppinen, Leclerc & Tubin, 2015). Approaches such as 'communities of practice' (Brown & Duguid, 1991), the 'learning organization' (Senge, 2006), and 'professional learning communities' (Hord, 2009) have all been drawn on as means of developing 'nested' learning systems (Resnick, 2009). Studying the effectiveness of different approaches to connecting aspects of a system and developing its capacity requires an expansion of the pre-existing research agenda to consider how such efforts are affected by broader system level factors (Hairon, Goh, Chua & Wang, 2015), particularly when considering their longer-term sustainability (Hadfield & Chapman, 2009).

This chapter focuses on the Welsh education system's experience of trying to establish national networks of PLCs, consisting of groups of practitioners working within and between schools, as a key strand of their improvement efforts (Harris & Jones, 2010). The chapter considers two different phases of PLC development and the system level conditions that affected the effectiveness of the implementation strategies that were adopted.

PLCs and teacher leadership

The nature, and perceived importance, of the inter-relationship between PLCs and teacher leadership, as a subset of distributed leadership, is neatly summarized by Harris and Jones (2010):

> The idea of professional learning communities is underpinned by the concept of distributed leadership ... within professional learning communities, distributed leadership is characterized by teachers working together on a shared area of enquiry (Harris, 2009). Distributed leadership provides the infra-structure that holds the community together, as it is the collective work of educators, at multiple levels who are leading innovative work that creates and sustains successful professional learning communities.
> (Harris & Jones, 2010, pp. 173–174)

The interdependence stressed by Harris and Jones (2010) raises the questions as to the nature of the interaction between PLCs as social sites that support professional learning and as arenas in which teachers' professional agency as leaders can be developed and enacted. The nature of the interaction between learning and leadership has been discussed in numerous empirical studies and reviews. The following list provides a brief summation of how distributed leadership, including forms of teacher leadership, have been linked to collaborative professional learning:

- As a logical precursor or condition for the development of a learning organization and supportive of PLCs (York-Barr & Duke, 2004;

Department for Education and Skills [DfES], 2005; Hipp & Huffman 2010).

- An essential part of the infrastructure for sustained mutual and deep professional learning (Harris & Jones, 2010; Jäppinen et al., 2015).
- A significant contributor to, and correlate of, professional learning in that the conditions that support a learning organization also support teacher leadership (Silins & Mulford, 2004).
- As symbiotic in that teacher leadership is an effective form of professional development, and leadership as collective learning is part of a learning organization (Poekert, 2012).
- Treating professional learning as an arena in which teacher leaders can exert their influence (Smeets & Ponte, 2009).

The study of PLCs as sites that develop teacher leadership, rather than as requiring the support of teacher leaders, was relatively under-represented in the early literature (York-Barr & Duke, 2004) and is under-theorized in the later (Hairon et al., 2015). In Wales PLCs were seen not just as a mechanism for developing teacher leadership but as key in developing the forms of distributed system leadership required to create a self-improving system (Hargreaves, 2012).

PLCs as socio-culturally determined knowledge communities are a means of generating human and social capital based on new collective understandings and inter-relationships, which form the necessary 'collaborative intentionality capital' (Engeström, 2005) to bring about wider changes in schools and systems. In the case of Wales, the development of networks of PLCs was intended to develop sufficient collaborative intentional capital, in the form of cohorts of teachers leaders prepared to work between schools, to bring about system level improvements. Networks of PLCs would act as mediating structures that would give opportunities for teachers to engage in cross-school improvement activities, provide supportive environments in which teachers could develop their identities as leaders, and which would change the local system's receptiveness to the idea of teachers as system leaders.

The theory underpinning how networks of PLCs can create collaborative capital is based upon a particular interpretation of how individuals' engagement in collective endeavour affects their professional agency, including the re-negotiation of aspects of their professional identities (Eteläpelto, Vähäsantanen, Hökkä & Paloniemi, 2013; Vähäsantanen, 2015). Teachers working in a PLC based around utilizing inquiry based approaches are given opportunities to not only develop key leadership skills and dispositions but also to engage in the types of internal conversations and professional dialogues that engender reflection on their professional concerns, intentions and preferred educational outcomes. Working in newly formed professional networks presents teachers with a range of possible 'socially suggested' professional identities (Vähäsantanen, 2015) in which they might invest newly acquired capacities and capital. In the case of Wales, amongst these possible future identities was included that of a teacher leader working on improving aspects of the local system. While a single PLC might provide an individual teacher with opportunities to develop their agency, renegotiate their identities and effect change within a school, a network of PLCs and cohorts of teacher leaders have the potential to develop sufficient collaborative intentional capital to change an education system as a whole.

PLCs and system level change

The development of multiple networks of PLCs was an attempt to re-structure and re-culture the 'practice landscape' (Kemmis & Grootenboer, 2008) of the Welsh education system. From Kemmis's perspective, an education system consists of nested sets of individual practice architectures that are 'bundled together in characteristic ways into practice landscapes and practice traditions' (Kemmis, Heikkinen, Fransson, Aspfors & Edwards-Groves, 2014, p. 157). Classroom practices are nested in departmental architectures, whose practices are set within a school's architecture and so on through groups of schools to whole education system. As different architectures are 'nested' within each other, changes in practices within one can affect others, and in doing so form new educational landscapes. Attempts to change the educational landscape in Wales by creating networks of PLCs was premised on the idea that, by creating multiple new architectures, free from certain traditions and norms, it would be possible to sustain new practices and innovations for long enough and at such a scale that they reconfigure, or as it might be termed restructure and re-culture, the landscape in which they operated.

Studying the effect of networks of PLCs on educational landscapes requires a consideration of how they are affected by, and are successful in changing, each of the three 'spaces' that together constitute the practice architectures that form such landscapes. A PLC as a support for social learning needs to re-configure the *cultural-discursive* space within a department's or school's practice architecture by challenging the values and beliefs that currently underpin practice and by changing the language used, and the discourses drawn upon to describe, legitimate and normalize existing practices and the pursuit of certain sets of educational outcomes over others. A PLC as an additional source of capacity within a school needs to reconfigure the *material-economic* space, that is the time, resources and practical arrangements provided to support practice innovation. Finally, as a new hub in the networks of relationships within a school a PLC needs to influence the *social-political* space, formed by the interactions between both formal and informal leaders, and by doing so shift how the outcomes being pursued in the school are determined and the manner in which different practices are legitimated. If PLCs are able to affect all three spaces, and can sustain these effects over time, they create new practice architectures within a school that will influence how practitioners innovate, learn from these innovations and develop their identities as leaders who can challenge existing school norms and traditions and disrupt established networks of power and influence.

A single PLC might be able to challenge the practice architecture of a department or even a whole school. Changing a system's practice landscape requires multiple architectures to be transformed by sustained and coherent shifts in practice that disrupt existing cycles of prefiguration and reconfiguration. Networks of PLCs, if they generate coherent new practices and sufficient teacher leaders, potentially have the capacity to bring about such wide scale transformations.

Policy and practice context

The different phases of PLC development in Wales need to be viewed against the backdrop of an education system that was, and still is, undergoing a rapid process of decentralization. Central government in Wales has struggled with the relative under-performance of the education system over the last decade (OECD, 2014) and has explored various policy options with regard to school improvement before settling on its current collaborative approach, heavily influenced by the notion of a 'self-improving' system (Hargreaves, 2012). Central government's encouragement of PLCs in Wales has become intertwined with the various policy initiatives required to turn a system seen as fragmented and bureaucratic into one where collaboration and partnership working would become the norm (Hill, 2013).

There have been two distinct phases of PLC development in Wales. The first phase was driven by central government and was an attempt to build local and regional networks of PLCs, based upon a national model (Harris & Jones, 2010), that would address the perceived failings of a fragmented 'middle tier' created by the 22 local authorities in Wales. PLCs were seen as key to the implementation of a new national school improvement framework. Networks of PLCs were to provide the capacity, and be the infrastructure, to develop the new practices required by the framework and share these across historical bureaucratic boundaries.

The second phase of PLC development, some five years later, was brought about by the emergence of a new middle tier structure based around four regional consortia, formed by the merger of the school improvement services of groups of local authorities. This second phase was marked by regionally distinct approaches to school improvement and professional learning. Across the regional consortia commitment to 'PLCs' varied but one consortium, Central South, focused on collaborative learning and joint practice development, and to facilitate this placed each of its schools in school networks called School Improvement Groups, or SIGs. The majority of SIGs tackled shared areas of interest or concern by forming groups of practitioners into 'siglets' that shared many of the characteristics of PLCs.

In the first phase of their development, PLCs were assigned a key role in the central government's school improvement policy (Harris & Jones, 2010). PLCs were constructed as a key means of implementing a National 'School Effectiveness Framework' (SEF) (Welsh Assembly Government, 2006a). The framework was composed of what were then seen as the key aspects of a comprehensive school improvement agenda. In the framework PLCs, operating within and between different levels of the system, were both an intended outcome and a means of implementation.

> The School Effectiveness Framework requires the development of professional learning communities at school, local authority and national levels to build collaborative capacity and engage leaders and practitioners at all levels in meaningful professional debate and learning.
>
> (Welsh Assembly government, 2006b, p. 12)

To develop the necessary collaborative capacity to achieve the scope and level of change envisaged in the SEF framework, the Welsh Government funded a number of pilot projects, involving over 100 schools across the country. The implementation model was based on appointing 'associates', senior school leaders, in each region who helped groups of pilot schools form school-based PLCs. The PLCs would develop responses to school based issues before sharing these solutions amongst their networks. This 'depth-to-scope' approach to implementation adopted was based on developing capacity within pilot schools, and then their networks, before developing PLCs across the system as a whole.

Two years after the launch of the SEF, and partly in response to disappointing PISA tests, this time in 2009, the then Education Minister launched a new 20-point improvement plan. The effects of this plan were to be wide-reaching particularly because of its emphasis on increased accountability. The plan represented a step back from locally defined partnership working and marked a return to more central government prescription, represented by a distinct shift in the policy discourse surrounding PLCs:

> The Professional Learning Communities can offer grounded practical examples of what works to teachers and head teachers as to how they source best practice. The implementation of best practice is essential. Those who refuse to implement it will be told 'adopt or justify'. We need to move from theory to practice. By the end of this school year, the School Effectiveness Framework will have been fully implemented and Professional Learning Communities (PLCs) will be in operation across Wales. We will be far more prescriptive about what those PLCs can focus on. They will not be allowed to be laissez-faire in their operation. They will have a clear focus on literacy and numeracy and tackling disadvantage.
>
> (Andrews, 2011, p. 9)

PLCs, at least in policy terms, had shifted from being a means of supporting school-led innovation to local solutions to one in which central government would prescribe their overarching foci and 'kite-mark' the teaching strategies they promoted.

Professional Learning Communities will focus on literacy, numeracy and tackling disadvantage. We will expect a strong focus on high reliability teaching practices and I want to see a new focus on the content of teaching within the School Effectiveness Framework. Provision of effective practice is not prescriptive, it is about ensuring that we have the best skilled teaching workforce continuously developing.

(Andrews, 2011, p. 9)

In 2011 the Welsh Government published its national model for PLCs (Welsh Assembly Government, 2013) but in the following years the idea of networks of PLCs moved from the centre to the periphery of government policy. By 2015, when the Welsh Government announced its 'New Deal' policy on career long professional development, PLCs featured as only one of a number of 'collaborative activities' that would form 'circles of collaboration' that ranged from a school department to the 'Global' (Welsh Assembly Government, 2015).

During the first phase of PLC development the regional consortia were just emerging, framed as an 'arrangement' that would *provide an excellent base on which to build a culture of shared working and innovation, taking into account local contexts and circumstances'* (Welsh Assembly Government, 2006b, p. 19). As the centrally driven policy ran out of steam, the development of PLCs was left to enthusiastic school head teachers. By 2014, four regional consortia had been established and their leaders and local head teachers began the next phase of PLC development.

The largest regional consortia, Central South, a partnership of five local authorities and some 408 schools, launched the Central South Challenge, a strategy to develop a 'self-improving school system' based on six 'principles':

- Schools are communities where collaborative enquiry is used to improve practice;
- Groupings of schools engage in joint practice development;
- Where necessary, more intensive partnerships support schools facing difficulties;
- Families and Community organisations support the work of schools;
- Coordination of the system is provided by school leaders;
- Local authorities work together to act as the 'conscience of the system'. (Central South Consortium, 2016, p. 3)

The strategy, whose implementation was overseen by a group made up mainly of school leaders, resulted in the launch of multiple collaborative improvement initiatives. One such initiative was to place all the schools in the region into School Improvement Groups (SIGs). Schools were allocated, by the consortia, into 43 SIGs, with an average size of 11 schools in the primary phase and seven in the secondary phase. The consortia used a range of criteria when building SIGs, including trying to ensure that schools from each of the five local authorities were represented. A strategic aim in developing the SIGs was to break down historical barriers between schools and so form an infrastructure capable of supporting school–led improvement across the consortium.

The SIGs were led by the head teachers of its constituent schools; in addition, each SIG appointed a convenor. They were free to select their own foci, means of sharing and developing practice, and to design their own structures and action plans. Each SIG convenor received training and support from the consortium in designing inquiry based approaches to professional learning and joint practice development.

Convenor training, run by the Consortium, focused on evaluating the effectiveness of SIGs' different approaches to professional learning and encouraged the sharing of their experience and this began to cohere an overarching approach to SIG working. The approach was based upon SIGs breaking down into smaller 'siglets' consisting of groups of practitioners focused upon a particular area of interest. Multiple siglets, ranging from 2–8 in number across SIGs, ensured that an improvement foci of interest to all the schools in the SIG was covered and allowed for the adoption of a range of approaches to professional learning; both of these were key factors in keeping schools engaged in collaborative working.

The Central South Challenge resulted in a large number of siglets, many of which became inquiry based PLCs, whose focus on changing classroom practices gave increased opportunities for teachers to take on leadership roles. By 2016 when the consortia were externally inspected, schools in the Central South region were not only showing better than average national improvements in pupil attainment but had formed over 200 siglets which, in combination with other forms of collaborative working, had created according to the national school inspection service,

> well-structured opportunities for schools to work together on improvement priorities that are specific to their context, and to share best practice. Engagement in this work has promoted productive school-to-school working across the region.
>
> (Estyn, 2015, p. 5)

The SIG implementation strategy adopted by the consortium was to move from scope-to-depth in that it initially aimed to involve as many schools in collaborative working as possible and then gradually increase the depth of this work. The consortium implementation strategy differed significantly to that used in the first phase of PLC development, where the initial focus was on establishing a small number of pilot schools who demonstrate good practice which would then be shared more widely – a process that was based on moving from depth-to-scope. The main differences between these two implementation strategies are summarized in Table 12.1.

The re-positioning, and re-emergence, of PLCs within the Welsh system in phase two reflected the influence of both top-down changes to the structure of local systems, the imposition of regional consortia by central government, and

Table 12.1 PLC implementation strategies

	Phase 1 Depth-to-Scope	Phase 2 Scope-to-Depth
Policy discourse	Tri-level reform based around a national network of PLCs working within and between schools to implement a national school effectiveness framework.	Part of a regional strategy to develop a self-improving system that would be school led.
Nature of the middle tier	'Fragmented' with 22 local authorities and an emerging consortia arrangement.	Established, but still temporary, regional consortia partly led by local head teachers.
Approach to collaborative system improvement	Based around a national network of PLCs operating within and between schools that would adopt a shared inquiry based model that focused on pedagogy.	Based around regionally based SIGs formed by the consortia to ensure their membership crossed traditional boundaries and which adopted a range of approaches to professional learning and joint practice development.
Degree of professional autonomy	Initially PLCs identified their own school based pedagogical foci but were then required to focus on national improvement areas of numeracy and literacy.	SIGs were free to identify shared areas for improvement, resulting in the growth of siglets that covered a range of priorities.
Approach to capacity building	Regional associates supported an 'inside out' approach which started with school-based PLCs that then shared practice across networks moving towards developing between school PLCs.	An 'outside in' approach based on funding convenors and SIGs to commence joint work on shared agendas often within smaller siglets, the results from which were then taken back into schools.
Going to scale	Moving from 'depth to scope' as small numbers of pilot schools develop high fidelity examples of utilizing the national model of PLCs to improve pedagogy. The examples produced by pilot schools are used by all schools when designing how to develop their PLCs.	Moving from 'scope to depth'. All schools placed in SIGs engage in some form of collaborative learning. Via sharing practice between SIGs, training for convenors and use of evaluation data, approaches gradually deepen so that they become more effective in improving classroom practice.

bottom-up cultural shifts, the emergence of increasing numbers of head teachers prepared to take on system leadership roles, from shaping regional strategy to leading a range of collaborative initiatives, including convening SIGs.

The Welsh practice landscape and the development of PLCs

The following analysis of the two phases of PLC development in Wales is based around the three constitutive spaces of a practice architecture. The analysis considers the key features of each space that supported, or hindered, the growth of system wide networks of PLCs.

The cultural-discursive space

The issues that dominated this space in the Welsh landscape were the lack of engagement by school leaders, at all levels, in collaborative forms of inquiry and joint practice development. In the first phase of PLC development, collaboration between schools had tended to be superficial and restricted to existing networks. As the evaluators of the implementation of the SEF observed,

> The networks that have developed suggest that many are focused upon sharing ideas and good practice rather than operating as true 'professional learning communities' … This is likely to have limited their impact to date, because rather than focusing upon changing the fundamentals … they have focused upon what might be regarded as more superficial solutions.
>
> (Holtom & Lloyd-Jones, 2009, p. 39)

The lack of engagement of school leaders with inquiry and joint practice development contributed in phase one to a gradual 'dumbing down' of what constituted a PLC once it moved beyond the pilot schools. Professional expectations amongst many school leaders were low with regards to the depth and quality of collaborative working as were expectations about the likely impact of PLCs on practice and school improvement. The 'dumbing down' process so affected the first phase of PLC development that the Welsh government published a warning to practitioners to stop over-applying the term PLC to any form of collaborative activity.

> There is a risk that PLCs could be misrepresented as a convenient 'catch all' for any form of collaboration, partnership or networking however effective or ineffective. Unless PLCs are properly configured using the national model, they will not have an impact on the learning outcomes desired.
>
> (Welsh Assembly Government, 2013, p. 5)

The strategy adopted by the Central South Consortium in the second phase of PLC development was to engage as many school leaders as possible in some form of collaborative learning. All schools were to be in a collaborative SIG, schools with an understanding of inquiry were appointed as 'Hubs' and funded to engage in joint practice development with networks of local schools, and cohorts of head teachers were trained and supported to undertake 'Peer Inquiries' into each other's schools. The strategy was to move from 'scope to depth' by initially encouraging widespread engagement in cross-school working then gradually 'deepening' the approaches being used. The advantage of this strategy was that it gradually reconfigured the cultural-discursive space by developing school leaders' understanding of the nature of inquiry based approaches and their role in school improvement; it gave time for the impact of SIGs and siglets to emerge, and for the practices of more effective partnerships to be discussed by those who were leading them at different levels. The range and scale of collaborative reform efforts gradually reconfigured the professional learning landscape from one dominated by training programmes provided by local authorities and central government to one based around the practice of collaborative inquiry and joint working.

The social-political space

The issue that dominated this space was the lack of trust between leaders at different levels of the system in Wales. The lack of trust affected leadership relationships both 'horizontally', between those at the same level, and 'vertically', between those at different levels of the system. A recent review by the Auditor General for Wales (2015) on the conditions that limited partnership working had, for example, highlighted the lack of trust between regional consortia and central government.

The lack of trust in the Welsh system had a number of sources. Practice traditions, that had their basis in how different local authorities had operated, had historically limited school leaders' mutual knowledge of each other's approaches and ways of working. Newly introduced centrally driven accountability systems had led to an increased sense of competition between schools that further inhibited leaders' willingness to share practice ideas and concerns. Waves of centrally driven policy initiatives had undermined many leaders' sense of professional autonomy and agency, limiting their willingness to grapple collectively with the shared issues they encountered.

The Central South Consortium response was to draw head teachers, and other leaders, from the region into its own leadership structures and by doing so model the form of distributed system leadership that was required. Local school leaders were appointed at all levels, they formed the majority of the 'Strategy group' that oversaw the development of the Challenge, co-led major collaborative initiatives, and of course initially convened the SIGs, which over time handed the leadership of 'siglets' to middle leaders and teachers from their own schools. This modeling of a distributed form of system leadership by the

Consortium engaged large numbers of leaders in a collective movement, that was both 'interest' based, in that their collaboration focused on improving the system and outcomes for pupils, but was also 'identity' based, in that it drew together leaders that saw themselves as part of the collective 'self' that was to take responsibility in a self-improving system.

The incorporation of school leaders into the structures of the Central South consortium, and the wider engagement of middle and teacher leaders in the SIGs, was a means of re-establishing their professional autonomy, encouraged authentic engagement with and ownership of the collaborative reforms, while ensuring that the focus of these collaborative efforts was meaningful in relation to individuals, schools and the local system as a whole.

Adopting the role of a system leader required a degree of identity renegotiation that even head teachers committed to working collaboratively found difficult at times. This process of renegotiation was not limited to just seeing themselves as system leaders; it also involved an increased identification with the success and needs of other schools. As one convenor commented, the school leaders in their SIG now felt that they *'belonged to one big school'*.

The material-economic space

Prior research into large scale reforms has highlighted the delayed impact of using inquiry based approaches as a means of building organizational capacity (Vargo, 2004). In the first phase of PLC development there was a clear disjuncture between claims that a series of pilots, involving less than 5 percent of schools nationally, had within a year increased capacity across the system (Andrews, 2011) and an external evaluation of the SEF which indicated a lack of depth in cross-school collaborative working (Holtom & Lloyd-Jones, 2009). The disjuncture highlighted the need for time, consistent levels of resourcing and a stable policy environment for PLCs to develop and function effectively across a system, as one SIG convenor commented,

> Often we start these projects and they don't get finished because of time or financial constraints. With our SIG we have been able to see things though. It is all about consistency with the SIG and that's really important.
> (Head teacher, Research Study Report 1, p. 15)

Uncertainty amongst leaders as to whether competition might increase in the future has been shown to limit collaborative efforts (Lacomba, Lagos & Neugebauer, 2011). Developing a middle tier organization co-led by school leaders provided a means of countering the uncertainty created by central devised policies that had previously swung between encouraging local collaboration and autonomy and enhancing accountability structures that have led to greater competition (Andrews, 2011).

The strategy adopted in Central South Consortium to SIG development was based on moving from 'scope-to-depth'. The SIG programme started with all

Table 12.2 School and system level conditions supportive of PLCs

Practice architecture	School conditions	System conditions
Cultural–discursive space Ideas, cognitions, semantics discourses	Teacher empowerment Teacher creativity Active promotion by leadership Creative conflict Authentic commitment of teachers A school culture that embraces inquiry Culture of risk taking and innovation Mutual respect Critical mass of people who are self-efficacious about their teaching practice	Drawing leaders at all levels into forms of collaborative engagement Increase leaders' mutual knowledge of each other's schools Develop a collective identity amongst leaders Changing the discourse around professional learning to one of school-led engagement in inquiry and joint practice development
Social-political space Roles, relationships, power, solidarity	Teacher autonomy Trust Positive staff relationships Goal setting Access to external partners and expertise More staff directly involved in teaching Senior leadership participation in inquiry and professional learning Links with other PLCs	Creation of new networks of informal leaders School-led middle tier structures Consistency and coherence of policy focus High levels of agreement on key issues faced by the system Professional autonomy with regard to dealing with systemic issues Low levels of competition Trust between leaders operating within and between different levels of the system
Material–economic space Physical, practical resources	Time Frequency and rhythm of meetings Professional development infrastructure Location of school Site facilities that support collaborative working Smaller school size	Co-coordinating structures to support horizontal and vertical integration of PLCs Removal of structural barriers between schools Consistent level of funding and support over time Opportunities to work in and across small groups of PLCs

schools being part of a network, depth was achieved when SIGs made the move from being sources of ideas and support for head teachers to becoming sites of joint practice development for teachers. For SIGs to develop in this way required a consistent level of funding over an extended period of time to allow first head teachers, then middle leaders and eventually teachers, to work collaboratively in a sustained manner.

Conclusions: school versus system conditions

Viewing schools and education systems through the theoretical lens of practice architectures and landscapes allowed for a comparative analysis of the conditions at different levels of a system that supports PLCs to develop. Table 12.2 compares the findings of research into the Welsh system attempts to create networks of PLCs with earlier research into the school conditions that supported PLC development (DfES, 2005; Stoll, Bolam, McMahon, Wallace & Thomas, 2006; Vescio, Ross & Adams, 2008; Darling-Hammond, Wei, Andree, Richardson & Orphanos, 2009; Mindich & Lieberman, 2012).

Concluding thoughts

The practice landscape of the Welsh education system has prefigured attempts over the last decade to develop system wide networks of PLCs. The emergence of regional consortia has led to a radical re-structuring of local systems that has given new impetus and direction to these attempts. In one consortia, at least, PLCs are making a distinct contribution to supporting teachers to become part of a distributed approach to system leadership.

The role of networks of PLCs in system reform is based on their potential to reconfigure the different spaces that form the 'architecture' of an educational landscape. The nature of the reconfigurations required in each system and the roles PLCs can play will depend upon the existing architecture and the improvements being sought, but in the case of Wales the following were significant.

- The Welsh system as a relatively small system has a policy focus upon a limited, but important, number of systemic issues, such as the impact of social deprivation upon pupil attainment. Networks of cross-school PLCs provided a means of finding a workable balance between ensuring sufficient improvement efforts are brought to bear on these systemic issues while providing leaders and teachers with opportunities to exert their professional autonomy in how these issues are addressed locally. Enhancing teachers' sense of autonomy, and efficacy, in challenging persistent and widespread issues supports the process of identity realignment required to become teacher leaders, both in and beyond their own schools.
- Teacher leaders' sense of identity, and agency, is bounded by the dynamic between their 'internal' identities, dispositions, and competencies and the

'external' socio-cultural conditions of the local system. The Welsh system was organizationally fragmented into small local education authorities but also marked by cohesive personal professional networks, especially between existing school leaders. PLCs provided new structures with the potential to disrupt existing networks of formal leadership and to develop new networks of 'informal' leaders.

- The Welsh system has been marked by a lack of trust, a limited history of cross-school working and the absence of a critical mass of practitioners with substantive experience in collaborative professional learning. Networks of PLCs, as sites of joint inquiry and co-construction of practice, have been significant in challenging mistrust as to the 'quality' and 'warrant' of new practices, increased the likelihood that such practices are examined critically and supported the adoption and adaption of classroom practices found to be effective.
- The Welsh experience has emphasized the need for teachers to be provided with sustained opportunities to adopt system leadership roles. Networks of PLCs can offer teachers the necessary support to take part in a more distributed form of system leadership but they require a degree of stability and coherence in national, local and organizational policies that currently appears to be missing in some of the education systems in the UK.

Bibliography

Andrews, L. (2011). *Teaching makes a difference*. Cardiff, UK: Welsh Government (Speech at the Reardon Smith Lecture Theatre, Cardiff, 2 February 2011). Retrieved on 1 July 2015 from http://wales.gov.uk/topics/educationandskills/allsectorpolicies/ourevents/teachingmakesadifference

Auditor General for Wales. (2015). *Achieving improvement in support to schools through regional education consortia – an early view*. Cardiff, UK: Auditor General for Wales.

Brown, J. S. & Duguid, P. (1991). Organizational learning and communities-of-practice: Toward a unified view of working, learning, and innovation. *Organization Science, 2*(1), 40–57.

Central South Consortium. (2016). *Central South Consortium Business Plan*. Ty Dysgu: Central South Consortium Joint Education Services.

Claeys, S., Jempron, J. & Paterson, C. (2014). *Regional challenges: A collaborative approach to improving education*. London: Centre Forum.

Coburn, C. E. (2003). Rethinking scale: Moving beyond numbers to deep and lasting change. *Educational Researcher, 32*(6) 3–12.

Cochran-Smith, M. & Lytle, S. L. (1999). Relationships of knowledge and practice: Teacher learning in communities. *Review of Research in Education, 24*, 249–305.

Corry, D. & Stoker, G. (2002). *New localism: Refashioning the centre-local relationship*. London: The New Local Government Network.

Cowan, D., Fleming, G. L., Thompson, T. L. & Morrissey, M. S. (2004). Study description: Investigating five PLC schools. In S. M. Hord (Ed.), *Learning together, leading together: Changing schools through professional learning communities* (pp. 15–19). New York: Teachers College Press.

Darling-Hammond, L., Wei, R. C., Andree, A., Richardson, N. & Orphanos, S. (2009). *Professional learning in the learning profession*. Washington, DC: National Staff Development Council.

Department for Education and Skills (DfES). (2005). *Creating and Sustaining Effective Professional Learning Communities, Research Report RR 637*. London: Bolam, R., McMahon, A., Stoll, L., Thomas, S., Wallace, M., Greenwood, A., … Smith, R.

Engeström, Y. (2005). Knotworking to create collaborative intentionality capital in fluid organizational fields. In M. M. Beyerlein, S. T. Beyerlein, & F. A. Kennedy (Eds.), *Collaborative capital: Creating intangible value*. Amsterdam, NL: Elsevier.

Estyn. (2015). *Improving schools through regional education consortia*. Cardiff: Estyn.

Eteläpelto, A., Vähäsantanen, K., Hökkä, P. & Paloniemi, S. (2013). What is agency? Conceptualizing professional agency at work. *Educational Research Review, 10*, 45–65.

Fullan, M. (2009). Large-scale reform comes of age. *Journal of Educational Change, 10*, 101–113.

Fullan, M., Rolheiser, C., Mascall, B. & Edge, K. (2004). Accomplishing large scale reform: A tri-level proposition. In F. Hernandez, & F. Goodson (Eds.), *Social geographies of educational change* (pp. 1–13). Dordrecht, NL: Springer.

Furlong, J. (2015). *Teaching tomorrow's teachers: Options for the future of initial teacher education in Wales*. Oxford, UK: University of Oxford, Department of Education.

Furlong, J., Hagger, H., Butcher, C. & Howson, J. (2006). *Review of Initial Teacher Training Provision in Wales: A report to the Welsh Assembly Government (the Furlong Report)*. Oxford, UK: University of Oxford, Department of Education.

Glendinning C., Powell, M. & Rummery, K. (Eds.). (2002). *Partnerships, New Labour and the governance of welfare*. London: The Policy Press.

Hadfield, M. & Chapman, C. (2009). *Leading School Based Networks*. London: Routledge.

Hairon, S., Goh, J. W. P., Chua, C. S. K. & Wang, L. Y. (2015). A research agenda for professional learning communities: Moving forward. *Professional Development in Education, (52)*, 1–15.

Hargreaves, D. H. (2012). *A self-improving system in international context*. Nottingham, UK: National College for School Leadership.

Harris, A. & Jones, M. (2010). Professional learning communities and system improvement. *Improving Schools, 13*(2), 172–181.

Hill, R. (2013). *The future delivery of education services in Wales*. Cardiff, UK: Welsh Government.

Hill, R., Dunford, J., Parish, N., Rea, S. & Sandals, L. (2012). *The growth of Academy Chains: Implications for leaders and leadership*. Nottingham, UK: NCSL.

Hipp, K. K. & Huffman, J. B. (Eds.). (2010). *Demystifying professional learning communities: School leadership at its best*. Lanham, MD: Rowman & Littlefield Education.

Holtom, D. & Lloyd-Jones, S. (2009). *Development and implementation of an evaluation programme for piloting in schools of the School Effectiveness Framework for Wales*. Cardiff, UK: Welsh Assembly Government.

Hopkins, D., Stringfield, S., Harris, A., Stoll, L. & Mackay, T. (2014). School and system improvement: A narrative state-of-the-art review. *School Effectiveness and School Improvement, 25*(2), 257–281.

Hord, S. (2009). Professional learning communities. Educators work together toward a shared purpose – Improved student learning. *Journal of Staff Development, 30*, 40–46.

Jäppinen, A. K., Leclerc, M. & Tubin, D. (2015). Collaborativeness as the core of professional learning communities beyond culture and context: Evidence from Canada, Finland, and Israel. *School Effectiveness and School Improvement, 15*, 1–18.

Kemmis, S. (2009) Action research as a practice-based practice. *Educational Action Research,* *17*(3), 463–474.

Kemmis, S. & Grootenboer, P. (2008). Situating praxis in practice: Practice architectures and the cultural, social and material conditions for practice. In S. Kemmis & T. J. Smith (Eds.), *Enabling praxis: Challenges for education* (pp. 37–64). Rotterdam: Sense Publishers.

Kemmis, S., Heikkinen, H.L., Fransson, G., Aspfors, J. & Edwards-Groves, C. (2014). Mentoring of new teachers as a contested practice: Supervision, support and collaborative self-development. *Teaching and Teacher Education, 43,* 154–164.

Lacomba, J. A., Lagos, F. & Neugebauer, T. (2011). Who makes the pie bigger? An experimental study on co-opetition. *New Zealand Economic Papers, 45*(1–2), 59–68.

Mindich, D. & Lieberman, A. (2012). *Building a learning community: A tale of two schools.* Stanford, CA: Stanford Center for Opportunity Policy in Education.

OECD. (2014). *Improving schools in Wales: An OECD perspective.* Paris: OECD Publishing.

PISA. (2012). *Programme for International Student Assessment.* OECD: Bradshaw, J. Retrieved on 4 September 2015 from www.oecd.org/pisa/keyfindings/PISA-2012-results-UK.pdf

Poekert, P. E. (2012). Teacher leadership and professional development: Examining links between two concepts central to school improvement. *Professional development in education, 38*(2), 169–188.

Resnick, L. (2009). Nested learning systems for the thinking curriculum. *Educational Researcher, 39*(3), 183–197.

Rincon-Gallardo, S. & Fullan, S. (2016). Essential features of effective networks in education. *Journal of Professional Capital and Community, 1*(1), 5–22.

Senge, P. M. (2006). *The fifth discipline: The art and practice of the learning organization.* London: Broadway Business.

Silins, H. & Mulford, B. (2004). Schools as learning organisations – Effects on teacher leadership and student outcomes. *School effectiveness and school improvement, 15*(3–4), 443–466.

Simkins, T., Coldron, J., Crawford, M. & Jones, S. (2015). Emerging local schooling landscapes, the role of the local authority. *School Leadership and Management, 35*(1), 1–16.

Smeets, K. & Ponte, P. (2009). Action research and teacher leadership. *Professional Development in Education, 35*(2), 175–193.

Stoll, L., Bolam, R., McMahon, A., Wallace, M. & Thomas, S. (2006). Professional learning communities: A review of the literature. *Journal of Educational Change,* 7(4), 221–258.

Vähäsantanen, K. (2015). Professional agency in the stream of change: Understanding educational change and teachers' professional identities. *Teaching and Teacher Education, 47,* 1–12.

Vargo, M. (2004). Choices and consequences in the Bay Area School Reform Collaborative: Building the capacity to scale up whole-school improvement. In T. Glennan, S. Bodilly, J. Galegher & K. Kerr (Eds.), *Expanding the reach of education reforms: Perspectives from leaders in the scale-up of educational interventions.* Santa Monica, CA: Rand Education.

Vescio, V., Ross, D. & Adams, A. (2008). A review of research on the impact of professional learning communities on teaching practice and student learning. *Teaching and Teacher Education, 24*(1), 80–91.

Wales Audit Office. (2015). *Achieving improvement in support to schools through regional education consortia – an early view.* Cardiff, UK: Wales Audit Office.

Welsh Assembly Government. (2006a). *School effectiveness framework.* Cardiff, UK: Welsh Assembly.

Welsh Assembly Government. (2006b). *The learning country.* Cardiff, UK: Welsh Assembly.

Welsh Assembly Government. (2013). *Professional learning communities: Guidance.* Cardiff, UK: Welsh Assembly.

Welsh Assembly Government. (2014). *National model for regional working.* Cardiff, UK: Welsh Assembly.

Welsh Assembly Government. (2015). *Effective collaboration.* Cardiff, UK: Welsh Assembly.

York-Barr, J. & Duke, K. (2004). What do we know about teacher leadership? Findings from two decades of scholarship. *Review of Educational Research, 74*(3), 255–316.

Conclusion

Improving schools and school systems is a complex, fraught and complicated business (Whelan, 2009; Hargreaves, Lieberman, Fullan & Hopkins, 2012). Ultimately, the task of improving any education system is fundamentally dependent on changing what happens in classrooms (Hattie, 2015; Wiliam, 2016). This book has outlined how teachers in different contexts, cultures and countries are working together, collaboratively, to change their professional practice for the better. Through the PLC examples in this book, the four tests of *authenticity, implementation, impact and sustainability* are well illustrated and supported.

In addition, from the various chapters, it is possible to discern ten common features of successful PLCs' practice, whether at the macro, meso or micro level and irrespective of scale, scope, nature or context. These common denominator features of successful and effective PLCs are:

1 *Clarity of purpose*: shared understanding of the core purpose of the collective work, clarity that their central intention is to improve learner outcomes and a relentless focus on improving professional practice.
2 *Shared PLC model*: a common, operational model that ensures that teachers know *how* to initiate, develop and sustain a PLC. A model that goes beyond a set of aspirational statements.
3 *Professional will, skill and persistence*: teacher development and training that focuses on developing collaborative and inquiry skills in preparation for the PLC work. The willingness and persistence to work through several PLC cycles so that the impact upon learners is apparent.
4 *Disciplined collaboration:* focused, purposeful and rigorous professional collaboration rather than loose cooperation.
5 *Expert facilitation:* external intervention and support that is timely, respected, trusted and knowledgeable.
6 *Fidelity of implementation:* adherence to a PLC model in ways that ensure that implementation is coherent and consistent.
7 *Understanding and diagnosing data:* the ability to understand data and to engage in inquiry and data analysis.

8 *Political support:* appropriate political (or micro-political) support for the PLC process to legitimize and reinforce it.
9 *Authentic teacher agency and leadership:* opportunities to exercise genuine teacher leadership and teacher agency.
10 *Trust:* building and establishing trust within the PLC through transparency, continuous communication and honest reflection.

The chapters in this book represent, in many cases, PLC work in progress and there is no suggestion or implication that any one PLC model or approach is endorsed or supported over another. Armstrong (2012) suggests that while system leaders can always learn from each other it is always critical to consider the local context and social structure to design problem-solving processes that relate to systemic change. The reality of professional collaboration, on the ground, is that it is hard, dedicated work and context and culture inevitably influence and shape the professional practice (Jones & Harris, 2014).

In these various accounts of PLCs in action one feature that stands out far more than others is the presence of high levels of *trust* (Hord, Roussin & Sommers, 2010; Huffman et al., 2007). In essence, the chapters in this book are accounts of initiating, building and sustaining professional trust. In some cases, they are also examples of attempts to reverse low-trust situations. It is no accident that many of the better-performing education systems exhibit and exemplify high trust in teachers and their professional practice (Fink, 2016).

In Finland, for example, there is a culture of trust where 'education authorities and political leaders believe that teachers, together with principals, parents, and their communities, know how to provide the best possible education for their children and youth' (Sahlberg, 2011, p. 130). Finland also scores well on international transparency rankings that indicate the perceptions of corruption among citizens. In some of the poorer-performing education systems the opposite tends to be the case; there are low levels of trust with low levels of transparency (Harris & Jones, 2015).

In their seminal book on the topic of 'Trust in Schools', Bryk and Schneider (2002) highlight 'that among public schools in Chicago that have a similar intake of students, the ones that perform the best have higher levels of trust between students, teachers, parents, administrators'. As Hargreaves and Fullan (2012, p. 91) note, 'It's not just a correlation – it's a cause and effect'. Trust and expertise work hand in hand to produce better results'. As highlighted in the introduction to this book, professional capital, that includes social capital, does not just happen by chance but rather is carefully structured, coordinated and nurtured over time. In his latest book, *Trust and Verify*, Dean Fink (2016) argues strongly for trust as a major explanatory factor for the differential performance of schools, districts and education systems. He concludes:

> Perhaps two things stand out more than any others. The first is just how pivotal the role of the principal is in developing high-trust relations in schools, and in developing the relationship between the school and the

employing authority and jurisdiction it serves. The second thing is the significance of the overall levels of trust that exist between the political system and the broader society with the teaching profession. Levels of trust between the teaching staff and their principal in individual schools also reflect this in part, and in so doing influence each teacher's sense of professionalism.

(Fink, 2016, p. 230)

At the heart of any authentic professional learning community, in any context or jurisdiction, you will find high teacher self-efficacy and a strong sense of professionalism (Harris & Jones, 2010; Huffman et al., 2007). In their latest book, Lieberman, Campbell and Yashkina (2016) conclude 'when educators, policy makers and researchers' voices are heard and these groups learn to work together, there is tremendous potential for the good of students and the professionalization of teaching'. Reflecting on Finland's exceptional educational success, Sahlberg (2010, p. 77) notes that 'teachers expect that they will experience professional autonomy, prestige, respect and trust in their work'. So teacher-led reform not only seems desirable but essential if better, longer-lasting school improvement is sought.

At the start of this book we outlined that contemporary educational reform and change is located between what Fink (2016) calls the 'production paradigm' and 'professional paradigm'. The production paradigm is underpinned by a neo-liberal concern with the development and management of human capital. In contrast, the 'professional paradigm' is concerned with developing professional capital in its most inclusive sense. The net result of this dichotomy is a postmodern cocktail of push and pull approaches to educational reform and change that materialize as incoherent and inconsistent policy formation. Overlay this with the fact that too many education systems have a 'crisis of trust' (Fink, 2016, p. 184) in the teaching profession and the reasons for the failure of much contemporary reform is self-evident.

So is there an alternative? In their work, Evers and Kneber (2016, p. 5) ask 'if high quality education cannot, by definition, be produced through a managed version of the teaching profession how should the system position itself towards teachers, how should the profession position itself towards the system?' Their answer is to 'flip the system' or, in other words, to put teachers at the forefront of educational reform and change. They ask for a revolution, albeit a 'quiet one', and assert that 'through becoming research-literate, teachers become the guardian of their own profession' (Evers and Kneber, 2015, p. 257). On the latter point they are absolutely right; on the former point, it is debatable whether this revolution will be or should be 'quiet'.

At the heart of successful educational change and reform, at scale, is the critical task of changing pedagogy and professional practice for the better (Fullan, 2011; Muijs & Reynolds, 2010). As Wiliam (2016) notes, 'every teacher needs to improve, not because they are not good enough, but because they can be even better'. As the examples in this book clearly show, focused, systematic, supported and structured teacher collaboration has the potential to change learning, teaching and schooling for the better.

The evidence shows that, if implemented properly, PLCs in their various forms have the power and potential to generate teacher agency, teacher leadership and teacher innovation in ways that lead directly to improvement in learner outcomes. We readily acknowledge that PLCs are not the only form that professional collaboration should or could take but they are certainly one of the most potent ways to build professional trust and to generate professional capital. Ultimately, the question is not whether we need teacher-led reform but rather how quickly and effectively we can mobilize it, at scale, for maximum impact and improvement.

References

Armstrong, A. (2012). Key drivers fuel international successes. *The Learning System,* 7(2), 1–5.

Bryk, A. & Schneider, B. (2002). *Trust in schools: A core resource for improvement.* New York: Russell Sage Foundation.

Evers, J. & Kneyber R. (2015: 1) *Flip the system: Changing education from the ground up.* London: Routledge.

Fink, D. (2016). *Trust and verify: The real secrets of school improvement.* London: IOE Press.

Fullan, M. (2011). Whole system reform for innovative teaching and learning. *Innovative Teaching and Learning Research,* 30–39. Retrieved from www.michaelfullan.ca/wp-content/uploads/2016/06/Untitled_Document_5.pdf

Hargreaves, A. & Fullan, M. (2012). *Professional capital: Transforming teaching in every school.* New York: Teachers College Press.

Hargreaves, A., Lieberman, A., Fullan, M. & Hopkins, D. W. (Eds.). (2014). *International handbook of educational change: Part two* (Vol. 5). The Netherlands: Springer.

Harris, A. & Jones, M. (2010). Professional learning communities and system improvement. *Improving Schools,* 13(2). 172–181.

Harris, A. & Jones, M. (2015). Transforming education systems: Comparative and critical perspectives on school leadership. *Asia Pacific Journal of Education,* 35(3), 311-318.

Hattie, J. (2015). *What doesn't work in education: The politics of distraction.* London: Pearson.

Hord, S., Roussin, J. & Sommers, W. (2010). *Guiding professional learning communities: Inspiration, challenge, surprise, and meaning.* Thousand Oaks, CA: Corwin Press.

Huffman, J. B., Pankake, A. & Munoz, A. (2007). The tri-level model in action: Site, district, and state plans for school accountability in increasing student success. *Jsl Vol 16-N5,* 16, 569.

Jones, M. & Harris, A. (2014). Principals leading successful organisational change: Building social capital through disciplined professional collaboration. *Journal of Organisational Change Management,* 27(3), 473–475.

Lieberman, A., Campbell, C. & Yashkina, A. (2016). *Teacher learning and leadership: Of, by, and for teachers.* London: Routledge.

Muijs, D. & Reynolds, D. (2010). *Effective teaching: Evidence and practice.* London: Sage.

Sahlberg, P. (2011). *Finnish lessons.* New York: Teachers College Press.

Whelan, F. (2009). *Lessons learned: How good policies produce better schools.* Bodmin, UK: MPG Books.

Wiliam, D. (2016). The secret of effective feedback. *Educational Leadership,* 73(7), 10–15.

Index

Page numbers in **bold** denote figures, those in *italics* denote tables.